The
EVERYTHING®
Poker Strategy Book

Dear Reader,

I am a fortunate guy. No, I don't get better hands than everyone else, but when it comes to poker, I've been blessed. I naturally understood the logic and beauty of this intense game—and how to beat it.

My parents, skilled bridge players, always said I was born with a deck of cards in my hand, and my earliest memories are of being propped up on phone books so I could see over the card table. When my dad's home game was short-handed one night, little twelve-year-old me piped up and cajoled the tough, cigar-chomping neighborhood men into letting me sit in. When it was my "bedtime" a few hours later, I took some of their money with me, and a local legend was born. Ever since, no matter where I've been, where I've worked, or what I've done, I've always been a poker player first. And the lessons I've learned at the table—patience, determination, staying power, reading people, courage, bluffing, creating a persona, and using psychology—have served me well.

Eventually, I graduated to high stakes, but some of my card time is still spent in the games that you will start out playing: low-limit and middle-limit casino poker and tournaments. Why? Because those games are a blast—AND profitable! In a quarter century at the tables, *I have never had a losing year.* Read this book carefully, and you will have the same success—even if you weren't born holding a deck of cards!

"Big" John Wenzel

The EVERYTHING® Series

Editorial

Publishing Director	Gary M. Krebs
Managing Editor	Kate McBride
Copy Chief	Laura MacLaughlin
Acquisitions Editor	Eric M. Hall
Development Editor	Karen Johnson Jacot
Production Editors	Jamie Wielgus
	Bridget Brace

Production

Production Director	Susan Beale
Production Manager	Michelle Roy Kelly
Series Designers	Daria Perreault
	Colleen Cunningham
	John Paulhus
Cover Design	Paul Beatrice
	Matt LeBlanc
Layout and Graphics	Colleen Cunningham
	Rachael Eiben
	Michelle Roy Kelly
	John Paulhus
	Daria Perreault
	Erin Ring
Series Cover Artist	Barry Littmann

Visit the entire Everything® Series at www.everything.com

THE

EVERYTHING®

POKER STRATEGY BOOK

Know when to hold, fold, and raise the stakes

John Wenzel

Adams Media
Avon, Massachusetts

An Everything® Series Book.
Everything® and everything.com® are registered trademarks of F+W Publications, Inc.

Published by Adams Media, an F+W Publications Company
57 Littlefield Street, Avon, MA 02322 U.S.A.
www.adamsmedia.com

ISBN: 1-59337-140-3
Printed in the United States of America.

J I H G F E D C B A

Library of Congress Cataloging-in-Publication Data
Wenzel, John.
The everything poker strategy book / John Wenzel.
p.   cm.
Everything series
ISBN 1-59337-140-3
1. Poker. 2. Gambling systems. I. Title. II. Series.
GV1251.W45 2005
795.4'12—dc22
2004009919

795.412

Wenz

This book is available at quantity discounts for bulk purchases.
For information, call 1-800-872-5627.

Contents

Acknowledgments

To the poker players of Las Vegas, Nevada.
Thank you for your continued support.

Top Ten Pearls of Poker Wisdom

1. "I feel my skill at poker is good enough collateral for a bank loan."—Johnny Moss

2. "Never criticize another man's way of playing his hand. . . . A man who buys his chips is entitled to play them any way he wants to."
—Amarillo Slim Preston

3. "People want to fall in love. Players want to be in action. Even when they know it will cause them pain." —Big John Wenzel

4. "If you know how a man plays poker, you will know the man."
—Old poker proverb

5. "Vegas is a city based on numbers, math, and discipline; a paradox to what it seems to be offering—chance, hope, ease, and instant gratification." —Sean Pole

6. "All the evidence points to Him [God] being an inveterate gambler, who throws the dice on every possible occasion."
—Stephen Hawking

7. "To me, finding a fair challenge beats searching for suckers."
—Doyle Brunson

8. "At the poker table, you never believe what you hear, and only half of what you see." —Poker player at Bellagio

9. "I have enough money to last me the rest of my life, unless I buy something." —Jackie Mason

10. "Good poker is hard work . . . Great poker is courage."
—Rick Bennet

Introduction

▶ WELCOME! AND BE WARNED. By the simple act of opening this book, you have turned the page on the life you used to know and entered a new world—the world of poker.

It is a world of stealthy guerrilla warfare and epic battles, brute force and intellectual cunning, where friend can quickly become foe and no stranger is to be trusted.

While the monetary stakes range from pennies to a king's ransom, they are always high—because you are putting yourself on the line and taking a stand. You can gamble for quarters and beer with your buds, or sell everything you own and walk up to a table at the opulent Bellagio in Vegas, slam it down, and challenge the best players in the world.

Although outnumbered and alone, you must not waver, for to waver invites rout. You fight the good fight with some unusual weapons: courage, intellect, aggression, misdirection, discipline, patience, confidence, and a wad of cash. The weapons are few, but they are more powerful than you can imagine. It is psychological warfare with your opponents and with yourself. Just a game, you say? I think you know that it is so much more, or you wouldn't have made the fateful decision to explore this book.

If you weren't aware of the power of poker, stop right now. Reading this book is a life-altering choice. This simple "game" will seep through your pores, wrap around your heart, and envelop your soul, uplifting it or crushing it, depending on your skills or even your fortunes on a particular evening.

You must have the character to stand up to Chance when it does not smile on you and be strong enough not to blame luck for your losses. If you can do this, you will gain amazing talents that will enhance every facet of your life—business and personal—not just your card play. You will discover that those who have mastered the secrets of poker have also mastered life. This is a hobby that will saturate your life with fun, fascination, and satisfaction, and make you a bundle of cold, hard cash as well. Not many avocations can make such a claim.

There is also a darker side: Without discipline and self-knowledge, the game can sap your spirit *and* your bank account. Every good poker player has had a night when he busted out and felt like throwing himself into that flaming pit of lava in front of the Mirage casino on the Vegas Strip. How you handle that night will determine who you are, at the tables and in your life. For poker can slam you with some thunderous body blows, the lowest of lows, but the highs will be there too, just as intense. There is no feeling in the universe like the tidal wave of euphoria that sweeps you into your own giddy corner of heaven as you leave the casino with your pockets full, having just won big bucks in a hot game or finished in the money in a major tournament.

All that cash just slaps against your thighs, heavy with the weight of victory, and you're walking on air, not for what it will buy but for what it means. It doesn't matter if you're already a billionaire. There's nothing like it. Anywhere. Welcome to Poker.

Chapter 1

The Stone-Cold Basics

From the days of the first poker mania when fancy gamblers preyed on riverboat rubes to today's high-tech hysteria fueled by television and the Internet, players have sought one thing: the secret to winning. Winning means money. Winning means fun. But winning consistently takes more than just buying some chips and getting a hand, or anyone with a buy-in and a pair of sunglasses would be rich.

There Is No Magic Formula

You can't make winning poker with a recipe. You can't just pick up a cookbook and become a skilled player. The well-worn cliché about poker says that "It is simple to learn, but it takes a lifetime to master." How true that is. Any intelligent person can learn the rules and the different hands in a few minutes, but the nuances and subtleties only become apparent over time. You will find that at some point you will start thinking of yourself as a pretty fair player. Then, a few months or a year later, you will look back at the way you played and how you approached certain hands and situations, and you will just shake your head at how naive you were. This is especially true for Texas Hold'em. Its complexities continue to amaze even seasoned pros, who, like you, continue to learn new tricks. Even after many years, they sometimes look back and shake their heads as well.

Each poker hand is its own battle, a skirmish in a larger game. Not just the game you're playing on a particular night—I mean the ongoing poker game you are playing throughout your entire life. You must think long-term. There will be games when no matter how well you play, you won't come out ahead. But if you play correctly, over time you will be a winner, and that's what it's all about.

Take the Long View

If you are following sound strategies like those presented in this book, don't let a few losing sessions or crazy hands tempt you to change your style. Don't be seduced by the "I would've won if I hadn't folded" refrain. You might as well know up front that every good player has folded winning hands. Get over it. It happens. You fold to a couple of bets in Seven-Card Stud with pocket deuces and, lo and behold, it turns out you would've gotten a miracle card (a third deuce) if you had only called. Or you toss a trash Hold'em hand like 7-4 offsuit and get some crazy flop (like 7-7-4) that would have given you a full house. Your brain screams that you made a mistake, that you'd be *rich* if you'd just called those bets, but you must quash those thoughts. Let them go. They are for losers. That fortunate scenario won't happen again if you spread out a hundred flops—the odds are worse than one in a thousand—so don't start thinking you should play hands like that. Take the long view. A miracle flop doesn't mean you should've called that bet. In fact, quite the opposite is true.

Even as fortune ebbs and flows, as it must, good decisions over time will make you a winner. Don't be seduced by "what if."

Poker's Infinite Variety

The *New York Times* estimates that more than 50 million people play poker in the United States alone, and Europeans are going crazy for it too. With millions of possible hands and all these people to play them, you can clearly see that no two hands, no two games, will ever be the same. Because poker is "a people game played with cards, not a card game played by people," how you play a hand varies depending on who you're facing, the history of the game you're in, whether it is loose or tight, the stakes, and a host of other factors. Even Hold'em, which has only 169 possible starting hands, has infinite variations.

FACT

Poker's origins are a little fuzzy, but it can be traced back to the French games *Bouillotte* and *Ambigu* and the English game, *Brag*, all played in the 1700s. These evolved into the German game *pochspiel* ("the bragging game") and the three-card French bluffing game *poque*, which became "poker" after colonists brought it to New Orleans. Consensus is that the name comes from the French word "pocher," which means to bluff, and/ or the German word "pochen," which means to boast.

You might know your opponents like brothers, but they still may vary their styles *within the same game*. Sometimes this happens intentionally, and sometimes it's due to factors like whether they are winning or losing. The variables are endless. It's no wonder that poker is called the chess of card games!

All poker discussions must by necessity be laden with "what ifs" and "it depends." That's not a cop out. That's just the way it is. Relatives will try to pin you down on strategy. They'll ask stuff like, "What percentage of starting hands do you play?" and "Do you raise with small pairs?" You'll struggle. You'll wrack your brain for a clever answer, but in the end you'll have to tell them, "It depends." And it does. There is no way to answer questions like that for all situations. Reading this book will help make the infinite more manageable for you—and the learning less expensive—but there is no magic potion that will turn you into a winner and no secret formula for playing hands. There is no substitute for experience.

Every Hand Is a Lesson

Play, play, and play some more. Pay attention to every hand, even the ones you're not in. Watch the players—their mannerisms, their moves. Get a line on their style. Try to put them on hands. Learn from the good players. Do you understand what a good hand is in the game you're playing? Do you know what a good hand is in particular situations in the game?

ESSENTIAL

Until now, most books have encouraged play that is too conservative and cautious. This is called "tight" in poker circles, and tight players are derisively known as "rocks." Now, don't get the wrong idea. Tight is a good way to start. You don't want to lose all your money playing questionable cards before you have learned the game. But you can't stay tight. Tight is predictable, and being predictable is the surest way to lose a lot of money. You have to understand when and how to loosen up, especially in lower-limit games.

Rethink a hand after you've played it. When the game's over and you're back home, lying in bed, replay the game in your mind, every hand. And hang in there during your learning curve—everyone has some early losses. Here are some things to analyze later:

- How did you lose the most money? Was it on stupid bluffs, calling with second-best hands, or chasing with draws?
- Think about the players. How would you characterize each one? Loose or tight, knowledgeable or a hack?
- Who bluffed a lot, and who never did? Who was lying in the weeds with hands? Who was so aggressive that he was certainly buying pots?

- How did that player who bluffed you out look and act during the hand? How was he different the time he had you beat for real?
- Were you too aggressive, or too timid? Did you miss winning bets, or did you overplay your hands?
- What type of hand made you the most money? Which hands cost you the most? How will you adjust for next time?

Again, you're going to have some losses, some bitter nights, especially early on. Even the very best, like Doyle Brunson and Amarillo Slim Preston, have gone broke at one time or another. But they learned. Today they are millionaires.

What better place to begin than at the very beginning? The rest of this chapter assumes that you have never held a deck of cards in your hand and (therefore) have never played poker. What follows are the stone-cold basics.

The Cards

Poker uses a standard fifty-two-card deck. The cards have thirteen denominations and four suits: spades, hearts, diamonds, and clubs. Spades and clubs are black, and hearts and diamonds are red. The colors of the cards have no meaning in poker, and the suits have no rank: They are equal. Thus, if one player has an ace-high royal flush (A-K-Q-J-10) of hearts, and another has the same hand in spades, the pot is split. It is a tie.

The denominations, called ranks, from highest rank to lowest are as follows: ace, king, queen, jack, ten, nine, eight, seven, six, five, four, three, and two. Kings, queens, and jacks are called face cards because they are illustrated with pictures of characters. Some people call them "paints" because of their colorful inks.

Cards have pet names. A two is always referred to as a deuce, and a three is a trey. Queens are often called ladies, and kings are cowboys. Aces are colorfully termed "bullets," or, in Hold'em, a pair of aces in the hole are called "pocket rockets."

The highest card is the ace, although in some lowball games—where the low hand wins—it is used as the lowest card in the deck (in other words, as a "one"). The ace can also always be used as a "one" to make a low straight (5-4-3-2-ace), known as a "wheel" or "bicycle."

FACT

The four modern suits evolved in fifteenth-century France. Spades represented the state, hearts the church, diamonds signified merchants, and clubs, farmers. The kings were modeled after David (Israel), spades; Alexander the Great (Greece), hearts; Julius Caesar (Rome), diamonds; and Charlemagne (Holy Roman Empire), clubs.

There Is Always Another Hand

A session of poker consists of many hands. If you are playing Texas Hold'em online, you could be playing up to sixty hands per hour, even more if there are only a few players at your table. In a casino, you might get thirty hands an hour at Hold'em, fewer if the game is Seven-Card Stud. At home, you might play only ten or fifteen each hour.

Each hand is a small part of the overall game. (Curiously, the cards you hold during a particular hand are also called your "hand.") You can gain or lose money in every hand. The object is to go home with more money than you came with.

You win a poker hand by having more valuable cards than your opponents at the end of the hand. Players may drop out of a particular hand at any time. Once they drop out (called folding), they are out of that hand and do not figure in the outcome, even if they would have won had they not folded.

All poker hands contain five cards. In games where you are dealt more than five cards, you may only use five cards to make your final hand. The other cards are not used, even in case of ties.

Rank of Hands

What follows are the poker hands you are seeking. The hardest hands to obtain have the greatest value. The most valuable hand—the "highest" hand—wins the hand and the pot (the money that has been wagered). The hands are presented here in descending order.

Royal Flush

This is a combination of both the highest straight (five cards in a row) and a flush (five cards of the same suit, whether spades, hearts, diamonds, or clubs). It is A-K-Q-J-10 of the same suit. Only four such hands exist, one for each suit. It is so rare you may never get one. Your chance of being dealt one of these in five cards is 1 in 649,740!

ALERT!

You may have seen the casino game Caribbean Stud, where you are dealt a five-card poker hand. Notice how they always want you to put up that extra dollar to go for the progressive jackpot? The jackpot is usually in the tens of thousands of dollars, and you win it by being dealt a royal flush. But unless they're willing to pay you odds of 649,739 to 1, you're making a real bad bet!

Straight Flush

A straight flush is five cards in a row (straight) all of the same suit (flush). It is identical to the royal flush except that the straight is *not* ace-high. A straight flush can be anything from king-high (K-Q-J-10-9) to five-high (5-4-3-2-A). The higher the first card of the straight flush, the better the hand. Thus, a king-high straight flush would beat a five-high. There are thirty-six straight flushes that are not royal. The odds of getting a straight flush are 1 in 72,193 in a five-card game with no draw.

Four of a Kind

Four of a kind is just what it says: four cards of identical rank, like four jacks or four deuces. The higher the rank of the card, the higher the hand. The best four of a kind is A-A-A-A. By holding four aces, you have every ace in the deck. Note that since poker is a five-card game, you will have an odd card that must complete the hand, so you might have A-A-A-A-5 or 9-9-9-9-K. This odd card, called a *kicker,* is used to break ties in poker, but since two four of a kinds can never tie (unless there are wild cards or community cards), the kicker here is irrelevant. Odds of being dealt a four of a kind: 1 in 4,165.

Full House

A full house is three cards of one rank and two of another. Suits do not matter. A full house can be A-A-A-K-K, the highest, all the way down to 2-2-2-3-3 (the lowest). When determining which full house wins (if there are more than one), the rank of the three identical cards is the determining factor. Thus, a full house of 9-9-9-2-2 beats a full house of 8-8-8-7-7. A full house is often called a boat. When describing your full house, you say "Full house, eights over sevens" or "Eights full of sevens" or just "Eights full." The odds of being dealt a full house in a five-card game are 1 in 694.

Flush

A flush is five cards of the same suit, like five hearts or five spades not in a row. If two players have flushes, the one with the highest card wins. (Suit does not matter.) An ace-high flush beats a king-high flush. A flush of Q-J-8-7-5 beats a flush of 10-9-6-5-3. You describe your hand as a "queen-high flush," or "flush, queen-high." If two players both have ace-high flushes, you go to the next card to determine the winner, all the way down to the fifth card, if necessary. So a flush of K-J-10-7-6 beats K-J-10-7-5. If all five cards are identical, then it is a tie and the pot is split. Odds of being dealt a flush: 1 in 509.

Straight

A straight is five cards in a row of mixed suits. For example, A-K-Q-J-10 or 9-8-7-6-5 or 6-5-4-3-2. The higher the straight, the better the hand. The high card in the straight determines its value. An ace-high straight is the highest. A 5-high straight (5-4-3-2-A) is the lowest. There is no such thing as an "around-the-corner straight" (J-Q-K-A-2). Odds of being dealt a straight in a five-card game: 1 in 255.

FACT

Big John's Tips: In Texas Hold'em, if there is an ace on the board after the flop (the first three shared cards) and no pairs, a straight draw will always exist. Since the ace can play high or low, there will be two cards on the flop that when combined with two correct hole cards will produce four cards to a straight—a straight draw. Try it!

Three of a Kind

Three of a kind (also known as "trips") is three cards of the same rank, such as 8-8-8, and two unrelated cards, for a hand like 8-8-8-K-J. Suit is not a factor. Odds of being dealt a three of a kind in a five-card game: 1 in 47.

Two Pair

Two pair is, surprise, two pairs, and one unrelated card, for example, J-J-7-7-4. You have a pair of jacks and a pair of sevens. You say: "Two pair, jacks and sevens," or "Two pair, jacks up." The value of the hand is determined by the top pair. So J-J-2-2 beats 10-10-9-9. The lower pair is important only in case of a tie. For example, J-J-3-3 beats J-J-2-2. The kicker is also used for breaking ties when two players have two identical pairs. Example: J-J-3-3-9 beats J-J-3-3-8. Odds of two pair being dealt to you in a five-card game: 1 in 21.

One Pair

A pair is the most basic of poker hands, but it's also very important, for a pair gets you an early lead in many games that you can exploit. It also is a strong hand in Hold'em if your hole cards are a pair. In heads-up play (you against one other person), a pair is big, and it often takes the pot in Hold'em. If two players have the same pair, the other three cards determine the winner. Example: A-A-J-9-3 beats A-A-J-9-2. If two players have identical hands, the pot is split evenly. Odds of a pair on five cards: 1 in 2.37. That's a little less than one out of every two hands.

No Pair (High Card)

Half your hands will be no pair (nothing). This means you don't have a pair or anything ranked above it. The strength of the hand is determined by the high card. Example: A-J-9-8-2 of different suits is an "ace-high." 9-7-6-3-2 is a "nine-high." Ace-high beats nine-high. A-J-9-8-3 beats A-J-9-8-2. Identical hands split the pot (provided there isn't a better hand held by some other player, of course). Chance of being dealt nothing: about 50-50.

Five-Card Poker Hands		
Hand	**Number Possible**	**Odds in a Five-Card Game**
Royal flush	4	649,739 to 1
Straight flush	36	72,192 to 1
Four of a kind	624	4,164 to 1
Full house	3,744	693 to 1
Flush	5,108	508 to 1
Straight	10,200	254 to 1
Three of a kind	54,912	46 to 1
Two pair	123,552	20 to 1
One pair	1,098,240	1.37 to 1
No pair	1,302,540	1 to 1

The Game

Each poker hand is its own small game. The object of the game is to win the pot, which is all the money (or whatever you are playing for) that has been wagered and anted and placed in the center of the table. You win the pot by having the highest-ranking card hand out of all the players who have not dropped out (folded) and remain at the end of the hand. If only one person remains in the hand, and everyone else folds, he wins no matter what his hand is.

The winner is determined at the showdown, which begins after all remaining players have put their money in the pot in the final betting round. The last bettor turns over his hand first, followed by the remaining players, starting to his left and proceeding clockwise. The player who must show his hand first is *not* the last player to put chips in the pot. Rather, it is the last player who made a bet or a raise. (Players who match a bet are not betting; they are calling.)

The cards speak for themselves. A player may call his hand by saying "full house," for example, but if he has miscalled his hand, either high or low, it is the hand that counts, not what he says. If you called a hand "three eights" when you in fact had a full house and someone noticed it, you would get credit for the full house. You are not disqualified for miscalling.

After one of the final players has turned over a hand at the showdown, some other players may realize they are beat and concede the hand. They may then "muck" their hands, turning them over face down, not showing them and not contesting the pot. However, in casino play, anyone at the table has the right to see the hand of any player who called the final bet, just by requesting to see it. In home games, this is subject to house rule, so get it straight before the game starts. (The pile of discards, folded, and undealt cards is called the "muck." Thus we get the term "mucking.")

If only one person remains in the hand, that person wins the pot, regardless of what hand he or she has. This winning hand does *not* have to be shown, even if someone asks to see it. This is the origin of the phrase: "You want to see it, you pay for it." It is usually to your advantage not to show your hand.

After someone wins the pot, that person takes the money and a new hand begins.

Antes and Blinds

Blinds and antes get money in the pot so there is something to play for, and so players can't just sit and "play for free," waiting forever for a cinch hand. They keep the game interesting.

Antes are a fixed amount put in the pot by each player before the start of the deal, usually a percentage of the minimum bet. This gets a pot started. Most stud games and non–community-card games use antes.

Blinds are used in community-card games like Hold'em and Omaha. The small blind, located to the left of the dealer, puts half the minimum bet in the pot before the deal. The big blind, located to the left of the small blind, puts a full bet in the pot. This amounts to the big blind making a full bet "blind," without having seen his cards. After the deal, the action is on the player to the big blind's left. He must either call the big blind's "bet," fold, or raise. When the action comes back around to the small blind, he must complete his bet (put in the other half of this bet) and call any raises to stay in the hand for the next round. He also has the option of raising, as does the big blind, even if no one has raised him. On the next round, if they are still in the hand, the small blind will act first and the big blind second, but they are now just players like everyone else. Their role as blinds has ended.

Are both blinds and antes ever used in the same game?
In most Hold'em poker tournaments, when the limits get extremely high, there are blinds (two) and antes (everyone), so a large pot is out there right from the get-go. This leads to some frenetic final-table action.

In most casino Seven-Stud games, a "bring-in" is used in addition to, or in place of, an ante. The low card on the board after three cards are dealt "brings it in" for the minimum bet, or a fraction of it. In future rounds, the high card bets first. (In lowball games, it's the opposite, and the high card brings it in.)

The Art of the Deal

Hey, you can't play without cards, right? Casinos employ a dealer to handle this essential chore. In home games, except for the rare high-stakes ones that employ a house dealer, the deal rotates around the table in a clockwise direction, with each player getting a turn at dealing and, often, calling which game will be played. The dealer shuffles the deck three or four times, asks the player on his right to cut, and deals one card at a time. The player on his left is dealt first, and he deals himself last. Don't forget to offer a cut.

All play in poker goes in a clockwise direction, to the left. This includes dealing the cards, passing the deal, drawing cards, and betting. Players should always act in turn. The only thing done to the right is the cut of the cards.

When a professional dealer is used, as in a casino or serious home game, the deal still shifts around the table, even though no player ever actually deals. This is done by using a marker called the button. In casinos, it is a small, white plastic circle with the word "dealer" stamped on it. The button moves from player to player after each hand. The player "on the button" has the best seat in the house, because in many games, like Hold'em and Omaha, he is the last to act on every round, just as if he were actually dealing the cards.

FACT

A misdeal occurs when the dealer accidentally turns one or more of a player's hole (hidden) cards face up, thus exposing it to another player, a huge disadvantage, obviously. Misdeals also occur if someone is dealt too many or too few cards, players are dealt in the wrong order, or any situation where the normal order of the cards is disrupted. Handling of a misdeal is subject to house rule.

The dealer uses the button to determine where to begin dealing. Since the player on the button is the "dealer," the cards are dealt to the player on his left first. The deal then proceeds clockwise, ending with the player on the button. After the hand, the button moves to the left, and the player who acted first now is the "dealer" and acts last during the next hand.

The Betting

The prize in every poker hand is the pot, but where does it come from? You know about the blinds and antes. But that's just a start. When the action is on a player (that is, it's his turn to act), that player has the option of checking, betting, or folding. The pot is built through bets. A bet is how a player maximizes his profit on a hand, or at least presses a perceived advantage. To bet, he says, "Bet" or just puts money in the pot, within the limits of the game.

To fold (or quit the hand), a player simply says "fold," turns his hand over, and gives it to the dealer. If he is first to act, he should never fold. The only time a player should fold is if another player has bet and he does not want to call (match the bet, also known as "seeing," back in the day). If there is no bet for him to call, and he does not wish to bet himself, he can pass by just saying "check" or rapping the table. He is still in the hand, but has chosen not to bet. If someone has bet, other players must match the bet or give up the hand.

If everyone checks, play proceeds to the next round, where players will receive their next card "free." No matter how poor your hand is, don't throw it away until someone forces you to act by betting. The free card could change everything!

Betting Rounds

As soon as any player makes a bet, the option to check becomes unavailable, but a new option appears, the raise. Now you can either fold, call the bet, or raise. By folding, you are out of the hand. By calling, you are in the hand as long as no one raises. By raising, you increase the amount a player must pay to stay in the game and go on to the next round. To raise, you say "Raise" and put in the amount of all bets made so far, plus the amount of your increase (your raise). Just keep in mind that you cannot raise less than the amount the other player bet. If it's a $5 bet to you, and you raise, you would put in $10. Other players now have to match $10. If someone reraises (raises the raiser), he would put in $15 (unless larger bets are allowed). If that happens, you have another decision to make—call, fold, or raise, the same choices you had the first time around. This continues until all players have either called all raises or folded. The betting round is now over. Hold'em has four rounds of betting: after the deal, the flop, the turn, and the river. Seven-Stud has five rounds. Draw has only two.

There are limits on the number of raises allowed per round in almost all casino and home games. This is to protect a player from being "whipsawed" between two raising players (sometimes in collusion) to the point where he must fold or pour all his money in the pot. Most casinos limit raises to three or four per round. That's *raises,* not total bets. A bet and four raises makes five total bets.

Note that if you are heads-up (just two players left) in many casino games, and the round of betting began with just two players, there is no limit on the number of raises.

Betting Limits

Virtually all games have betting limits to keep the stakes at a desired level. In standard two-tiered limits, designated as $5–$10 or $10–$20 (and so on), players can only bet those specific amounts. In early rounds in a $5–$10 game, players can bet or raise only $5. In later rounds, they can only bet or raise in increments of $10. There are no other choices. In games like $2–$10, common for Stud, a player can bet anywhere from $2 to $10 any time. *No-limit* poker is just what it says: You can bet any amount you have in front of you at any time. In *pot-limit*, you can bet an amount up to the size of the pot any time. In pot-limit, your call is considered part of the pot. For example, if the pot is $10, and someone raises the pot size, there is now $20 in the pot. If you want to raise, you first call the bet ($10), making the pot $30. You can now raise up to $30, for a possible $60 pot, $40 of which is your money. The sky's the limit!

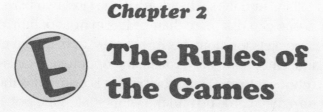

Chapter 2

The Rules of
the Games

By far the most popular poker games today are Texas Hold'em, Seven-Card Stud, and Omaha. The rules for these games are universal throughout the world and are presented in this chapter to get you started. Draw poker is also included, because it is a great introductory game and a good learning tool, along with Five-Card Stud because it is such a classic game.

Table Stakes

No matter what limit you play, in all casino and most home games, table stakes are used. That means a player can't bet more money than he has on the table. Once a player has put all the money he has on the table into the pot, he announces "all-in," and if it's a heads-up game (just two players), the betting stops. No one can risk more than he has in front of him; players cannot dig into their pockets for more, borrow money, or hand out checks or IOUs during a hand. Once someone is all-in, the opponent equals the all-in amount (if he chooses to call), and the betting is over. If it is the last round, players just turn their cards up and the winner takes the pot. If there are more than two players involved, the ones with money remaining can still bet. Their chips go in a side pot. The "all-in" player is only eligible for the main pot, but the other players are eligible for both pots.

Texas Hold'em

Texas Hold'em is a seven-card game with two hole cards, five community (shared) cards, and two blind bets. Hold'em generally uses a two-tiered betting structure with four betting rounds. The first two rounds use what's called a small bet. The second two rounds use a bet twice that size, termed a big bet. For example, if the limits are $5–$10, $5 is the only bet allowed during the first two rounds, with the designated number of raises, and in the second two rounds, there's a $10 betting limit. In most such games, $5 and $10 are the only bets allowed during their rounds, with nothing in between. There are no $2, or $4, or $7 bets, for example.

Even if the big blind's initial "automatic bet" has only been called, both blinds still have the option of raising, since they are "live." For example, in a $4–$8 game, if the big blind is $4, the small blind is $2, and two players call, the small blind can raise by adding another $6. The big blind can raise by adding $4, to make the total of $8.

To begin, each player is dealt two cards face down, after which a round of betting ensues, with the player to the left of the big blind acting first, and the action then proceeding clockwise. Since the big blind is a bet, the player next to him must match that bet (call), fold, or raise. Other players then have the same option. When the action returns to the blinds, they can call bets as necessary, fold, or raise.

When that first round is completed, the dealer places the "flop" in the center of the table. The flop is three face-up community cards shared by all players. Another betting round ensues. The dealer then turns a fourth card face up, called the "turn," followed by another betting round. Then the dealer turns up the fifth and final community card, called the "river." There is one last round of betting, then the showdown.

There are now five community cards all players can use to make their five-card poker hand. A player may utilize all five cards on the board, or may choose to use four board cards and one from his hand or three board cards and both his hole cards. High hand wins.

Seven-Card Stud

Seven-Stud (known simply as "Stud" in casinos and in this book) is a seven-card game with three hole cards and four up cards. There are no shared cards. Stud uses antes, not blinds. The antes are a fraction of the first bet and are put in the pot by all players prior to the deal. There are casino games, $1–$5 limit, for example, where the ante is as low as a dime. Some may have no ante at all. A dollar would be considered a high ante (in a $1–$5 game), but is great for a home game. The higher the ante, the more action.

FACT

Some Stud games are played with a "spread limit." In $1–$5 Stud, for example, a player can bet as little as a buck or as much as $5 at any time, or any amount in between, such as $2, $3, or $4. The only stipulation is that raises must be for at least the amount of the original bet. If someone raises you $5, you cannot then reraise him $2.

The first round of betting comes after players are dealt two hole cards and one face-up card. In home games, the person with the highest card showing has the option of betting first. Sometimes the bet is mandatory, and it must be for at least the minimum allowable bet. In a casino, to build a pot, the low card "brings it in." In a $1–$5 game, for example, the bring-in might be a dollar, a quarter, or fifty cents, depending on the casino. This is the only time a bet can be for less than the minimum.

If the high card brings it in, and two players both have the top card (like each showing an ace), then the suit of the high card (spades highest, then hearts, diamonds, and clubs) determines who acts first. This is true for later rounds as well, if two players have identical up cards that are high on the board. In casinos where low card brings it in, suit is used to settle ties, with clubs being lowest, then diamonds, hearts, and spades.

After the first round of betting, the dealer gives remaining players a second face-up card. This is the fourth card dealt, known as fourth street. (A street is the cards dealt on a particular round: the fourth card is known as fourth street; the fifth card is fifth street.) It is followed by another betting round. On fourth and remaining streets, the high hand showing on board acts first.

Another up card comes on fifth street, followed by a betting round. A sixth card, also up, is dealt on sixth street, then another betting round. On seventh street, players are dealt their last hole card, followed by the last betting round. High hand on board still acts first. The showdown follows, where players make their best five-card hand. (The two extra cards are not used—even to break ties.) In Stud games using a two-tiered limit, like $5–$10, the low limit is in effect for the first two rounds, the higher limit for the final three.

Five-Card Stud

During the first half of the twentieth century, Five-Stud was *the* high-stakes game. It is a game of pure bluff and guts, because it's pretty much laid out there before you.

FACT

The most famous poker hand of all time was a Five-Stud hand, when Nick the Greek won a half-million-dollar pot from Johnny Moss at Binion's Horseshoe Casino in Las Vegas in 1949. Nick caught a pair of jacks on the river; Johnny had a pair of nines.

Players receive one card down and then four up, one at a time. There are bets on second, third, fourth, and fifth streets. What is that one hole card? That's the question. With just one card hidden, threat and parry, moves and countermoves take place on a primal level. It's not played much in casinos anymore, but it is a good game for home players who want to learn to bluff and read opponents, if the stakes are high enough.

You are constantly presented with the decision to chase or fold in Five-Stud. A pair is strong. Pairing a hole card is especially strong. Aces and kings can take a pot unpaired, if they can stand the heat. Pros used to love this game before Hold'em came along.

Draw Poker

Draw was once the most popular poker game in the country. Many public card rooms in California featured Draw exclusively. Today, Draw poker is rarely played except in home games, but it is a good game to start with. It is also a great way to introduce kids to poker and to learn the relative value of the hands—and how hard it is to attain some of them.

Draw uses five cards, an ante, and two betting rounds. First, players are dealt five cards face down. For play to start, someone must "open" the betting for at least the minimum bet. In the Jacks-or-Better version of Draw, the traditional game, a player must have at least a pair of jacks to open. The player to the left of the dealer acts first, and play proceeds clockwise. Once a player has opened, other players may call his bet, fold, or raise, no matter what they have in their hand. (After someone has opened, other players do *not* have to declare whether they have an opening hand or not. And no one is obligated to open if he does not wish to, even with a pair of jacks or better. He can just check.) If no one opens, players put in a second ante and a new hand is dealt.

Bad Cards? Throw 'em Away!

After the first round of bets, starting to the left of the dealer, players have the option of discarding up to three cards and replacing them with new cards from the top of the deck. (In some home games, a player may take four cards if he shows an ace.) Taking no cards is called "standing pat."

If you are the opener, keep your discards near you, so opponents think that you've "split your openers"—thrown away your pair to go for a better hand. Sometimes you will. For example, you might have a pair of jacks but also four hearts. If you decide to discard a jack and take just one card and go for the flush, you need to keep that discard nearby. After the hand is over, someone might ask you to prove you had a legal opening hand (a pair of jacks or better).

After everyone has drawn, the final betting round begins, usually with a higher limit. The player who opened the betting in the first round acts first. The standard showdown follows this betting round, with the last bettor (or raiser) showing his cards first, and then proceeding to his left. Draw is a great low-limit home game. At higher limits, it can get conservative, but that version is also strategic and full of nuances.

QUESTION?

Are there other versions of Draw?
Yes. In one, you can open on *any* hand. In another, called progressive, if no one opens when it is Jacks or Better, then on the next hand a player needs queens to open. The next hands would require kings, then the next one aces. Then back to jacks and the cycle begins again until someone finally opens. Players ante again for each hand, so this game can build a pot.

Omaha High

Omaha is the most intense and unpredictable of the "big three" casino poker games. It will test your courage—and your bankroll. There are longtime Omaha players who say: "I've never seen a preflop Omaha hand I could raise with!" While others say: "I've never seen a preflop Omaha hand I didn't like." The game is played like Hold'em but with four hole cards instead of two. With a total of nine cards to choose from, anything can happen—and usually does. The catch is that you must use two hole cards to complete your hand. No more, no less. So a player could have four eights in the pocket, but he only has two eights to work with—he'll never even make trips. And if he has four cards to a flush, he really only has two—and the two extra flush cards actually hurt him, because that's two more cards to the suit that will never appear on the board. If your hole cards are two pair, you don't have two pair—you have one pair plus three cards on the board.

It is often difficult, especially for new players, to figure out exactly what their hand is in Omaha—especially in the high-low variation. Even if you think you've lost, turn your hand face up at the showdown and let the dealer call your hand. While he's reading it, double-check it yourself to make sure he's right.

Omaha Eight or Better

This high-low split game (written as "Omaha 8/B") is actually more popular than straight Omaha. The games are identical, except that a qualifying low hand (five cards eight-or-below unpaired) takes half the pot. Cards speak, and straights and flushes don't count against the low. Ace is the lowest card in a low hand, the highest in a high hand. Different hole cards may be used to make high and low hands. Because of the "must use two hole cards" rule, there must be three cards eight or below on the board for a qualifying low to be possible.

Low hands are "read" from high to low. An 8-6-4-3-2 is termed an "eight-low" or "eight-six" or "eighty-six." The 8-6-4-3-2 would beat 8-7-4-3-A, because the six is lower than the seven. Omaha 8/B can be a real action game, with many players seeing the flop and overflowing pots.

If you have four unpaired low cards in your hand, your chance of making a low is 49 percent. If two low cards flop, your chance increases to 70 percent, but if only one low card hits, your chance is down to 24 percent.

Big John's Tips: Unlike in Hold'em, where you shouldn't fear that someone has the nuts (best possible hand) against you, in Omaha, someone almost always has it.

Some Other Great Games

Here are a few other variations to try some time:

- **Razz:** This is Seven-Card Stud where the low hand wins. Straights and flushes don't count, so the best hand is 5-4-3-2-A.
- **Crazy Pineapple:** This is played like Hold'em, except you receive three hole cards and discard one after the flop.
- **Tahoe:** Played like Crazy Pineapple, except you do not discard a hole card and you only can use two of your hole cards.
- **Seven-Card Stud High-Low:** High and low hands split the pot. Low hand must be five cards eight-or-below unpaired, best being 5-4-3-2-A.
- **Thirty-Eight:** A home Seven-Stud split-pot game where the high hand must be trips or better and low must be eight-low or lower.
- **Deuces Wild:** Any game where deuces are "wild." That is, a two can be any card in the deck or used to make five of a kind (five aces is best hand).

Have fun with these crazy games—or invent your own!

Chapter 3

Skill, Not Luck

When you start your poker career, somebody—your mom, girlfriend, boyfriend, or buddy—sooner or later is going to pipe up in all their wisdom and declare: "It's all luck." But nothing could be further from the truth. What is termed "luck" can be a factor during a particular hand, even a particular week. On the other hand, the players who believe "luck" will bail them out are the ones who soon find their money in the pockets of those who don't—even if they're starting out in a friendly home game.

You Have the Right to Choose

You are not competing against an unrelenting roulette wheel that makes the House 5.26 percent of every bet, or emotionless dice whose probabilities can be figured to the nth degree by any kid with a calculator, or a slot machine that takes your coins and spits some back out according to a computer chip preset by the casino. The beauty of poker is that you are playing against people. And all you have to do to win is play better than they do. Your opponents are flesh and blood. They make decisions, many of them wrong. And more than in any other game, you can make your own decisions, too—good, sound, logical decisions based on reasoning and psychology that quite quickly will pay dividends. You are not a prisoner of a roll of the dice.

If you sit down at a Hold'em table with nine others, your odds of ending up big winner are *not* 9-to-1! Your chances are determined by how much better or worse you are than these people. If you're a lot more skilled, your odds could be just 5-to-1, 3-to-1 or perhaps as good as 1-to-1 (even money), given enough playing time. If you're playing against world champs, on the other hand, the odds might be 100-to-1 against you.

World Series of Poker champ Phil Hellmuth knows it isn't luck. In his book *Play Poker Like the Pros,* he writes, "Why do the same people, by and large, keep winning poker tournaments year after year? They win because they apply finely honed strategies and tactics, calculate and recalculate the odds, read their opponents well, avoid becoming predictable, and know how and when to make a good bluff."

Luck Is No Lady

Sure, even with perfect play, you won't win every session. Yes, the quality of your cards will vary from night to night, even hour to hour. But the hands even out. Over time, you will get about the same number of good and bad hands as anyone else. It's how you play them that will determine your fortunes, not Lady Luck.

Calling luck a "lady" leads people astray. It leads them to believe luck is something tangible, when it doesn't exist at all. Giving a name to something that is just an expected mathematical deviation doesn't make it real. The deviations, streaks of good and bad outcomes, exist. They must. It can be proven mathematically.

At the card table, some people call this deviation "luck." The deviation can drive you crazy over the short term, but as sure as the sun rises and sets in the sky, over time, with more and more hands, that deviation approaches the expected result. You can count on it. And you definitely can bet on it! In fact, it's the *only* way to wager.

It's Not Gambling if You're Good

Good poker players don't resort to superstition or "luck" because they are not gamblers, any more than a casino is gambling when it sets up a craps table and has a guaranteed advantage on every bet.

Take this example. Daredevil Robbie Knievel is going to jump a motorcycle over a row of umpteen buses. Looks like he'll kill himself, you say. Well, if *you* tried it, not having a clue about how to do it, you would indeed be "lucky" if you survived. It's a pure gamble, a roll of the dice.

But for Robbie—who has studied speed and distance and wind and knows his bike and has done it many times—while there is still danger, a whole lot of things would have to go wrong for him *not* to clear those buses. For him, it's not a gamble; it's a calculated risk, a small one. He knows he'll make it close to 100 percent of the time.

And that should be *you* at the poker table if you are to be successful. You won't clear those buses every time (win every game), but when you know what you are doing, you will be taking a calculated risk, not a gamble, and that risk will be minuscule. Once you're a knowledgeable player, you can get the math on your side, and a lot of bad things have to happen for you to lose money, even short-term. That's why it's not gambling.

How You Make Money at Poker

Being successful at poker isn't about winning the most pots. Instead, it's about winning the most money. You aren't going to win every hand, nor should you try to. You make as much money from folding at the right time as you do from raking pots. Pros pride themselves on what they call good folds, or "good laydowns." They know that money saved is the same as money won. It may sound obvious, but you win by being a better player than your opponents. Know more about the game and the odds; be more observant, focused, and patient; and keep improving your skills. Let others sit back and think they're good—you keep learning. Their mistakes are your profits. If you're more skilled, you are the favorite. It's like you're a mini-casino with a built-in house edge! Here's how you win:

- Make more with your good hands. Bet it up with the lead, and make others pay to try to catch up.
- Don't get "married" to a hand. Almost every hand can be beaten. Fold when it's obvious you're facing superior cards.
- Don't feel you have to "protect" chips. Chips you've already tossed into the pot are no longer yours.
- Don't play marginal hands. Hands that start out second-best usually end up second-best. Be patient.
- Don't throw in bets on a whim or to "keep someone honest." These losing bets add up quickly.
- Be unpredictable. Vary your play. Bluff once in awhile to keep them guessing.
- Be friendly. People mind losing to a nice guy a lot less than losing to a jerk, and it is a bad idea to make enemies at the table.
- Be fearless and (selectively) aggressive. Play at a limit comfortable for you, uncomfortable for others.
- Adapt your style to the type of game (mild or wild, and so on) you're in and the players you are facing.

Looking for the opposite of these qualities is a good way to spot weaker players. In short, if you can be all these things and play under control, keeping your ego and emotions out of it, you are on your way. As Amarillo Slim says, "You have to have a strong constitution, and no nerves whatsoever."

A Home Game with Your Homies

If you begin your poker life playing in "home games" with friends, family, and acquaintances, you are truly blessed, because these will be some of the most enjoyable games of your life, short of winning thousands on the World Poker Tour. Good players are in love with the game, and there is no place better than home to discover the joy of poker. Here's some advice on making house rules, so that fun game goes smooth and friendly week after week, and getting the money.

Setting House Rules

Without the casino floor people to settle disputes, you're on your own, and if you don't have the rules and etiquette straight, a joyous game can end in argument and bitterness.

Since you're on the honor system, you have to play with people you trust, and you must shun those who violate that trust. It is poker, so you are trying to win money—that is a big part of the fun. But that is not all of it. Camaraderie is important, too. There definitely is a place for quality players in a social game, but there is no place for angle-shooters and sleaze-balls. Don't let a game hurt a good friendship. Some of the following may seem complicated or needless, but you'd be amazed at how seemingly trivial matters can break up a good game.

Who Is the Bank?

The banker collects money, doles out chips and, most importantly, redeems the chips for cash at the end of the night. It is important that this person assume full responsibility for paying off all chips when the game is over. All chips should be bought from the bank. If for some reason someone must buy from another player, the cash should stay on the table, in play, not "rat-holed" in someone's pocket.

When Does the Game End?

Agree on a definite quitting time at the beginning of the night, and stick to it. In a casino or online, you can quit whenever you want, but not in a friendly game, where you are ostensibly playing to have fun with your buds as much as to take their cash. You're not there to take their money and run. With a definite quitting time, everyone knows the score and can adjust their play accordingly. There are fewer hard feelings, and the losers have received a fair shot to "get their money back."

If someone wants to quit early, have him announce it when he shows up, not hours into the game (after he's won a bunch of loot), and *make him stick to it*. Sometimes players will announce they're leaving early, but if they're losing, they hang around. If they're winning, they leave. That is not kosher.

Before you give someone a loan, even a pal, during a poker game, ask yourself this: Why would I lend someone money that I probably won't get back, and that he will use to try to take my money?

Stakes and Raises

Establish the buy-in amount, betting limits, and how many raises will be allowed (three or four is standard). Decide if there will be unlimited raises when the hand is heads-up. Remember that if you allow three raises, that means a total of four bets (a bet and three raises). Make the stakes high enough to be meaningful but not so high someone could "get hurt."

Once you have your limits, decide specifics. For example, if you're playing $5–$10, can you bet *up to* $5 during the lower rounds, and up to $10 on the higher rounds? Or can you *only* bet $5 on the lower rounds, and *only* $10 during the higher?

Will you play table stakes? Or will you allow players to dig into their pockets during a hand? How about borrowing money from others to play? Will IOUs be accepted? When will they be paid off? You can see the financial morass that can occur, even in a friendly game. IOUs have broken up the best of friendships, and they have a peculiar way of becoming worthless the morning after.

Decide if you are going to allow check-raising. Check-raising, also called "sandbagging," is one of your main weapons for maximizing profit on a great hand, but many home games ban this move because it seems too underhanded. New players interpret it as being so deceptive as to be unfriendly, designed solely to trick someone, then gouge him. Of course, it is nothing of the sort, it is just good poker. You're supposed to be deceptive and maximize profits. Any good home game should be able to handle the check-raise, especially if you hope to graduate to casino poker. Many groups put this to a vote.

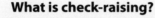

What is check-raising?
If you check, another player bets, and then you raise him, that is a check-raise. It is the ultimate deceptive play. You have feigned weakness, then hit back with power. It can demoralize or anger opponents, sometimes both.

Misdeals

Decide what constitutes a misdeal. You can follow casino rules or make your own. For example, if a player is given a card face up that should be down, in the casino he can't keep it. He gets a new card after that round of cards is dealt. In some home games, the player gets to choose if he wants the card. In most casinos, if a player has too many or too few cards, the hand is thrown in. At home, players may try to make it work, perhaps by giving him a card from the top of the deck or taking a card at random from his hand. The important thing is that everyone agrees (or at least a majority), and everyone knows the policy up front.

Getting Along

In addition to setting house rules, there are protocols that will keep a mutiny from occurring while you are seeking your bounty. These are common-sense things like saying "Call" or "Raise" loud and clear and staying out of disputes that don't involve you. These concepts hold true

not only at home but in the casino, too. The same goes for always acting in turn, being ready to act when it is your turn, keeping your cards in
sight and on or above the table, keeping your bets in front of you (don't
"splash" the pot by tossing them into the center), and not showing your
cards to others, whether they are in the hand or not. Playing "partners"
with another player or going easy on a friend is resented, and it's not a
good idea to talk about your hand, whether you're telling the truth or
lying. It causes bad feelings, and while it's a part of most home games,
this behavior is banned in most casinos.

If you're in a good game, you want to be invited back, so don't destroy
others' fun by acting like the game is life or death. Poor sportsmanship,
complaints, and boorishness can ruin a game. Everyone loses hands.
Getting angry, throwing things, accusing others of cheating, criticizing
someone's play, snapping at players, and being a downer can cast a pall
over the game and make it seem like you are only there for the cash.
People will feel bad about winning, and that's just no fun. You want to
treat people in a way that will make them want to come back for more,
win or lose.

FACT

Whining about getting bad hands is the sign of a loser. Good players
know it's the way you play the poorer hands that determines if you will
win or lose. By complaining about your ill fortune, you are admitting that
you are a bozo who needs to get lucky to win.

The Typical Home Game

What, you don't have a home game? Go organize one! Grab your buds,
watch a World Poker Tour (WPT) event together, and then start playing.
Have fun. And ladies, there are more and more "girls' poker nights" happening all over. Go for it.

You will be amazed at how similar home games are all over the
world. They're friendly, affordable gatherings with maybe one guy playing over his head, and one or two under theirs. There are really only two
variations: first are the games that are real loose, with a lot of people just

calling, and second are the games that are real loose, with a lot of people raising.

The first variation is definitely more plentiful. The common denominator is that there are a lot of people in every hand, even on the later streets, and tight players are thought strange. Folks have come to play, so they play a lot of starting hands—and stick with them. They want to be in action, not on the sidelines. Hunches are followed, not the odds. A miracle draw is reason enough to call a bet or even a raise. Bluffing isn't easy, and often players call with next to nothing just to "keep you honest." "Better to throw money away than be bluffed out!" is the prevailing philosophy.

In the best of the games, there will be drinking, smoking, eating, loose talk, and a lot of banter. Groups have been known to meet regularly for a decade or more.

Winning in a Home Game

While it's true that "luck" is a bigger factor in home games than in a casino, it's still the skillful players who win over time. You just have to adapt. You can still play solid poker, but you won't be as tight as in a casino. First of all, if you're too tight, you'll get abuse from your buds. Second, with more players in the hand and bigger pots, you will have the odds to play some marginal hands that won't hit as often but that will pay off big when they do.

Fold More Often Than Your Opponents

Even though you can play more starting hands, you're still going to fold more hands than most of the others, and you're not going to stay with the hand if it doesn't develop fast (unlike your pals). Even though others may be in with some real trash, with so many hands out there you're not guaranteed a win. *Money saved is money earned.* You *can* be patient at home—just try to play tight without appearing to. Complain about your bad hands when you fold. They'll understand.

Starting out with second-best hands is asking to be second-best at the river, and being second-best is where you lose the most money. Watch your home game, and you'll see for yourself: The loosest player at the table may win a lot of pots, but he'll be the big loser most often, because he's always finishing second. Better to drop out of the race than to be runner-up.

FACT

Even pocket aces, the best starting hand in Hold'em, are an underdog in a large field. Aces win 88 percent of the time against one player, but against six random hands staying to the river, they're lucky to win half the time.

When You Have It, Bet It

Don't worry about people folding when you have a monster hand, unless it's sitting on the board. No one's going to believe you have it. These folks came to play. They didn't come to fold. Your winning hand will get paid off, even on the river. You don't have to finesse people with check-raises. Just bet. In fact, check-raises might just *lose* you money, because that's one of the few times they'll believe you have the nuts.

Bluff Early

They say you can't bluff in a loose game, but unless the stakes are too low, you *can* do it selectively. Know your players. There always will be someone to bluff, either a player over his head financially, one afraid of losing, or one who analyzes too much. But there will be many more who would rather throw in that last bet than risk the "emasculation" of being bluffed out. And you can't bluff someone who isn't skilled enough to know what your bets mean and put you on a hand. In large pots, as in many casino games, someone will "sheriff" the pot when it gets huge. Someone will "keep you honest."

But getting caught bluffing isn't all bad in a home game. In fact, it is a good idea to bluff early and often, *until you are caught*. Make sure when you are nabbed that everyone knows it. The memory of this bluff will stick with them all night, and for many games to come, so stop trying to buy pots for awhile. Meanwhile, your opponents will pay off your big hands over and over again with nothing.

Easily Read Home Players

Some pros say that reading players is futile in a wild home game, but that couldn't be further from the truth. Home players are actually easier to read because they are less skilled and less guarded. Some are advanced enough to at least try to mask their feelings, but they never get beyond the "acting weak when strong, strong when weak" stage. You won't have to look too deep to figure a player out.

The few who bluff will act noticeably different during their bluff. The talker will suddenly be still, the quiet one will talk, the nervous one will be calm, the calm one nervous, the one who always looks around will look straight ahead, and the one who usually stares right at you will suddenly be looking anywhere but in your eyes. Bluffing is so rare it's easy to spot.

It's also easy to tell if someone's on a draw or just how strong his hand is. Players' bets are not consistent. The mannerisms and force vary. The vibe is not disguised. They are open books, and you can use this information to win at home.

Is He Bluffing, or Just Drunk?

Drinking and poker don't mix, unless your primary objective is to drink with poker as a little diversion. If you must drink, only do it at a home game, and at least be less impaired than your buds. Raking in pots is just as much fun as blindly throwing money around in a drunken stupor.

Watch for changes in style as players drink. Just when you didn't think the game could get looser, it does. Some players who never bet and never bluff might actually do both. Players will try to drive you out of pots, or refuse to fold, and you may take some bad beats from players who don't even know what hand they have. Just chalk it up to the charm of a home game!

ALERT!

Watch out for false tells with drunken players, and tells that have changed from when they were sober. Also, it can be very hard to read a player too drunk to know—or care!—what he has.

Know the Secrets of the Crazy Games

Part of the appeal of a home game is that the dealer can call any game he wants. Crazy community-card games like Criss-Cross, games where you pass cards to other players, games with one or more wild cards . . . it's enough to make a serious player throw up. But not so fast! Before you look down your nose at these games, think about what a gold mine they really are. Wild games build pots. And the pots are built by wishful thinking a good player can exploit.

If you are a student of poker and one of the better players at the table, you should easily be able to make money with these variations. It's quite simple. Most players don't understand that you need a monster hand to win wild-card games, and they wind up pursuing straights and flushes when someone always has a full house, or a full house in games where you know someone will get at least four of a kind.

Common Mistakes

To win home games, just avoid these bad plays your opponents will make frequently:

- Slow-playing strong hands. Giving free cards so other players will stay in and build a pot will get you beat.
- Not raising enough. Raise when you're ahead. Don't wait for a lock. And make sure you raise on the river.

- Being afraid to fold. You're not less of a man—or woman—if you fold. Play smarter than them.
- Not realizing that with more players in, it will usually take a better hand than usual at the river to win.
- Not having fun, win or lose. Be a good sport so you'll be invited back. Don't be a sore loser or a sore winner!
- Not knowing who the dangerous player in your home game is. He's the one to watch.

Remember these few pieces of advice, and your home game will always be fun and profitable.

Chapter 4

E Odds and Probability in Poker

Since you're not relying on luck, you know you will make money by playing hands that give you the best opportunity to win. Your aim is to face players with worse hands during play (so you can bet) and at the showdown (so you can win). Poker is bound up in precisely calculable probabilities that represent the likelihood of an event occurring, such as being dealt a specific card. Poker odds indicate the chance of making a particular hand, and the likelihood that your hand will be the winner.

Get the Odds on Your Side

Every expert poker player has two main sets of skills: the psychological and the mathematical. The psychological enables you to find patterns and weakness in your opponents and divine their hands; the mathematical helps you decide your chance of winning, and therefore how much money to invest. The mathematical—the subject of this chapter—cannot alone make you into a champion player, but without understanding probability you will surely be lost. You must be able to know quickly when a hand is a favorite or a longshot, and what your chances are. Without that, you cannot make the right decisions, even if you know your opponents' cards!

The Dream of the Mathematical Player

Players who rely on odds alone are never top players, but they don't lose much, either. In fact, there are players who are grinding out a small living with little more than odds skills right now. The math can help you when all else fails, like when you don't have a read on someone or when you're on a draw and don't know whether to try to chase someone down.

The paradox of probability in its purest form is that it can tell you with mathematical certainty what will happen *over time,* like how often you'll make your flush draw or inside straight, but it cannot tell you if you'll make it *this time.* This certainty/uncertainty is just one of the quandaries that keep people coming back to the poker table.

It is the dream of the mathematical players that they can use probability to make the correct decision on every hand, to use math alone to have a built-in edge like the casino has on a slot machine or craps. Alas, they often can't do this without knowing everyone else's cards (and in some cases, using a computer). Thankfully, most math-oriented players aren't as good at reading people, betting, or playing fearlessly as they are at figuring odds, or we'd all be in trouble.

The Anti-Gamblers

"Percentage players" are like anti-gamblers. While gamblers will play hunches and streaks, math guys seek to only bet when they have a mathematical advantage. For example, the Gambler says he'll pull an ace out of the deck, but wants odds. The Numbers guy thinks: "There are 52 cards and 4 aces. His probability is 4 out of 52, or 1 out of 13. So correct odds are 12-to-1. On average, he'll hit once for every twelve losses. If I give him 12-to-1 for $100 a pop, he'll lose twelve times for $1,200, but then get $1,200 for his win. It's a tie. But I'll come out ahead if I offer him only 11-to-1," the Numbers guy ponders, "and only have to pay him $1,100 when he wins, so I'll have $100 profit. I've got the best of it!" The Gambler, who may or may not know the real odds, takes the 11-to-1 because he's *sure* he'll pull that ace out, but of course, unless he is clairvoyant, he's going to lose, over time, $100 to the Numbers guy for every thirteen times he pulls a card. It's a bad bet.

Can you see how the Gambler might win over the short term? He pulls six cards, no ace, and loses $600. He finds an ace on the seventh try and wins $1,100. He's won $500, if he walks away. Do you know any gamblers who would walk away? Didn't think so, but the math guys would walk. Except that they wouldn't have taken the worst of it in the first place, would they?

The Gambler might do all right at poker, though, when he drives the predictable math major out of pot after pot. At poker, percentage players can get killed by streaky, fearless players, especially over the short term. The Numbers guys go through horrible times where the gods of math seem to have deserted them. The good ones take comfort in the long term and stay the course, waiting for the deviation to approach the midpoint. For players who rely *only* on math, however, that long-term breakthrough can be elusive in poker, because understanding probability is only a way to begin. Getting the best of it isn't a bad way to start out, as long as you realize that in poker, it isn't always clear who has the best of it. Having the best of it depends on much more than just the cards you hold.

Figuring Potential, Knowing Your "Outs"

During play, while your hand is still building, it only has potential. You either want your cards to be the best at every point in the hand (in which case you will often be betting like crazy), or you want them to have the potential to be the best hand at the end (in which case you *might* bet).

The probability that yours will be best, as well as your payoff if you make it, determines whether that hand should be played.

Every hand has a value, and you want to play hands that have the expectation of making you money over time. You don't play hands that will lose money. You'll learn good from bad by reading and playing, but good and bad are relative only to earning power. An A-K will win 41 percent of the time against four random hands going to the river, while Q-2 is only 20 percent. Still, poker being *situational*, there are times when you could bet, and win, with that Q-2, even against A-K! But you don't want to be on the chasing side of the odds if you don't have to be. You want to be the favorite and to bet it up in lower-limit games. The lower the limit, the more necessary it is that you have a real hand, rather than just skills, to win.

Sometimes odds can be difficult to figure, not because of the math involved, but because you're not sure what your opponents are holding. It is this uncertainty that makes poker interesting. As you progress, you'll get better at "putting people on hands," and this will make it easier to figure your odds of winning.

But there will be times when you just don't know if your hand is best, and other times when you know you're beat *right now*, but you have a chance of winning if you receive the correct cards. Figuring odds allows you to know how much of a chance you have and whether that chance is worth pursuing. Knowing the percentages is an essential tool when making your key decision: to bet, call, raise, or fold.

FACT

If someone says you have a 10 percent chance, that means you have 90 percent against you. The probability is 10 out of 100, so the odds are 90-to-10 against you, which simplified is 9-1 against. At 25 percent (25 out of 100), your odds are 3-1 against. At 50 percent (50 out of 100), your chance is 50-50, also called 1-to-1 odds or even money.

Calculating Your Outs

Poker players think in terms of "outs"—the number of cards left in the deck that will make your winning hand. If someone is chasing *you*, you're calculating how many outs *he* has so you can discover *his* chance of making his hand and beating *you*. You then compare the outs to the number of unseen cards in the deck to find the odds.

Say there's one card to come in Hold'em, you have pocket kings, and the board is Q-Q-7-2 rainbow (that is, different suits). You figure someone has a queen in the hole for trip queens. The only way you win is if a king comes. There are two left in the deck. (Yes, it's possible someone might have folded a king, but when figuring outs you must use *all* unseen cards, because you just don't know.) So you have two outs. There are only six seen cards: your two kings and the four board cards. Subtracting six from fifty-two leaves forty-six. Your probability is 2 out of 46, which is the same as 1 out of 23. You'll make your hand once in twenty-three tries. This makes your odds 22-to-1, or a true longshot. (If you're interested in percentages, divide 2 by 46 [or 1 by 23], and you arrive at 4.3 percent. You will make this draw only about four times out of a hundred tries!)

Seven-Stud Example

You are playing Seven-Stud. There's one card to come, and your lone opponent has Q-8-K-K on board. He bets. You're *sure* all he has is a pair of kings. You have an ace and believe that if you pair your ace you will win, as long as he doesn't make two pair or trips. (You hope he doesn't have a straight or flush draw hidden.) No other aces have appeared, so there are three left. To figure your probability of getting an ace, subtract the cards you have seen from fifty-two, then divide by three. You've seen your six cards, your opponent's four up cards, and six other up cards folded by other players. That's sixteen. Subtracted from fifty-two, that leaves thirty-six unseen cards, three of which are aces. Your probability of getting an ace is 3 in 36. Simplified, that's 1 in 12, or (in terms of odds) 11-to-1 against. You have just 1 chance in 12 of pairing the ace, but even then you're not guaranteed a win—your foe can also improve.

Hold'em Example

You're playing Hold'em, and you have pocket aces. The board is A-6-7-10, all spades. You're sure that at least one of your two remaining foes has a spade for an ace-high flush. There's a bet to you. Do you call? An aces-over full house would be a guaranteed winner. What is your chance of making it? (Actually, someone with trip sixes, sevens, or tens could make four of a kind to beat you. What is the chance of that? Subtract the known cards—four on board, two in his hand, and two in your hand—from fifty-two, and you get forty-four unknown cards. There is one card that would make quads, so his odds are 43 to 1—so remote as to be discounted. You're just going to assume no one's going to make quads.)

FACT

Odds versus probability: The probability of pulling a specific card, like the ace of spades, out of a fifty-two-card deck is 1 in 52 because there is one correct event out of fifty-two possible outcomes. There's 1 chance for, 51 against. In odds form, that's stated as "51-to-1 against" or "51-1 against."

Back to your problem: whether to call. First of all, you're drawing to the winning hand. You shouldn't draw to hands that might end up second-best even if you hit it. Second, how many outs do you have? You have one ace (to hit quads) and three sixes, three sevens, and three tens that will make your full house. That's ten outs out of an unseen deck of forty-six cards (you've subtracted the board and your two aces from fifty-two). The odds against you are 36-to-10. Simplified, that's 3.6-to-1. Not bad, especially since there's a nice pot built up.

But wait. If you are *sure* that an opponent has a set (trips) of sixes, sevens, or tens, then you have to subtract three cards from your outs and two from the unseen cards. (That's two from the pair in his hand that can't help you make your full house, and the fourth card of that rank that is in the deck and no longer an "out" because it would give him quads.) Now your odds are 37-to-7, or 5-to-1. (You get 5-to-1 by dividing 7 outs into the 44. You arrive at 6.3, which you round to 6, more than close enough. You have 1 chance in 6, so your odds are 5-to-1.) This is getting to be a longshot.

Pot Odds to the Rescue

You know you like to be ahead in a hand. You like to have others chasing you and praying for miracles, not the other way around. And if you feel that way, you know the conservative math guys feel the same way, double. But is it ever "right" to go for a draw, to chase a card, to go for a longshot?

Even the percentage players would answer this with a resounding "Yes!" And the reason is something that pros have known for years: pot odds.

When you use pot odds, you are simplifying a difficult decision by turning it into a standard proposition bet, like the Gambler and Numbers guy did when they bet on pulling an ace out of the deck. You compare how much it will cost you to call against how much is in the pot, and you can quickly see if you are getting a fair return. In the above Hold'em example, you are getting 5-to-1 to make aces full and win. Say the game's $10–$20 and it's going to cost you $20 to call. Sounds steep, considering you'll only hit the hand once every six tries. But then you look at the pot. There's at least $150 in there! The pot is laying you 150-20, or 7.5-to-1 odds, 50 percent better than the correct 5-to-1. So you definitely call. Think about it: Over many similar situations, you will lose your $20 five times for a total of $100, but you'll win one time for $150. You're up $50 for every six occurrences, on average! This is the elusive edge top players try to achieve on every hand. While you are a big underdog to hit your hand, the pot odds give you the best of it over time.

Taking less than proper odds from the pot is no different than going to the track and taking 3-1 odds on a horse that should be a 6-1 longshot. You'll be out of money very quickly, always taking the worst of it. Treat the pot as a bookie, and get better than correct odds, or don't bet.

Here's a Stud scenario. There is one card to come, and you have four cards to a spade flush, your only chance of winning. You're sure your lone opponent has no more than a high pair, but you know you won't be able to win on a bluff. Out of thirteen spades, you have four, but you've seen four others folded by other players. That leaves you five outs. You subtract the cards you've seen (your six, your opponent's four up cards, and seven folded cards) from fifty-two and get thirty-five. Your chances are 5 out of 35, which is 30-5, or 6-to-1 against. It'll cost you $20 to call, and there's $60 in the pot. The pot's laying you just 3-to-1 odds. You need at least 6-to-1 to break even in the long run, so you fold. It's a sucker bet—there's not enough in the pot to make chasing worthwhile. For every $60 you would win, you would lose $120 chasing!

Using Pot Odds Before the River

Using pot odds prior to the river is a little trickier. First of all, it's harder to be sure that the hand you're drawing to will be unbeatable at the showdown. If you're not drawing to the nut hand, that changes your odds completely because you have to allow for times when you will hit your hand and don't win. Pot odds become a much less useful tool if you can be beat, so much so that they often can't be used. If you are going to pour money in on a longshot, make sure it is a winner. If you're chasing a straight and there's a flush draw present, that is not a nut draw. If you are seeking a flush and the board pairs, someone might have a full house, so that is not a nut draw.

If there's more than one card to come, pot odds must be figured one card at a time. Say you're playing $10–$20 Hold'em with A-J, both spades, and the flop is 10♠, 6♠, and 5♥. There are four of you in the pot, and it's $10 to you. You have a nut flush draw. You get excited because you know you have a better than 2-to-1 chance of hitting it by the river. You think the nut flush will be a sure winner. But you have forgotten that unless you're going all-in, you will face a bet on the turn also. When figuring pot odds, you have to use your chances of making your hand *on the next card only*. The bet after the turn will entail a different set of odds. There's now $50 in the pot, your odds of hitting the flush *on the turn* are 4-1 (9 out of 47). You're getting 5-1 from the pot, so you can justify a call, but everyone else folds. Not good. Now you're stuck chasing against one player.

Should I keep track of how much is in the pot?
Yes, so you can quickly figure pot odds. An easy way is to total it up in terms of "small bets" on early streets, "big bets" later on.

The deuce of diamonds hits on the turn, and your opponent bets $20, which makes the pot $80. You're getting 4-1, a borderline call, but you grudgingly do. (For the record, a 4-1 shot is a 20 percent chance, 1 in 5. Your chance of rivering the flush is 19.6 percent.) The pot is now $100, but $40 of it was yours. You could make your hand on the river, bet, your opponent then folds, and you've risked $40 on a drawing hand just to win

$60! Pot odds before the river can be a risky proposition. Too many players use it to justify throwing in money on longshots.

The river is the five of spades. You hit it! Now three scenarios could occur. One, you bet and he folds, having correctly figured you for a flush. Two, you bet and he calls to keep you honest. Three, he makes a full house on the river. He bets, you raise, he reraises, pushing your total loss on the hand to $100. He had flopped a set of tens and now has tens full of fives. Where you went wrong was figuring your outs. You didn't have nine spade outs—you had seven. The five and deuce of spades were not outs, as they gave him a full house. So your odds were 5-1, not 4-1, and they were not good enough to call.

Don't chase draws against just one player. First of all, you will rarely get proper pot odds to call. Second, if you hit a draw, like a flush or a straight, you want a big payoff to make up for all the times you missed. If you must chase, wait for a larger field.

Another nightmare for you would have been if one or two players had raised and/or reraised on the flop. Raises reduce your pot odds. Meanwhile, those players have hands while you have just a prayer, and you'll be facing more bets on the turn. You don't want to be calling raises with just a draw. The pot odds rarely justify it, and you end up taking a big loss on a speculative hand. That's what you want *them* to do!

The hard lessons here are these:

- Don't chase with borderline odds. Get a good overlay from the pot.
- If you are going to justify calls with pot odds, make sure you're going for the nuts.
- Be careful using pot odds to call with more than one card to come, unless you're going all-in.
- Realize that if someone raises, the pot odds might no longer be there to call.

Other Applications for Pot Odds

You will encounter some real loose games, both at home and in the casino, if you start out playing lower-limit poker. In some games, almost the whole table will see fourth street in Stud or the flop in Hold'em. But you're smart. You don't want to invest in trash starting hands that drain your chips. So what do you do? Pot odds can help here. Sure, you still want to be selective, and you don't want to just throw money in with everyone else and turn the game into an exercise in luck. But with so many players in there, it actually becomes correct to see a lot of flops in Hold'em and a lot of fourth streets in Stud.

In Stud, you could easily call with any three relatively high cards, any three to a straight, even any pair. In Hold'em, against six other players, you're obviously getting 6-1 odds preflop, so you can conceivably play any hand that has more than a 16-percent chance of winning. Those would include about any ace, K-7 and above, Q-9 and above, J-10 and above, and of course all the pairs and suited connectors. But don't just play any two suited cards, even though everyone else is. Have a little pride! And patience. Remember, playing questionable hands is valid only if you're sure you won't be raised, with the exception being if you're positive *everyone's* going to call that raise.

ESSENTIAL

When counting your "outs," ask yourself if someone could be holding one of your cards. Consider the board and the other player's betting pattern. If he does have one of your cards, that changes your odds and impacts your decision to call or fold—and might be the difference between winning and losing.

If you're new to the game, pot odds can also help you decide whether to call that final bet on the river. If you're playing well, you have the lead, and you're the one who's bet on the river. But now that someone's bet into you and you don't have much, you're stuck. You have to go over the hand, the betting, and how the cards fell, and meld it with your knowledge of the player. Does he bluff? Could he have missed his draw and now be betting because it's his only chance?

If your poker skills haven't solved your dilemma, use pot odds. If you're facing a $10 bet here, and the pot's just $30, that's only 3-to-1 odds. If all you can beat is a bluff, he'll have to be bluffing one out of four times for you to break even calling. With a pot this small, it's probably not worth it. You don't want to risk a lot to win a little—you'd like it the opposite way.

But say it's a $100 pot. That's 10-to-1. The size of the pot and the odds have your attention. If chances are greater than 9 percent that he's bluffing, you should call. If you catch someone trying to buy one just one out of eleven times, you break even. If you catch someone twice out of eleven times, you're up $110!

Don't just throw in river bets to sheriff the pot. River bets saved here and there really add up. But if analyzing the player doesn't solve your dilemma, then look to the pot. If you're getting big odds with no chance of a raise, the pot odds favor a call.

The Seductive World of "Implied Odds"

You'll hear players talking about "implied odds." Implied odds are a fancy way of saying that if you hit a big hand, you believe you'll get a big payoff, with some raising and reraising on the river. Many feel you can use these future bets—if you are sure they will occur—to justify a call even if the pot odds are below what they should be. The future rewards will be that great.

For example, take this Hold'em scenario. You have K♥ and Q♠. After the turn the board is K♠, J♠, 2♠, Q♥. You feel that one opponent has a straight, the other an ace-high flush. The full house you hope to get will blow them away. You have four outs out of forty-six cards, or about 10-1 odds. It's a $5–$10 game. It's going to cost you $10 to see the river, and there's $70 in the pot. You're getting 7-1, but you need 10-1. You feel, however, that if you hit the nuts, you can get $20 out of each of them. With implied odds, you are getting $110 for that $10 call on the turn (11-to-1), if your "feeling" is correct.

Notice the judgment calls that are involved with implied odds, and be aware that you have left the realm of mathematical certainty and entered the realm of speculation and, often, wishful thinking.

Used correctly, pot odds can be a faithful ally, not a surreptitious enemy. But pot odds and implied odds can be misused if players are just looking for an excuse to stay in a hand. A good player, in general, is wary of chasing—despite the odds, he is still a longshot, and the payoff will occur over the long term, over many games. In the near term, chasing four-flushes and four-straights could put you in the hole. For the mathematical player lost in poker's deep ocean of uncertainty, pot odds are a distant ship on the horizon, a refuge, a life raft. But while they may keep his head above water, they alone won't make him a great player or a big winner.

A lot of players use "implied odds" to justify calling with speculative drawing hands just because they want to stay in action, not because the future payoff justifies it. Don't fall into that trap.

Chapter 5

On to the Casino!

Home games are fun, but every good poker player eventually yearns for the adrenaline rush of a casino game. The casino atmosphere is electric. There is always a game, day or night. You choose the game, the table, and the stakes. You leave whenever you want, and you'll always get paid. But beware! There are some big differences between casino poker and your home game.

Your First Casino Game

Starting out, you will have an easier time if you are not pegged as a rookie right off the bat. There may be a time later in your career when you want others to think you're clueless, but your first casino game is not that time. It'll be hard enough without having a bull's-eye on your chest and sharks trying to run you over. Learn as much as you can about the protocols before you hit the cardroom, so you can act like you belong. If you act like a pro, people just might think you are one.

Stepping Up to the Plate

Whether you start in a California cardroom with hundreds of tables or a small casino with just a few, walk in like you own the place. If your heart's not beating fast, check your pulse. You may be dead! There will be a sign-up board on the wall listing all the games, or a sign-up sheet at a desk. (Sometimes the sign-up for higher limits is in a different area than lower limit.) Don't wait for a floorperson to ask you what you want; they're always busy. Interrupt him if you have to. He won't mind. Tell the floorperson which game you want and the limit, and he'll take you to your table or put you on the waiting list.

ALERT!

Casinos play "cards speak." At the showdown, just turn over your hand and let the dealer call what you have. But make sure he is right about your hand and your opponent's! You'd be surprised at how often they are wrong. And turn over all your cards.

If there's a wait, ask where the tables are with your limit, so you can start observing play. This will put you way ahead of the game when you do sit down to play. Watch who's controlling the action, whether it's tight or loose, and start looking for tells, which are often easier to spot when you're away from the table. The floorperson will page you when a seat is available. If you're not near him, raise your hand—quickly—so he can see it, or he'll give the spot to someone else. The floorperson may ask how many chips you want, or you may have to get them from the dealer.

There are four main poker-room employees:

- The manager, who is the head administrator
- The shift managers, who is responsible for the overall room (one per shift)
- The floorpeople, who settle disputes and keep the room running
- The dealers, who, of course, deal the games and run the individual tables

Oh yeah, and don't forget the cocktail waitresses!

Read the Rules

At home, you establish house rules. In the casino, the basics will be posted on the wall. Read them, without drawing attention to the fact you're doing it, which would tip everyone off that you are new. The rules will cover such things as limits, number of raises, buy-ins, the rake, profanity, and the like. If you still have questions, quietly ask a floorperson or dealer on break.

All casinos play table stakes—you cannot bet (or lose) more than you have on the table. When you put your last chip in the pot, announce that you are "all-in." All casinos allow check-raising.

Casinos don't allow "string bets," that is, putting some chips in the pot, then reaching back to your stack to get more to raise. If you do this, you will not be allowed to bump it up. To avoid this faux pas, simply have enough chips in your hand to cover your raise, or, much better yet, just announce "Raise," then it's fine to return to your stack for the chips you need.

Poker-Table Protocol

You can get away with a lot at home, but this is not going to be true in a casino, where your cards must stay on the table. You can't look at anyone's else's hand, you can't comment on the hand if you've folded, and in many rooms you can't even discuss your own hand. You can't stash cash in your pocket if you've sold someone chips, which should only be done after checking with the dealer.

And follow the common-sense etiquette from your home game: Act in turn, be ready to act when it's on you, don't slow down the game, don't splash the pot, don't abuse other players or the dealer, and be a good sport. Try not to whine, complain, or criticize someone who has beaten you out of a pot. And you don't have to say anything when you win a pot. Just rake in the chips.

Choosing a Seat

If you are fortunate, there will be more than one seat available. Ask for a chair that is at one end of the table, not across from the dealer. From the end, you can see the entire table in front of you. It's easy to watch the action and easy to spot tells. Across from the dealer, you can't see anything but the dealer's mug, and you're constantly swiveling your noggin around. You end up seeing the side of a lot of heads. If you get stuck in one of these seats, tell the dealer you want to change seats when someone leaves. If a new dealer comes in, tell him too. And always be on the lookout for a more profitable table. Just quietly tell the floorperson you want a table change.

FACT

The seats at a poker table are numbered, starting to the dealer's left and going clockwise, ending with the seat on his right. There are ten seats at a Hold'em table, eight for Stud. The most advantageous seats are 2, 3, 8, and 9 for Hold'em, and 2, 3, 6, and 7 for Stud.

Posting

In some casinos, you must "post" some chips when you first enter the game, like a "live" blind, on your first hand. Your "post" acts as a second big blind, and it's "live" (meaning you can raise). In other casinos, you are dealt in like a regular player from the start. Ask someone (privately) before you sit down what the posting procedure is, because it might save you money to sit out until the big blind comes around to you. Or, it might be better if you let the button pass before playing your first hand. Check it out.

Tipping

Yes, tip the dealer. How much is, of course, up to you. Most casinos used to have quarters and fifty-cent pieces in the game for tips, but that is becoming rare. Today, with the $1 chip usually the lowest denomination, you will tip a buck. This means you, not the casino, are paying the dealer's salary. Is that right? No, but you're stuck with it. Remember, to you, the "toke" is just another rake—it's more money out of play. But don't take it out on the dealer: It isn't easy making a living a dollar at a time. And you definitely want him or her on your side.

The world's worst tippers aren't low-rollers playing $1–$2, $1–$5, $2–$4, or $4–$8. These players tip a dollar or more when the pot is only twenty or thirty bucks. Any dealer will tell you that they dread dealing the big-money games, $100–$200, $300–$600 and higher—because they're lucky to pry a buck out of the "big boys"! Sometimes they get nothing.

Bad Beat Jackpots

Here's something you won't find at home, the chance to win tens of thousands of dollars by *losing*! Many casinos rake an extra buck from each pot and put it toward a jackpot that builds to huge heights. In most rooms you win the lion's share by having an aces-full-of-tens hand (or better) *beaten* by four of a kind or better. The winning hand gets a share, as do the other players in the hand. To bring in players, some rooms will bump up the jackpot to $100,000 or more during certain hours. Needless to say, these jackpots are nearly impossible to win, but they're easy to contribute to. They are just another rake, and good players hate them. In fact, many of the high-limit games are not included in the jackpot.

Some rooms will also pay a smaller, progressive bonus for high hands, like straight flushes and four of a kinds. Again, good players hate this stuff. Those looking to get lucky love it. Just remember, you're paying the bill. Casinos aren't giving anything away.

Drinking

It's okay to have some beers with your buds, but in the casino, players take no prisoners, and you have to be sharp. Alcohol is a depressant, and even one drink slows most folks down. Real poker takes stamina, and you don't need anything making you tired. And if you think you can hide tells when you're drunk, you're probably drunk. Drinkers are your prey—don't be one.

Be Wary When "Mucking" Your Hand

Here is a tip that will save you a lot of heartache, recrimination, and money. Unless everyone else has folded, just turn your cards face up and let the dealer read them and call your hand. Even if someone has flipped over a better hand, do it anyway. Someone may have miscalled his holding, or you could have misread your hand or your opponent's. If you throw your cards into the muck pile, or never turn them face up, your hand is disqualified and you cannot win. A hand turned face-up must be read by the dealer.

And if you have won the hand, whether against other players or because everyone else folded, do not throw away your cards (called mucking) *until the dealer pushes the pot to you*. Too many bad things can happen when you start flinging cards around. Even in cases where you do not have to show your hand (such as when everyone else has folded), don't do anything with your cards until the pot is actually passed to you. By the way, if you show your hand to one person, any other player can ask to see it as well.

If even one of your cards so much as touches the bunch of discards and unused cards called the muck pile, your hand is dead and you cannot win. Don't act hastily.

Beware of someone calling out that he has a "full house" or "flush," and so on, especially before he's turned the cards over. An unethical player sometimes will call out a huge hand he doesn't really have, hoping his opponent will impulsively throw away (muck) his cards, making his hand dead. In that case, the original player wins the pot automatically.

Protect your hand. Keep chips or some heavy "lucky charm" on top of your hole cards to keep the dealer from mistakenly grabbing them and to keep others' mucked hands from accidentally hitting them. If those other cards touch yours, your hand is dead. The way some players fling cards around, it's a good idea to keep those hole cards well protected.

Beating the Rake

Poker is one of the few games in a casino where you are not playing against the House. Not having to buck that inexorable House edge, as in blackjack or craps, is a big part of its lure. You don't have the House, with all its power and resources, aligned against you. But the House has to be paid. It's running the game, giving you drinks, giving you space, buying equipment, paying employees, and, most importantly, ensuring you'll be paid when you win and not mugged when you leave the table, even if you quit while you're way ahead!

The payment to the House is called the *rake*. To a casino, the dealer's most important job is to remove chips from the pot and put them in the drop box. Standard rake is 5 or 10 percent up to a certain amount, such as $3, $4, or even $5 per hand. Don't ever play anyplace where there is no cap on the rake. As a rule, $3 is fair, $4 is borderline, and $5 or more is too high to beat.

As a player, you want the rake to be as low as possible. The rake is your enemy. A rake that is too high—more than 5 percent of the pot, for example—will sap the stacks of everyone at the table and keep you from winning. Just as there are casino games, like roulette, where the House edge is just too high (5.26 percent) for you to ever show a long-term profit, so it is with an exorbitant rake.

Seek out a *low percentage.* If the rake is $3, but the average pot is just $30, you're paying 10 percent! No one can win that way. If the pot is $60, and you're paying $3, that's 5 percent, the most you should pay but still too high. If the average pot is $120 and you're paying $3, that's just 2.5 percent. Now you're talking! That's manageable. You want high pots and a low rake, not the other way around! This starkly illustrates one reason why you should not play stakes that are too low: The rake is too high compared to the size of the pots.

Does the rake really matter?
Yes! Keep in mind that if there is a $3 rake, and the dealer is tipped a buck a hand, and you play thirty hands per hour, that's $120 taken out of play every sixty minutes! That's money that you will never see again. If eight players each started with $100, in less than seven hours the House would have every penny.

In many higher-stakes games, a "seat charge" replaces the rake. These are games where pots are routinely in the hundreds or thousands of dollars. Players pay a fee ($9 per player, for example) every half hour to play. That's $90 per half hour in a ten-person game, about twice what rooms make from a $3 rake. But because the pots are so large, the players are willing to pay the seat charge.

Remember, you have to be good enough to beat the rake to be a winner at casino poker.

Decisions, Decisions! Texas Hold'em, Stud, or Omaha?

The three most popular casino games are drastically different. Which one is for you?

Well, the one that is *not* for you is Omaha, and its cousin, Omaha 8 or Better (written as Omaha 8/B, a high-low-split game). Omaha is fun to learn at home, and as with the other two, it will require some adjustment when you play it in the casino. But Omaha—with *nine* cards—is just too unpredictable, too wild, and too difficult to get a handle on when you are new. The fluctuation in bankroll that Omaha players must endure is not a good way to start your casino experience. Even some veteran Omaha players say they've never seen an Omaha hand they could raise with preflop. Omaha is an action game, and to win you're going to have to bet some well-calculated draws—and hit them. More crazy things happen on the river in Omaha than in any other game, and it can eat you up. Start with the other two games first.

Seven-Card Stud (called simply "Stud" in the casino) and its many variations are king in most home games. If you're comfortable with Stud, start there. But be aware every moment that you are not in your home game and that your strategy needs to change. It's easy to slip into home-game mode if you're not careful. Stud is great for players who can keep track of up cards and folded cards, who can figure odds, and who can put players on hands based on their betting patterns and board. Stud has one more betting round than Hold'em, and it's harder to know when you have the nuts. Stud can be fun in the casino, as long as you're not against a tableful of guys in their eighties who've been playing for fifty years.

Big John's Tips: Don't eat a huge, heavy meal before you play serious poker, as it saps your strength and concentration. Instead of rushing to your brain, blood is rushing to your stomach. Eat light!

Hold'em is a much faster game than Stud. Unlike Stud, where you spend a lot of time watching other people play and the dealer deal, in Hold'em, even though you fold a lot of starting hands, there's always another hand coming right up. The community-card nature of the game makes it easy to figure what the nut hand is, and the key skills are betting, analyzing the flop, understanding position, and reading players. Mistakes are punished quickly in Hold'em, and there are fewer surprises. Hold'em doesn't work so well at home, because proper play requires folding so much. But it's perfect for the casino. Find a game that isn't over your head and dive in!

Are You Really Ready to Play?

This is a question too many players fail to ask: "Am I ready to play poker?" Not "Do I have the skills to play?" You know your skill level. What players (even some very good ones) misjudge is their emotional readiness. You cannot play an intense game like poker, which requires focus and retention, if you are distracted. If you're worried about your girlfriend, boyfriend, spouse, job, the big loss you suffered yesterday, an argument, money problems, or anything that has you depressed or concerned, you will be off your game. Don't play disturbed, sick, drunk, or tired.

You know how hard it is to concentrate when daily woes keep creeping into your consciousness. Why risk making a bad situation worse by going out and giving money away? There is real money at stake, lots of it. Be sharp, or stay home.

Chapter 6

Show Me the Money!

Your bankroll is your strength. Money talks, and the more money you have for poker, the more successful you will be at the table. This doesn't mean you take money from your food budget or use the rent check. The only good bankroll is money you can afford to lose. You cannot bet effectively, take risks, and play aggressively and fearlessly if you are worried about the cash or have fewer chips than your opponents.

Buying In: How Much Is Enough?

The secret to buying chips is simple: Don't be short-stacked. Chips are power in poker, and you want a lot of them right from the start. You can't play aggressively if you're hurting after one bad hand. You may not want to buy as many as the big winner in the game, who's likely been raking in pots for hours, but you should certainly get as many as the runner-up. If it's a new game, or an average game, a good rule of thumb is to buy a minimum of thirty times the small bet in Hold'em, forty times for Seven-Stud. In a $9–$18 Hold'em game, buy $300 worth. In $4–$8, many start with just $100. In $6–$12, a $200 buy-in is pretty standard. Starting with $500 in $15–$30 works, and it never hurts to put some Benjamins (hundred-dollar bills) under your chips. If you have a lot of chips, sharks may be less tempted to try to push you around. Better too many, than not enough!

Make sure you find out if "money plays," that is, if those $100 bills can be used to bet with. In some casinos, money can be used like chips, although you still have to buy in. Some casinos allow only Benjamins to be used like chips, while others allow $20 bills and higher.

QUESTION?

Should I leave my chips in the plastic chip rack at the table?
No, take your chips out of the rack, place them on the table, and get rid of the rack. Playing out of a rack slows down the game. Some casinos won't allow it.

At the Table, It's Play Money

The best players are those who, once they sit down, think of their chips only as "play money," a way of keeping score but no more valuable than currency from a Monopoly game. Everyone's faced someone who is underfunded. It is a miserable place to be—for him. It is nearly impossible to win when you're worried that every time you bet, you're taking food out of your family's mouth. You wind up playing conservative and predictable—just waiting for the nuts. Slowly, the chips are nibbled away as sharks catch on and drive you out of pot after pot. They're willing to take a risk, but you're not. It is Rule 1 that you play only with money you can afford to lose.

Don't Be the Table Pauper

Rule 2 is to have sufficient money on the table so that you aren't the short stack—you don't want to be a target for sharks who think you might play scared. You need enough chips to sustain some losses and to be able to wait for good cards to come around. You must have the funds to bluff, play your game, and avoid panic when you're behind. You need enough chips that when you get a great hand, you can bet it up big. The worst scenario is to finally get that monster hand and then have no money to bet with. When you become short on chips (less than five big bets), either buy more or leave the game. If you can't play strong and without fear, don't play.

Protect Your Stake

Rule 3 is not to risk a large percentage of your bankroll at any one session. How can you play right if your whole wad is on the line? A general rule is to risk no more than 10 percent of your total poker capital. (For pros, the percentage is much lower, because they must be able to withstand a losing streak of more than ten games.) So if you're buying in for $300, you need a grand total of $3,000. Seven-Stud expert Roy West suggests a bankroll of at least 300 times the big bet. Knowing a loss won't break you makes for confident poker.

Big John's first three rules of money management:

1. Have enough money behind you to be able to play fearlessly.
2. Don't be the short stack. If you get low on chips, buy more or leave.
3. Don't risk more than 10 percent of your bankroll at any one session.

Playing the Rush, Cutting Your Losses

There are two schools of thought on streaks, both winning and losing. Play like they're going to continue, or play like they won't. Winning several hands in a row is called a rush, but getting on a rush is not easy. In a ten-person Hold'em game, you're a 9-to-1 shot to win any particular hand. So even if you've bucked those odds and won a pot, winning the next one is a 9-1 shot again. Since good players toss so many starting hands, your work is cut out for you. Of course, if you're better than the field, your chances are better than 9-1, but no matter how good you are, you are never as good as 50-50 to win the next hand. Even speculating that you are a 2-to-1 or 3-to-1 underdog would be stretching the chances of even the best player winning a given hand.

Don't Get Stupid When You're Winning

But rushes *do* happen. Despite the odds against, many seasoned poker players fear rushes, and they get out of the way of anyone who appears to be on one.

If you find yourself on a hot streak, you are in poker heaven. Your blood is rushing, your senses tingle, the world fades away, and time stops. You enter an almost Zen-like state, what surfers call "stoked," and you just play the hands, almost without conscious thought. You're "in the zone." You *know* the cards will come, and they do! Suddenly, you have a mountain of chips. The problem occurs when you begin "thinking" again. You may start believing you're invincible, or maybe you get the crazy idea that you're playing with "their" money—you can take all sorts of chances and gambles and play some marginal hands because you just know you're "lucky" tonight. Or you may think the opposite: "I'm way up, so I'm not taking any chances," and just sit on your pile.

FACT

Cashing in: Most casinos have a cashier in the cardroom just for poker players. You do not cash your chips in at the table.

Anyone can see what's coming next. Playing borderline hands leads to costly second-best finishes; tightening up makes you predictable. Changing the style that won the chips leads to losses. First thing you know, you're telling yourself: "I'll quit as soon as I get back to where I was." Too late. This gets back to the popular axiom, "You don't count your chips when you're sitting at the table." The best strategy is to simply play well, and not play any looser or tighter solely because you are up.

Because the majority of your starting hands are "unplayable" in poker, don't bet that your winning streak will continue. And for the same reason, if you're on a losing streak, don't bet that that your string of "bad cards" is going to change either. This is not roulette or craps, those "luck" games where pros say to "press" (increase) your bets when you're on a roll. This is poker, a skill game. Unless you're the kind of player who has to get lucky to win, just keep doing the things that won you the money in the first place!

Don't Get Stupid When You're Losing

Learning what to do when you are losing is one of the most critical skills in poker. You face busting out of the game, or worse, suffering a serious blow to your bankroll and confidence. The secrets to playing from behind are patience, lack of ego, and analysis. *Patience* means stick to your game plan, for hours if necessary, until things swing your way. *Lack of ego* means admit that it may be your own play that's the problem, realize that this particular game might not be beatable, and accept that a small loss may be a moral victory when lesser players would have lost a bundle. *Analysis* means to dispassionately figure out what's going wrong and, if need be, leave the game and come back another day, fresh and with bankroll intact.

The worst thing to do when losing is to try to win it back all at once. This is the classic mistake of a player who is steaming. Frustrated, getting bad cards and bad beats, he doesn't realize that his loss at this point is probably quite manageable. Instead of taking it in stride, he blows up, if not externally, then internally. He starts playing too many hands, betting wildly, making obvious bluffs, chasing a lot of draws, and staying in too long, hoping for miracles. Suddenly, he's the fish at the table, and the good players can see he's on tilt. Even if he's not slamming his cards, cussing out the dealer, and screaming, they feel his desperation. There's blood in the water, and the great whites are circling. A player on tilt is as easy to beat as a drunk.

More money's been lost trying to "get even" in poker than trying to win, so don't be a sucker. If you're losing, play tighter, not looser. The cards are bad, so wait for them to turn, but don't keep sticking money into the game. If things don't change, have the guts to take the small loss. It's only a big loss that can hurt you. In poker, you want to live to fight another day. Frankly, the cards probably won't get better, and your losing play is making you predictable and the table target.

ALERT!

Every poker player has at least once prayed to the poker gods: "If I just get back to even, I'll quit!" Few make it back, and fewer keep the vow when they do, and they live to regret it. If you are one of the fortunate ones to recoup, quit the second you get "even." No excuses!

Take Your Money and Run

Poker is about "booking wins," that is, leaving the table a winner. Have the discipline to ensure that once ahead, you do not wind up a loser. The best way is to set limits for yourself. Since it can be demoralizing to be way up and then have to leave only a little ahead, you must not be tempted to now try to build your chips back to stratospheric heights. You had your chance, so take the win before you go in the red and feel down on yourself.

Big John's last two rules of money management are these:

4. Set a profit target and quit when you reach it, to book a big win.
5. Set a limit on your losses to prevent a small loss from becoming a disaster.

Don't Lose It All Back

Set limits *before* you start play, and stick to them! To ensure a big win, tell yourself you'll quit when you reach a certain plateau, like being ahead 100 times the small blind. This is a huge win in limit poker, so don't expect it to happen often. But when it does, unless you're in the world's easiest game, just book that big win and go play some golf. You're supposed to quit while you're ahead in a casino.

You might try setting a limit on your hours at the table, based on knowing how long you can concentrate effectively. This will only work if you are honest with yourself and have the discipline to stick to your vow. The least effective way would be to tell yourself that you'll quit when you get tired—it's too easy to kid yourself with this one! When you're up a good amount and have not been playing long, try vowing that if you lose, say, 20 percent of your winnings, you'll quit immediately. The important thing is that you stick to your promise! Don't play games with yourself. That's for losers.

Set a Loss Limit Before You Begin

Don't kid yourself that the cards are going to turn around if you go in the hole. More often, you'll run out of money first. If you lose your buy-in, you might purchase one more full buy-in, or perhaps half a buy-in, but that's it! You can justify a rebuy if it's an easy game and you are positive you can beat it, but be honest. Ask yourself, Are you losing because of some freak hands, or do you just not have it today? Are the cards telling you something like, "Tonight's just not the night"? Is the game too tough? Don't keep pouring money into a game you can't beat.

World Series of Poker champ Stu Ungar, one of the best players of all time, once said: "I have no chance at all in a $5–$10 Hold'em game. No chance whatsoever." Why? Because the stakes were so far below his usual game that he could not adapt. His high-limit moves just didn't work in low-limit games.

Stu Ungar's story underscores one of the most essential poker skills: analysis. This is more than analyzing the game—it's analyzing yourself. You have to know yourself and your limitations to win. You must be brutally honest. Lack of self-knowledge, or wishful thinking, creates poker's biggest losers. These are the saps who tell endless "bad beat" stories, whine about their "bad luck," and run to the ATM machines to get back in the game because it's "loaded with fish." There's your lesson. If you have to run to the ATM, *you're* the fish! Take cash to the game, and when it's gone, so are you. *Don't ever bring an ATM card*—it's just too easy to lie to yourself and say you can beat the game that's already beaten you. Usually, there's a good reason you're losing. So go home, or you'll hate yourself in the morning.

The Stakes Should Help You, Hurt Others

The stakes—how high or low you are playing—have a huge impact on the game. Obviously, there would seem to be a big difference between $2–$4 and $50–$100, and between $50–$100 and $300–$600. But is there? The real difference isn't the stakes but in the players' reaction to the stakes. For example, a down-on-his-luck gambler risking his last $20 in the world will be sweating more in a $4–$8 Hold'em game than some billionaire oil sheik playing $300–$600. More than the stakes, it's how your opponents handle the stakes that concerns you. You want the stakes just high enough to keep you focused, but you'd love the level to be either too high or too low for your opponents. Too high, and they play too conservative; too low, and they play too loose. Watch closely for those out of their element.

No-Limit and Pot-Limit: For the Crazy

The basic question about no-limit and pot-limit poker is this: Why would you want to play in a game where you can lose every cent on one bad beat or one clever play? These games—which are grouped together because you can easily have your whole stake in the pot on any given hand—give a huge advantage to the big-money boys with nothing to lose, no fear, and big expense accounts. The all-or-nothing nature of no-limit and pot-limit favor those who like insane—rather than calculated—risk. These games take years of experience to play well, and the learning curve can be an expensive one. Unless you are Bill Gates, save these stakes for tournament play (if you absolutely must play them), where at least your loss is limited to the entry fee and the playing field is more level.

What stakes *should* you play? Pros say to play the highest you can comfortably afford, but on any given night you should pick the game where you have the greatest chance of winning, regardless of stakes.

Give yourself this test: If you have not called a bet because of the stakes, you are playing too high. If you have called a bet solely because it was "just a few bucks," you are playing too low. You'll feel it in your gut when you are "just right." Keep in mind that the higher the stakes, the more serious the game.

FACT

Benny Binion invented the poker tournament in 1970 when he got a bunch of the best road gamblers in the country together at his Horseshoe casino in Vegas for the first "World Series," to settle once and for all who was best. Today, the tournament format is used all over the world.

Games Change over Time

"I'm winning big. Why should I quit?" you ask. Well, if you haven't been playing too long, and the game is still a gold mine, you should keep playing as long as you are sure you can still beat it. But this isn't usually the case. You can only stay sharp for a few hours, and you may have become tired without realizing it. It's easy to kid yourself when you're winning. And the cards may be turning, your rush over.

You can be pretty sure of one thing. If you are an unfamiliar face, the regulars will think you have won that big pile of chips by getting lucky. The sharks will converge on you in the blink of an eye. Sometimes they're even contacted by players, or casino personnel. Some rooms employ "shills" to play for the House. Suddenly, the fish who fed your pile of chips have busted out and have been replaced by some seasoned locals who have shown up for no other reason than to take *your* chips. That's right, *your* chips. Do you really want to play against people targeting you personally?

There is a lot be said for not sticking around when you are way ahead, feeding the House rake and bucking tougher and tougher opponents. After they've finally gotten themselves into this "fat" game, it'll be sweet to get some racks and slowly, methodically, clang all those chips into the chip holders, stack them up, and carry them off to the cashier.

As their jaws drop and they mutter to each other, just nod, wave, and say, "Thanks, fellas!"

Chapter 7

Casino Poker: You're on the Pros' Turf

You know it's casino poker when you look around and notice no one's smiling or talking, you have two callers instead of seven, and no one's spilled beer on you recently! Okay, though you won't find your home game in a public cardroom, you can still find some fun—and profit—if you choose your table carefully. Here's how to recognize a good game when you graduate from the kitchen table to the bright lights and glitz of the gambling hall.

Switching Gears from Your Home Game

There are more differences between home and casino games than just the size of the chandeliers. One you play with your buddies, the other with strangers—90 percent of whom think they're experts. While a home game is a wonderful place to learn and have fun, you have to unlearn a few things when you hit the casino, where you will usually be competing against better players. You can't expect to make as much money from the mistakes of others—you're going to have to earn it. It will be much more difficult to be dominant. The players are more experienced, and you're folding many more hands. You won't be a winner all the time, either. Among your friends, you can play a little looser and use your (hopefully) greater knowledge of the game to take over, but that's much harder to do among strangers.

Patience to the Fore!

At home you can play more hands. Not only is it expected, but with everyone else in, the pots are big enough for you take some chances. In most casino games, folks play tighter. You're going to be facing strong hands, so you must have a hand yourself. That means waiting for good cards. Patiently. Not waiting for a little while, then starting to play trash. Waiting for a long time, if need be, so that when you take the plunge, you can do so with confidence—with a raise, not limping in on a prayer.

QUESTION?

What is "limping in"?
"Limping in" means entering the hand by calling someone else's bet, rather than by raising. Limping is a questionable play because though you've thrown money in the pot, you've shown weakness in doing so. Someone will bet at you on the next round.

A Raise Means What It Says

Unlike at home, where a raise could mean anything, in the casino a raise usually means what it says: I've got a hand. There are players who will bluff, sure, but they pick their spots. You need to quickly get a line on the players who will and won't, but for the most part, unless someone's targeting you as a "new guy" and trying to run you over, a raise means what it says. That goes double for reraises and triple for check-raises. You might go years without seeing a check-raise bluff in a lower-limit game, so don't assume everyone's trying to bluff you. A raise is sending you a message—figure out what it is. Don't be like all those guys in your home game who keep throwing money in to see "one more card."

This is one of those many "It's true, but…" poker axioms. Yes, a raise means you're facing a good hand in the casino, but the higher the limit, the more you will face bluffs and semi-bluffs (bluffing with outs). The difference from your home game is that casino bluffers know *when* to bluff—they don't just throw in a prayer out of the blue. They will bluff when they know you have nothing—and often win—even when their "nothing" is even worse than yours.

In addition to the raises having more behind them, you'll face more strategic raises. Good players would rather cut off a toe than let you just limp in and see cards cheaply. If you're on a draw, you'll have to pay for it. If you haven't taken control of a hand by showing some power, someone else will.

Reading Players: Home Versus Casino

Even the sober home players have many unguarded moments and transparent tricks. The tricky homies will act the opposite of what they have, but there's nothing more obvious than someone who acts all sad and then suddenly raises you! Players love to talk at home, and the more they talk, the more they give away. All the movements, the loose talk laden with clues, the changes in body language when they are strong or weak, the failure to vary their play—all these giveaways are money in your pocket. Rarely will players cross you up by changing styles or mannerisms, especially as the evening wears on. Have a tough decision? Look to your left. You'll see a few players getting ready to toss away their hands, and not trying to hide it.

If you are playing any kind of reasonable limit, you will rarely find these mistakes in the casino, where players are making a conscious effort not to give anything away. The clues to their holdings are much more subtle. You won't hear a lot of talk or see players ready to fold before their turn. The good ones have gone beyond the poker face. They have poker bodies. When there is movement, they strive to make it controlled and consistent. Your opponents will have seen it all before and will be watching you.

ALERT!

Don't be a "calling station"—a timid player who keeps calling bets, but never takes control by raising. Such a player is seen as weak. He rarely wins because he needs to hit his hand to take the pot. Bettors can win by sheer force. Callers cannot.

Other Differences: Home Versus Casino

Your home game may have some players who lose almost every week, but you'll be indeed fortunate if you find a "live one" in a casino game. In a casino, even one or two weak players can make a game profitable, but more often than not you'll be facing players who know the game as well as (or better than) you do. Here are some things to watch for:

- Casino players will test you. They'll invest chips to feel you out.
- You will be facing better hands. Players don't toss in chips to be "in action." You'll have fewer callers.
- In the casino, folks will call you with a draw (for example, a four-flush) if the pot is large. At home, they'll always call you.
- If you don't bet, someone else will. Someone will try to run you out if you show any weakness.
- The higher the stakes, the better the players, though some weak players can be found at every level.
- You can't give "free" cards. "Luring people in" with a big hand is a recipe for disaster. Take the sure thing.
- Home players are always looking for the big score. Good casino players just want a score.
- You won't find many drinkers at the table. Good players know better and seek out drunks to beat them, not join them.

- Your cardroom opponents aren't your pals. They're after your money and don't feel they have to be nice about it.

Don't be daunted by casino players or think they are all experts just because they talk a good game. They have their tells and weaknesses, otherwise they'd be playing $300–$600 limit in Vegas. Their weak points are just a little harder to find.

FACT

Big John's Tips: If someone's staring at you in a home game, it's because you've forgotten it's your turn. In a casino, it's because he wants your money. Or he wants to see if your pupils dilate when you look at your cards!

Choose Your Tablemates Wisely

Always keep your two goals in mind when choosing a game: Have fun, and win money. You don't have to settle for whatever the floorperson gives you. If you're stuck in a game where it's obvious everyone knows each other, why stay? Why be the target? Why be the outsider in what amounts to someone else's home game?

Watch Your Back

It isn't a bad idea to have someone covering your back during your first forays into the casino. Have a buddy with you. You don't have to hide that you know each other. It's perfectly all right. But don't play partners—that changes the whole game. Don't take a "piece" of the other guy's action. That's just one more thing you don't need to clutter your mind with. You can be friendly to your bud and have fun, but avoid bad feelings around the table and bet against him the same way you would any other player.

Most strangers you'll encounter are decent people, but you're going to hear some horror stories about being stuck at a table with jerks. These unsavory types can range anywhere from gruff, ornery old men who bark at anyone who starts up a conversation, to people who won't shut up.

There will be whiners who complain about any hand they don't win and about the horrible luck that has afflicted them for what seems like their whole lives. Even winning a hand doesn't bring a smile to their faces—they just think it's their due. Others are mute except when they win, when they'll give you a detailed postmortem on the hand. You'll find those just trying to supplement their Social Security who will criticize your every raise, while others will try to drive you out of every pot. Still others consider every hand they lose a bad beat, and will loudly tell you how you "never should've played" the hand you beat them with. There are hordes of obnoxious mediocre players who think they're experts, but for every bad apple, there's a real peach.

You're Not Glued to Your Chair

The good news is you can change your seat any time you like and never see these people again for as long as you live. It doesn't matter what they think. You don't have to like them, and they don't have to like you, but you're not put on this Earth to be miserable. Feel free to stand up to these people, even get mad if someone knocks your play. It's common for a little tiff or two to break out, and some players will use their mouths to try to intimidate and to take over.

Remember, aggression is rewarded in poker. So give it back, if that's your style. You'll find that most of the other players will be with you. You don't have to suffer in silence. Or if you prefer, let your cards speak. But for many, it's harder to play if someone's upset them and they haven't hit back. They begin to feel weak and then, sometimes, to play weak.

If the players are too strong and there are no obvious big losers in the game, change tables. Everyone's heard the old poker chestnut: "If you haven't spotted the sucker at the table in the first half hour, the sucker is you." In other words, someone's got to pay the rent. If there aren't a few weak players (be honest), switch tables. And if you're surrounded by jerks, unless the game is a real bonanza, find a better table or better casino. Just ask the floorperson for a table change, and always be on the lookout for greener pastures. Spend your time with good people, not losers who criticize others to mask their own failings. The poker world is chock-full of interesting people to meet and compete against. Introduce yourself to your tablemates!

Playing in a Loose Game

As much as anything else, it's whether the game is loose, tight, or in between that will determine your play. You should know the type of game you'll be embroiled in before you even sit down so you can adopt the correct strategy from the very first hand. So watch first, and then sit.

QUESTION?

What is "under the gun"?
The person under the gun is to the left of the big blind and is first to act during the first betting round in Hold'em. He must call the big blind's "bet," raise, or fold. In future rounds, the big and small blinds act before him if they have not folded.

What Is a Loose Game?

Loose games are easy to spot. They are more animated, with much raising and reraising before the flop and frequent capped pots. When there's not a lot of raising, many players are limping in. Whether it's a "raise-fest" or not, the common denominator in loose games is a lot of players seeing the flop—and big pots. You'll notice a "snowball effect" in many loose games. The player "under the gun" limps in, perhaps with 10-9, a marginal early position hand. Had he raised, this would have made it two bets to go from early position, and many might have folded their borderline hands, fearing still another raise. But since he limped, the next guy decides this might be a big pot building, so he limps in too, also with a questionable early position hand like K-10. Others limp as well, dreaming of a big pot. The pot is now to the point where two things happen. First, no one in late position is going to fold preflop—with so many players, it is correct to limp in with almost any two hole cards. Second, no one expects anyone in late position to raise, as no one will fold for one more bet due to the pot size. Even pocket aces in Hold'em are an underdog to a huge field, and A-K is an underdog (41 percent) to just four players. This is the perfect scenario for those looking to "get lucky." And even in the raise-fest loose game, raises won't always drive players out. Sometimes they will "drive them in"!

Strategy in Loose Games

The most important decision to make in a loose game is a fundamental one: Do you want to play in it in the first place? Many good players avoid these games. They feel that with so many players in every hand, they cannot use their skills—like forcing people out, bluffing, and jamming their big hands—and the multiple limp-ins actually make it correct for poor players to call with many of their questionable hands and draws. But if you can handle the bankroll swings, these games can be quite lucrative. Think about it. There's always a ton of chips up for grabs, and because so many players play marginal starting hands, they overrate their hole cards and don't fold soon enough on later streets. They get in the habit of playing bad hands and draws, and most continue their questionable play even after the game tightens up, as it inevitably will.

Realize you are going to have some money fluctuation in a loose game. You are not going to be as loose as the others—not even close—but you are going to be looser than usual. You *are* going to limp in for one bet with many more starting hands. You *are* going to chase open-ended straight and flush draws, even if there are raises, and you'll be playing second pairs (that is, the second highest pair possible on the board, not only the top pair). As with a loose home game, you still will be one of the tighter players—you just have to play solid without others finding out how tight you really are. You are going to make money by folding sooner than the wild men, not playing as many starting hands, and avoiding that dreaded second-best finish.

Some of your strategy is similar to a loose home game, so make sure you advertise how you're staying in pots. When you bet, act as wild as they do. Even in loose games, most players are very aware of who's tight. If you sit waiting for a monster hand, you probably won't get paid off. But realize that "monster" starting hands aren't as strong against a large field, especially in Hold'em, where there are five cards to come. If you can't drive people out early, you're going to be just calling with any pair except (maybe) aces, and you will fear straight and flush draws on the board. You can be sure that if there are two to a suit on the flop, someone has a flush draw. Three to a suit, someone's holding a flush. Call with all pairs, connectors (suited or not), and even hands like 8-6 suited. Just get away from them quickly when they don't hit on the flop, or your play will deteriorate into the crapshoot style of your loose opponents.

QUESTION?

What is a rock?

"Rock" is a somewhat derogatory term for an unimaginative, conservative, cautious player. While such players often think of themselves as "solid" and are proud that they only play the very best hands, other players deride their unimaginative play and take advantage of their predictability. Rocks are often called "weak-tight"—weak for their failure to raise enough, tight because they play so few hands.

The battlefield is littered with solid players who think they can jam it with A-K offsuit or pocket queens or jacks in a loose game. Other players just laugh and gladly toss in their money and build a pot. A-K is an underdog to a large field, and many a good player has left muttering "I can't play in this game" after his A-K has drained his chips and his opponent, while raking the pot, has laughed and said, "Ace-king no good!" If you are tighter than most of the field and are getting nowhere, and/or you're tired of battling the six or more players who see every flop, realize that you're probably playing stakes that are too low. Stay patient, or look for a more profitable game.

Recognizing a Tight Game

Tight games are as easy to spot as loose contests. Here are some dead giveaways:

- Players are generally older, and there isn't a lot of talking or smiling.
- Players look serious and want to get on to the next hand.
- Players spend a lot of time making sure their chips are in neat stacks.
- Reraising and check-raising are almost nonexistent.

- Few players see the flop. Fewer see the turn.
- Often, everyone folds to the blinds, who then "chop."

If you see a tight game, besides asking yourself if you're going to have any fun there, ask yourself if you have the time and patience needed to pry chips loose from these cheapskates. Your goal is to make money, and there's always another game right around the corner.

FACT

"Chopping" a pot means to split it, as in the case of a tie. The blinds can chop when everyone else has folded preflop. If both agree, they simply take their blinds back and the hand is over. Smart players chop because the House gets no rake. They avoid a hand in bad position and avoid paying a blind. If someone asks, "Do you chop?" say "Yes!"

Strategy in a Tight Game

A winning strategy in a tight game is the opposite of a loose-game strategy. While you sometimes have to hunker down in a loose game, in a tight game you can be the aggressive one. With so many players just waiting for huge starting hands, you can raise and reraise with marginal hands and drive people out. Blind-stealing is easy, and an early raise will often get you heads-up. Realize if you're called that your tight opponent might have better cards than you, but you have a stronger weapon than cards—you have control of the hand, and you're facing someone whose first instinct is to fold, not take chances. If the flop in Hold'em shows lower cards or fourth street in Stud gives him a blank (useless card), you bet it up and drive him out. If the flop or fourth street is stronger, you usually should bet even if you haven't improved. If your opponent beats you in the pot or raises(!), you simply fold. If someone shows you strength, drop out. Don't be stubborn if a rock finally gets the big hand he's been praying for. Just fold.

If they catch on that you're buying pots, watch out for a bluff. Generally, though, it is against the nature of supertight players to risk their chips trying to buy one, especially against someone who shows strength. After awhile, your aggressive style will have the fringe benefit of getting your good hands paid off. Look for the threshold when they begin to catch on. They'll start calling you more often. *Switch gears* at that point, playing only quality hands that will take their chips "legitimately." Watch out for others using this same strategy.

Beware! There is a big difference between an overcautious rock and an expert just playing solid. The rock will be pushed around as he waits for the nuts. The expert is just waiting for quality hands and will push back if you confront him. Don't wake the sleeping bear. He knows your tricks and will set traps for you.

The Ideal Game

The best games, of course, are those where you're the best player at the table. The worst game is where everyone is better than you. You can, however, do all right if there are *a few* better players, as long as you can quickly identify who they are. Most games have a few loose players, a few tight, and the rest in between: tight but not ridiculous, aggressive when need be, loose when appropriate. This pretty much should characterize your own play. If the majority are quality players, ask yourself if you can make money in the game. Often, even with good players at the table, a few weak players will be enough to give you a profit if you play smart.

Remember: If the other players are more skilled than you, the only way you can win is by getting lucky.

Chapter 8

Betting: The Language of Poker

The language of poker isn't spoken with your lips; it's spoken with your chips. How and when you put your money in the pot says volumes about you and your hand and these actions are a key to maximizing your profits. Betting is one of the supreme skills—and art forms—in the game. Bets send a message. It's imperative that the message that comes through is the one you want opponents to hear.

The Safety Zone

Betting is how you control the game or, at least, increase your take in the hand you're trying to win. Your mathematical and psychological skills, along with your knowledge of the game, are all put in action through betting, just as a hitter in baseball brings all his skills and training to bear when he finally swings at the ball. Poker is an American game, so it's all about the money, and through betting you force your opponents to a decision. Do they want to put their hard-earned cash in there, or not?

Poker isn't a friendly game of Parcheesi, and it isn't chess, so cerebral and complicated that it can be appreciated solely for itself. No, poker is all about psychology, guts, and most of all the money—and having the courage to risk it. Risk is the key word. It can't be stressed enough: You have to be competing for something of real value, some significant amount of bling-bling, or there is no reason for anyone to ever fold a hand. If no one folds, you don't have a poker game—you just have a bunch of people sitting around seeing who's going to get lucky.

Play Stakes Where Their Hearts Are Racing

Unless you're playing socially, where poker is a secondary activity to drinking and talking, you should *never* play stakes so low that most people are just calling bets without thinking because they have nothing meaningful at risk. If you are just starting out in poker, *don't* play ultra–low-limit games like $1–$5, $1–$2, $2–$4, and $3–$6. You learn nothing in these loose games where people have nothing to lose; in fact, you'll pick up some bad habits, like just throwing chips in on a prayer. A borderline limit would be $4–$8, maybe okay until you get your feet wet, but graduate to $5–$10 or $6–$12 quickly, then $8–$16 and $10–$20. Keep moving up as long as you're winning.

To use poker skills, your bets must have some bite. They must put your opponents to the test. Make them think. Give them a chance to make a mistake. Therefore, you cannot use your skills in a game where the stakes are so low that calling a bet is meaningless.

Loose games can seem tempting, with so much poor play, but most good players hate them because they can't effectively use their skills: aggression, betting strategies, and reading players. If you are to bring your skills to bear through betting, your bets must put people to a decision, make them choke up, make them think—and fold. If the limits are too low, none of that will happen. You keep *your* focus by playing stakes that mean something to you, too, so you choose the highest limit where you can still play smart and fearlessly. But what you are seeking most is a game where others are over their heads, where they are uncomfortable, where losing the money will hurt. You want them outside of where they feel safe and secure, their safety zone.

The Easiest Money

Outside the zone means "scared money" in poker, and playing with scared money is the quickest way to lose. Playing against scared money is a piece of cake—just be aggressive. Every bet is a big decision to scared money, and it's written all over their faces. Scared players go into a shell and fold hand after hand they could've won, and only come out with a monster hand, at which point you will fold.

This is an extreme case. For your bets to be effective, you only need to be sure players seriously care about the chips in front of them. They must be concerned about losing them and be at the higher end of their comfortable limit, which is where many people play. It's easy to spot. Those who agonize and worry too much are out of their safety zone, while those who call bets too fast and too often and don't seem too concerned about much of anything are too far within theirs. Find a game where they're nervous—no matter what the stakes—and take over.

Making a Statement

A bet is first and foremost a declaration: *I have a better hand than you.* If no one ever tried to bluff a pot, most hands might end right there. Everyone would fold to the better hand. The conflict occurs when someone believes the bettor's full of hot air or thinks he has a better hand—or will have by the river. Anyone who disagrees with your declaration can argue the point by raising you, and if you think he's wrong, you can tell him so by reraising. If he's still not convinced, he can raise you back. And so it goes, a struggle for control, with players butting heads, back and forth, neither wanting to back down. It boils down to *convincing* the other guy you have the superior hand. If you ever watch two good heads-up players go at it, you'll see this reraising frequently—often when *they both have trash hands*—because it's become about who will blink first, not the cards.

Dominance on the Green Felt

The primary purpose of a bet is to establish dominance in the hand. Once control is established, the bettor will often win the pot without a fight—and without the good hand his bet claimed he had. Later, with skill and some good cards, that dominance can spread to the game as a whole. In most games, to attain a dominant position you'll need to bet up and show down some good hands at first. This gets folks used to thinking your bets have something behind them. It is a tremendous psychological advantage to be dominant in a game, as it is in life. But just as in life, you have to watch for the cunning types scurrying around the edges, trying to trap you and bring you down. Don't let your ego get in the way here— you don't have to win every hand, and even the sheriff is allowed to fold.

ALERT!

Don't keep betting to establish dominance if it's obvious your opponent isn't going to drop and has a better hand than you. Back off and save your money. Plowing money into a lost cause will just make you look foolish and hurt you on future hands.

Bet with the Lead

To maintain dominance, you want to be betting it up, making other players think. But they've got to "respect" your raises. They can't just laugh at them or all pile in because they think you're a clown who's just thrown dead money in the pot. Your opponents must believe there's power behind your play. So when you've got the best hand—at any point—you bet it up big and keep the pressure on. This goes for before the flop in Hold'em relentlessly to the river, from third street in Stud to the last wager. You bet your hand strong—don't mess around. Betting is how you take over, so you seek every opportunity to bet it up. And the best time of all is when you're leading.

ALERT!

To avoid giving yourself away, the best way to bet is in a smooth, controlled, consistent manner, not too fast or too slow, the same way every time. Getting cute with different betting styles usually backfires. Focus your eyes on one thing. Don't look all over the place.

When you're the favorite to win the hand, you bet to win the pot *right now*. Your lead is often more tenuous than you know, so you are satisfied to win whatever's there. Every hand begins as a struggle for the antes and blinds, and you're happy with those and any other sure thing this table will give you. Most times, of course, you'll have callers. Then betting is your way to either drive people out or maximize your profit—or both. If you have top pair and top kicker on the flop, and everyone else just has overcards or draws, you're favored to win unless you're facing a huge field. So you bet and take their money, whether they stay or drop. If it's a big field, you still bet, this time to push people out.

Make the inferior hands pay to chase you. Don't ever let them do it for free. When in doubt, bet it out! Siphoning money from drawing hands is one of the most profitable moves in poker, and you must take advantage of it mercilessly.

Bet Like You Mean It

Whether it's true or not, when you bet, you're stating that you have the best hand, so bet with power. Don't pussyfoot around. It makes no sense at all to pretend like you're weak with some sad expression, or to whine about your hand and then bet. It's incongruous, and all it does is get good players thinking and watching you. A bet indicates strength. So when you bet, bet strongly and forcefully. You don't have to slam your chips down, but you are stating you have a hand, so act like it. Putting chips in meekly either means you're playing your first game and are unsure of yourself (not something you want anyone to think), or you are pretending to be weak when you are strong, another rookie move. If you are weak, why are you betting?

A bet means a hand, so be confident. Then, when you are betting with nothing, you can bet the same way, and you have conditioned others to recognize that that betting style indicates a good hand, and they will be more likely to fold. This makes a lot more sense. Maybe you're one of those who wants to keep people in a hand to build a pot. Well, first of all, you shouldn't be playing casino poker thinking like that—in a casino, you want to drive people out and grab the sure thing. Second, don't worry, because there's usually at least one rube who doesn't believe you and will call, at least for a street or two. Remember: Pros look for reasons to fold, but average players look for excuses to play, to call.

It's important to keep this in mind. Unless you have an unbeatable hand, you *want* people to think you have a top hand when you bet. You *want* them to fold. If your raises aren't respected, you may get some hands paid off, but you won't be able to bluff. You'll also be facing a larger field than you want—a field that will run you down hand after hand.

QUESTION?

What are "rolled-up" cards?
In Seven-Stud, if your first three cards are three of a kind, you are said to be "rolled-up." If you have three aces, for example, you are said to have "rolled-up aces." This is obviously an incredible hand.

When Not to Bet

There are a few situations when you should not bet a big hand. One is when you are so far in the lead that your odds of being caught are microscopic, and if you bet, everyone will fold. For example, you flop a full house in Hold'em, and you've got all the cards. If the flop's K-K-Q, and you have K-Q, what can anyone else have? So check, and let them catch up a bit. Hope someone will bet into you, catch a second-best hand, or bluff at the pot!

Or if you have rolled-up high trips in a tight Stud game, you may want to play it coy. Same with flopping top set (three of a kind is also called a set) in Hold'em against a small field if the board's not scary. But be wary. Except for when you have the mortal nuts, you will rarely go wrong betting, but you can go horribly wrong giving free cards to drawing hands.

Besides having a monster, there are a few other times you wouldn't bet a decent hand:

- You have a drawing hand and are trying to see cards cheaply, and betting will not enable you to bluff successfully if you miss.
- You have the lead, but there is a huge field against you that will likely overtake you, and betting will not get them to fold.
- You plan to check-raise or are trying to trap an aggressive player you know will bet into you.

As you can see, there are very few situations when you should not push the top hand. You should bet when you feel you are favored to win to make the pot larger. You must maximize profit from your winning hands (bet), and minimize losses from your losing ones (don't bet).

FACT

A straight-flush draw in Hold'em has fifteen outs, giving you a 54-percent chance of hitting a straight, flush, or straight flush with two cards to come. If you have two overcards that could win for you, that's six more outs! This is one of the few times when a draw could actually be favored to win.

Either Raise or Fold, but Rarely Call

A lot of good things happen when you bet, and a few things can happen when you don't—most of them bad. That's why as the limits get higher and the poker becomes more skilled, you'll realize that your best options are to bet or fold, not just call. Calling is weak. You're just reacting to someone else, so the only way you win is if you have the better hand. If someone's betting into you, that is no sure thing. This is one reason pros get so upset if they've lost a lot of money—or a tournament—"calling off my chips." It's a weak play, the antithesis of dominance.

Amateurs believe calling is an option between betting and folding on the value scale. Actually, calling is worse than folding because folding saves you money, while calling has shown weakness, which will make you a target and cost you money.

If you bet or raise, you give yourself an extra way to win. You know you can win with the best hand, but your aggression also allows you to win by making your foe fold a better hand or potential winner, either right now or on a later street. Pros seek this edge on every hand. That's why they'd rather fold than just call someone who will have control of the hand on the next round.

If you are going to call anyway, and you're not facing a raising hand, it's better to just bet rather than check and call someone else's wager. But don't call just because you have put some chips in the pot. That money belongs to the pot now. And if you've made some mistakes in the hand, don't make it worse. Don't use a past bet to justify a future call.

Give Them a Chance to Guess Wrong

You put your opponent to a decision—an expensive decision—by betting. Your bet must threaten him with the loss of something dear to him—his money—and he must know that future threats will be coming. He must know you as someone who isn't going to just fire one bullet—there's going to be a barrage. Now he's in the hot seat, not you.

ALERT!

If you consider not calling a bet because you are dwelling on what the money you are risking will buy, you are playing too high. If you risk any money not earmarked for "recreation"—like rent or food money—you are making a big mistake. Using that money will hurt your game and your life.

When you make him sweat, good things happen. You've put him under pressure, and you've forced him to make a decision—a decision that might be no more than a guess. When people guess, they often guess wrong, and that's another way for you to win.

Good things happen when you bet. You establish a strong image, make opponents react to you, and take control. You give yourself multiple ways to win, and you get an idea of the strength of other hands. You force others to act. In return, you obtain information.

What's the worst that can happen? Someone has a hand? Then you fold. There's no shame in that—that's just being smart. But more often than not, he *won't* have a hand, but he will think *you* have one because you're putting your money where your mouth is and doing it strongly and fearlessly.

Not Betting Invites Rout

There are a host of bad things that occur if you just call or limp in:

- You lose control of the hand.
- You create a weak image.
- You don't drive others out of the pot.
- You invite bets and bluffs.
- You become a target on future streets.
- You allow drawing hands to beat you.

By just calling, you send a message that your hand is not to be feared. Unless you get real lucky, you're just throwing money away.

Hammer Your Foes with Raises

A raise is a bet—on steroids! You can send a message with a bet, but a raise is special delivery. If they still don't get it, a reraise or check-raise will hammer your point home like a telegram delivered by Sammy the Bull. There are tight games where raising is rare and reraising nonexistent, where players won't bet with A-K. You'll find aggressive games where folks not only raise with A-K, they will reraise with it or even cap the pot. It's all relative to the style of game and the hands your opponents are playing.

But one thing remains the same. A raise is a club you use to bludgeon your opponents who have popped their heads up into your line of fire by daring to bet. You slap them down with a raise. A raise can be so unexpected that the momentary unguarded look on your opponent's grill will tell you everything you need to know about his hand. With some players, the look won't even be guarded—they'll just start whining!

All that goes double for a reraise. A reraise (raising someone who's already raised) not only slaps him down, it stomps him into the dirt. Be careful, though, with a reraise if the person who raised you is the type to never bump it up without a huge hand.

QUESTION?

What is the "nuts"?
The "nuts" is the best possible hand based on your cards and the cards of all the other players still in the hand. An unbeatable hand. For example, if the board in Hold'em is 2-2-J-9-6, the best possible hand is four deuces—two deuces on the board and two deuces for someone's hole cards. If there are three spades on board and no pair, the nuts is an ace-high flush. Anyone with two spades in the hole, one of which is the ace, has the nuts.

Check-Raising

Check-raising can be the most devastating bet of all. A check-raise flat out tells the whole table that you have such a monster that you could afford to sit and wait for someone else to bet with the sole purpose of sucking more chips out of him. Its power is demoralizing and its element of surprise is devastating. This is so true that in tighter games, it can even be used as a bluff if you are against thinking players, as the check-raise is stating unequivocally that you have the nuts. The check-raise always gives away your hand, so decide first if it is the best way to maximize your profit or if you should be more straightforward.

The same can be said of the re-reraise. In most games, this would cap the pot, and in many games you won't get a cap without someone having pocket aces or sometimes kings preflop. A re-reraise is like a check-raise in that the re-reraiser is saying he has the nuts, and you should probably believe him. If you're in a position to cap it, think first. If it's not the river, sometimes it's best to hold back that last bet to disguise your hand and make more money on later streets, as long as your hand is not in danger.

It is important to make your opponents aware that you will check-raise and slow-play. If they don't believe you'll ever use these moves, then whenever you check, you invite an automatic bet from someone behind you.

"Tells" are cues shown by a player that either give away his hand (a big smile when he hits), some trickery (playing a hand differently than expected), a bluff (always tugging on an ear when he's lying), or his personality (counting his chips after every hand).

Send Out a Probe

Bets can do more for you than just intimidate your opponents and send them a message. They can act as expendable probes scouring an alien landscape, or unmanned drone planes flying low over the mountains of Afghanistan, searching for terrorists. If they're shot down, no harm done, but the information they gather could keep you from getting massacred.

Early in a hand, when the limits are lower, sending out a feeler bet will help you get a line on your opponent in a hurry. For example, say you have pocket kings in Hold'em. You've bet them preflop, have two callers, and then a dreaded ace flops with a six and a four. If you're first, you must bet. If you are raised, you have your answer—someone has aces. So you fold. If someone else bets first, and that isn't enough of a sign he has aces, then raise. If you are raised back, you know.

In Seven-Stud, feeler bets are even more important. Expert Stud players often say it's all over by fifth street. Why? Because top players send their chips out on a mission. Someone has an ace up early? Well, everyone bets an ace. But good players will bet into that ace, or raise the ace's bet, to "see where he's at." The response to this feeler dictates the rest of the hand. Watch the emotional response—not just the monetary response—to your probe. These feelers are like your personal lie detector, and you're paying for this information, so pay attention and use it wisely. It's going to cost you a few chips, but the information could either save you from a huge loss or clear the way for a big win. The higher up you go in limit poker, the more of these bets you will encounter.

If someone tries to counter your probe by slow-playing, that's okay with you—you'll take a cheap card.

QUESTION?

What is "capping the pot"?
When the maximum number of bets and raises has been used up in a betting round, the pot is said to be "capped." If a bet and three raises are allowed, the fourth bet would cap the pot. If the limit is $10, all players in the capped pot would owe $40. Often, players will say "cap" or "cap it" when they make that final bet.

Bet into Weakness

All bets can bring you information, whether feelers, bluffs, or straight bets. Who's weak or strong in a specific hand is what you most want to know, but you also can get a line on who's weak or strong in general, who you can push around. Your bets are a less effective tool on those who won't be pushed around or intimidated. A good way to get an aggressive player off your back is just to push back, preferably with a hand, but if not, just betting back at him will put him on notice that you won't be run over.

You have to make a stand and show people you're willing to protect your turf. When you stand up, it is hoped you won't do it the one time the bully actually has a hand, so use your skills to pick a good spot—just don't wait too long to do it. And if you're in the lead, you must protect your hand. If you've bet preflop in Hold'em, you must in most cases bet after the flop. If you have the only pair on board in Stud, you have to bet it like you have two pair or trips—even if you have total hooey. If you don't, you should fold, because you've just told the table your hand sucks, and you will be run over.

If you detect weakness during a hand, you bet—no matter what you hold. If you detect weakness on the river, you bet to pick up the pot. Good players pound on weakness. It's like that in every sport. You must be the strong one, and in poker, betting is your weapon of strength. You use bets to manipulate how your hand is perceived, and it is the perception that counts. Other players will act according to their perception of your hand.

Once you know how players will respond to your bets, you massage them into the right mindset and rake in the chips.

Chapter 9

The Weapons of Position and Isolation

The Greek mathematician Archimedes said, "Give me a fulcrum and a long enough lever, and I will move the Earth." A poker player has his own lever and fulcrum: position play and isolation. Position at the table is such a powerful advantage that a decent player with position on every hand would be virtually unbeatable, and a mediocre player with position would beat some pretty good pros. Mastering position play can help give you an edge on every hand.

What Is Position?

"Man, I'm glad I don't have to act first!" You'll probably be only a few hands into your poker career when you first mutter this "sigh of relief" to yourself. What a difference it makes when your opponents must act before you. Since good poker is based on information, it follows that having other players make decisions first is an advantage. That is the essence of position.

Your "position" is the point in the betting round when you must act relative to the other players. If there's a full table and you're one of the first to act, you're said to be in early position; if you're in the middle bunch, that's middle position; if you're in the final few, that's late position. Those who have acted before you are said to be in front of you, while those acting after you are behind you.

In some types of poker, your position will be fluid. With Stud, since the high card on the board bets first, you might be in early position on one round, but if the player to your left suddenly gets high hand on board, you will be last to act. Position can be unpredictable as long as board cards are coming. In Draw, you will be under the gun if you are to the left of the dealer, but if the player to your left opens, on the next round you will be last.

But position play is most critical in community-card games. In Hold'em and Omaha, your position remains constant, which makes this another factor you have under control—one more reason the pros like these games so much. They don't like surprises. If you start out in fourth position, you will stay in fourth position—until someone folds, of course. If you're on the button (the dealer), you're in last position, and everyone acts before you. And they will continue to act before you all hand long. If you're one of the blinds, you're in the earliest position, but in the first round, since you've already put money in, the third-position player is first. In later rounds, the blinds act first. Before the flop, the two players to the left of the blinds are considered in early position, the next three are in middle position, and the final three are late.

Why Position Is Crucial

Your poker life is a perpetual search for clues on which to base choices. Since every bet, check, raise, or twitch (or lack thereof) sends out waves of information, if you're last to act, you have it all spread out before you like a casino buffet. Your opponents must cast their lot in the dark, not knowing what you will do. By the time it's your turn, you will have seen and analyzed their actions. The only thing left is to know your foes well enough to divine whether anyone is being deceptive. Positional advantage increases on a sort of sliding scale. The more players you have acting before you, and the fewer acting after, the more positional advantage you get.

Advantages of Late Position

You're in the driver's seat in late position, especially if you're dead last. If you have a strong hand, someone may bet into you, so you hammer him with a raise, increasing your profit. Or someone may try to bluff, not having a clue that the last card made you strong. You make him pay. If those in front of you show weakness, then you try to buy the pot. You can just sit back and watch it all unfold, quiet and safe in the corner of your web, waiting for the unsuspecting flies.

QUESTION?

What is "sandbagging"?
Sandbagging is a strategy of "lying in the weeds," where a player doesn't bet a sure winning hand. Instead, he hopes another player will bet into him. Then he check-raises, and doubles his profit.

On the river, if your hand is borderline, you may be able to call without fearing a raise, and this could be the difference between winning and losing. If you are in middle position and call a bet, you risk a raise after you. You know that if someone raises, your hand is not a winner, so you've just thrown money away. If you're in late position, the borderline hands fear *you*. Strong late position hands get paid off more. In early position, if you bet your big hand, everyone may fold. In late position, someone may bet into you, or if it's checked to you and you bet, they may think you're just trying to buy the pot.

With starting hands, you're in the catbird seat. You can limp in with marginal hands on the end because you won't be raised, and during the hand you can get free cards when others fear a raise, or fold cheaply. In last position, you can check with less fear of others taking advantage of your weakness. As the hand progresses, you can give yourself free cards or call a bet without fear of a raise.

Are there any disadvantages to late position? Only the rare check-raise.

Early Position: A Nightmare on All Streets

While you're calm, cool, and collected in late position, early position is the opposite—a total nightmare. Take the best-case scenario: You have the nuts. Unfortunately, you're first to act. What do you do? If you bet, the others, thinking you must be super-strong to bet in early position, probably fold. Unlike late position, you have little chance of anyone betting into your monster. If you play it coy and sandbag it, the rest of the table might just check right along with you. Then you suffer the embarrassment of missing bets or, on the river, turning over the nuts without having made a bet.

At the other end of the spectrum, if you have a horrible hand, you won't have the option of bluffing on the river if everyone checks, as you would in late position. Where you travel the roughest road is with the borderline hands, those "possible" winners. Having little information, you will usually be stuck with a weak check, thus ensuring a bet from someone else. Then you're stuck again.

With borderline hands, not knowing others' strength makes you weak. You check much more than you should early in the hand, thus inviting people to run over you. You often violate the edict "Bet or fold, but don't just call," because you can't always risk a bet on just a "possible" winner with so many players still to act.

Whether to enter a hand in the first place is one of the most critical decisions in poker, and as much as any other factor—including the cards themselves—position determines which starting hands you should play.

You can't play as many hands from early position, either. Starting hands that aren't worth a raise have to be thrown away, or you might find yourself in the untenable position of either putting in a bet and then having to fold, or wasting two or even three bets on a hand barely worth one, such as low pairs and low suited connectors in Hold'em. Not knowing the number of opponents you'll be facing makes starting-hand decisions an expensive headache.

There are many hands that might be worth calling a single bet with, but not two (such as 10-9 offsuit); and others that are worth a preflop call against a large field, but worthless against just a few opponents (3-3; 7-6 suited). In early position, you don't know the field size or if you will be raised, so you must dump many more hands.

Advantages of Early Position

Believe it or not, there are a few. First, many knowledgeable players are afraid of a starting-hand raise from early position. "Book play" states that you need very strong starting hands to call the big blind's bet early— and you do. Unless they think the raiser is a yahoo, they might fold some good preflop hands in later position. If you're at a table riddled with tight locals, aggressively betting some marginal hands from an early spot might pick up the blinds, or the pot after the flop or turn—if they think you've read the book.

If you have a starting hand you want to steal the blinds with or get heads-up, early position is primetime for you. You raise the big blind, making it two bets to go. This is a sound strategy for any pair, from deuces to queens. Someone's going to need a hand to call you in an average game. You'll win the blinds or maybe gets heads-up with the button or big blind. If it gets heads-up, your pair is anywhere from a 55-percent favorite (deuces) to 88 percent (aces). But if you just *call* the big blind, you'll be faced with a field large enough to ensure that someone will hit an overcard pair (it's better than 50-50 an overcard hits the flop if you have jacks), but probably not large enough to justify chasing a set (8-1 against flopping it).

One final early position advantage is you might get some check-raise opportunities, but you want to be sure someone will bet, because, as stated earlier, you run the risk of everyone checking after you. Realize that these early position "advantages" are a rarity.

Stealing Blinds, Stealing Pots

When it comes to taking control and reaping the financial rewards of that power, position is king. One of your key moves is stealing the blinds in late position, either on the button or one off. Raising to get the blinds to fold is essential if you have a good hand late, and just as essential if you have nothing and there is only one caller (or none) to you.

If you have a good hand late, you want the blinds out so they won't suddenly beat your A-Q by limping in with a trash hand and getting a low flop, like 8-6-3. Your A-Q doesn't look so good now, does it, if you let the blinds in free with their 7-5 or 8-2 or 6-5? If you bet again with that flop, a good player probably will call you down. You're going to need to pair up, and your chance of that is only 25 percent on the turn, 13 percent on the river. Good luck!

Raising in Late Position

So get the blinds out at all costs. You know that if anyone called in front of you, they have some kind of hand, but you want the wild cards out—the blinds. If you allow them to limp in, they literally could have anything, which makes your post-flop decision a nightmare. If a blind bets right out after the flop, how can you call unless you hit a hand, which in most cases you will not? By being timid here, you've gone from favorite to underdog.

> "Buying the button" is a sophisticated move that can get you position. If you are one or two to the right of the button, putting in a strong raise will often force the players after you to fold, giving you position on the rest of the field.

Raise at least three out of four times in late position unless there are many callers, and always if you have a hand and believe a raise will fold the blinds. The ideal scenario, though, is when there are few or no callers to you. Then you raise and steal the blinds. If they call, it's all right, because they will now understand that you will make this bet whether you have a top hand or not. This gets your better hands paid off. If you get called, so what? You have position on the next round, when you *should* bet again, unless you feel it in your bones that you're facing a hand. In that case, maybe you'll get a free card. If someone bets into you, you can easily fold. No harm done. That's the advantage of acting last.

Stealing the blinds is your gateway to stealing pots. You've built an image as being a little reckless by always betting in the last two positions, when in fact it's a calculated move and you are anything but loose. Advertising this play can only help get your big hands called. Not making this move could have the opposite effect: You will be perceived as weak.

Speaking of weak, if you are in last position on the river and no one has bet, it is *expected* that you will make this *position bet*. Forcefully. Everyone has told you they have nothing. They are giving you the pot. Take it. If you don't make this bet, don't ever expect to have a bet called on the river when you have a strong hand. The same goes for the flop and turn if it's checked to you: Give them the excuse to fold they're looking for.

Paying attention to what others do—and don't do—before you must act is an advantage you *must* push.

Do Your Opponents Know Position?

The value of position grows with the stakes. When big money is at risk, every edge is magnified. At higher limits, many players are rock solid as far as position, particularly when it comes to starting hands. Fortunately, this makes them somewhat predictable. It is easier to put them on hands. You know there are hands they simply will not play in certain positions. That's the good news. The bad news is the hands you put them on are usually quite formidable.

There is a time-tested truism in poker that you should "sit behind the money." In other words, you should sit with the players with the most chips directly on your right. This is because during a game, money flows in a clockwise direction, and you will have those with the most power acting before you.

At lower stakes, many players won't understand position, and they'll play the same hands from anywhere. It is up to you to spot these players and adjust. As a fringe benefit, you'll have them betting right into the teeth of your big hands.

Even in a wild game, position will help you. You won't be able to steal pots, but with good position you can observe all the craziness and then simply fold. When you have a great hand, you can hammer those who made the loose bets earlier. In a tight game, you can kill people with position bets. If the world's biggest rock finally bets, you can quietly fold from late position without giving him or her a cent.

Curiously, in early position, the strategy is similar in both loose and tight games: check and fold a lot of hands.

The Concept of Isolation

The more you play, the more you will realize that your lead in a hand is hanging by a slender thread, and even the best starting hands are vulnerable. This is the case in Stud, where you receive 43 percent of your total cards before you must act (three of seven), but it's especially true in Hold'em, where you start with only two (28 percent). This makes the game highly unpredictable. Even with great pocket cards, a lot of water has to go under the bridge before you bring that pot home.

With the exception of small pairs and straight and flush draws (where you often wish to chase a longshot payoff against a large field), starting hands in Hold'em demand isolation. You must thin the field. Sure, if you have a high rolled-up set in Stud or aces in Hold'em against rocks, you may want to be coy, but even aces will only win 34 percent of the time against nine random hands (as shown in **TABLE 9-1**), and 44 percent of the time against six. The second-best hand, pocket kings, is also vulnerable. If you don't believe that, let people in cheaply sometime and see how you feel when an ace flops. You now have just two outs and an 8-percent chance of winning, all because you got greedy and let someone in cheap with A-4, instead of forcing a fold.

Multiple Opponents Are Powerful

The more overcards there are to your hand, the more tenuous your lead. If you have A♠-10♠ and the flop is 10♥-9♥-3♣, you have to bet like crazy. If you have the chance to make it two bets to go, do so. There are three overcards to your ten that will kill you, and the larger the field against you, the greater the chance that someone will hit. For example, if the players against you combined have a jack, queen, and king, all of which beat you if paired, they have nine outs and a 35-percent chance of hitting by the river. If someone has Q-J or J-8 for a straight draw, you can add four more outs, making thirteen. Now your chance of winning is down to 52 percent. If someone's paired the board (J-9), that's trouble, as there's now a two-pair draw, and if there's a flush draw as well (e.g., K♥-Q♥), you are now at least a 2-to-1 *under-dog* to win. You could have this whole arsenal against you in the hands of only three foes!

When you are in the lead, you must look at the field cumulatively. You don't treat adversaries as separate entities and say, "I have the best hand." You might very well have the best hand, and the best chance of winning against any *one* of them, but against the *field* you will lose more often than not.

FACT

To "straddle," the player to the left of the big blind puts up double the big blind's "bet"; in other words, he "raises" the big blind before he's been dealt a hand. The player to the straddle's left is now first to act, and the "straddler" may raise his own bet when the action comes around to him.

Look at how the odds change relative to the number of opponents. Say you have pocket jacks in Hold'em. What are the chances that someone has aces, kings, or queens in the hole? With seven foes it's 8-1 against; with eight it's 7-1; and with nine it's down to 6-1. Say you have an ace in the hole. The chance of someone else having an ace is 42 percent five-handed, but ten-handed it's 75 percent!

Isolate Early and Often

Isolation begins with your starting hand. You must get the field down to a manageable number so that when you have top pair on the flop (the most likely way you'll be in the lead), you can drive it home. Betting before the flop sets up plays *on* the flop. That's why if you bet preflop, you should almost always bet post-flop. Get others in the habit of seeing you do this. This is an expected play. It makes sense: If you are strong before the flop, you want them to think you are strong after as well. If you show weakness here, you invite rout, and having a small field is advantageous on every street. Naturally, you must examine your options if you meet resistance, but if you have top pair on the flop—either with tens, as in the example above, or with an overpair like pocket jacks to the 10-9-3 flop— you must make it as expensive as possible for those draws to chase.

This isn't a home game, where you're "sucking people in" with a top hand to build a pot. This is real poker, where you don't want any surprises and the pot is just fine the way it is, thank you.

It is an overlooked concept that the more players there are in a hand, the better hand you will need to win. This begins with the starting hands and is true all the way to the river. In a heads-up game, you don't need much. But in an eight- or ten-player game, you need a *very* good hand. The chance of someone getting pocket aces in a ten-player game is 22-1 against; in heads-up, it's 110-1. It's 8-1 against any one of the ten players being dealt A-K, but it's a 41-1 shot heads-up. (In Seven-Stud, odds are 5-1 against being dealt a pair in the opening three cards. In an eight-person game, you can be sure someone will have one, but in heads-up, the odds say neither will have a pair.)

The more players at the table, the better the chance *someone* has a top starting hand. The more players, the more hands seeing the flop, and the better those hands are. And with more seeing the flop (or fourth street in Stud), there are many more combinations to fear.

TABLE 9-1 shows the winning percentage for some pocket pairs against random hands when all players stay to the river. By the way, you will end up with a set about 20 percent of the time. You'll flop a set one out of nine tries (11 percent).

Table 9-1 Hold'em Pocket Pairs Against Multiple Opponents							
Number of Players	**AA**	**QQ**	**TT**	**88**	**66**	**44**	**22**
2	88%	82%	77%	71%	65%	60%	55%
4	68%	58%	50%	43%	36%	30%	22%
7	44%	34%	27%	23%	20%	17%	15%
10	34%	26%	20%	16%	13%	11%	10%

A note of caution: Charts like this are a general tool. You face random hands in a simulation, but in actual play the hands will be better than random. The betting, of course, changes everything, because while in the simulation everyone plays to the river, in actual practice this isn't the case.

Who to Target for Isolation

Some players are just asking for you to get them alone. The following player types are the most vulnerable, if you have any kind of early hand at all:

- **Wild players.** This breed loves to raise, build a pot, and try to take over, but they do it with less-than-premium hands. You build on their raises by reraising, making it too expensive for others to stay. You know they have nothing, so your raise not only isolates them, it allows you to bet them out of the pot if they don't get lucky on the flop or turn.
- **Loose players.** They don't raise as much as wild players, but the strategy against them is similar. Since you know they stay with many mediocre hands in all positions, if you can isolate them, your higher card—any ace, king, or even queen—should make you the favorite over their 10-8, J-9, 9-8, and all the small suited hands they love to play. The fact that you've raised also makes you a cinch, unless they get a draw on the flop. Then you make them pay to the river.
- **Poor players.** This one is pretty obvious. Any time you can get it heads-up against an inferior or inexperienced player, you're the favorite. They play poorer quality hands, don't understand isolation, and have trouble discerning your hand. Your raise puts them on the defensive, and they will often fold if they don't hit top pair.

- **Straddlers.** What a gold mine these gamblers are! Raising without seeing their cards—what are they thinking? You know full well the odds are against them being dealt a hand, so you bet it up with anything to isolate them preflop. Then just drive their trash out. Look at it this way: Out of 169 possible starting hands, J-9 offsuit is ranked fortieth. It's 4-to-1 against getting this hand or better, and it's still mediocre. Make the straddlers pay!

The best way to isolate someone is if you can raise or—even better—reraise him or her. If you can make it two or three to bets to go to the rest of the field, you'll get it heads-up most of the time.

Isolation in Action

Here's a typical example of why you must isolate with most top hands. You have A-Q preflop. You believe it's the best hand. Heads-up you're in good shape, but against three players you win just 39 percent of the time, and 25 percent against six. The problem is the flop—your chance of pairing is just 27 percent. This is okay against one player—you can still bet whether you hit or not because you can assume he hasn't improved either. But facing three or more, you know someone's paired and has you beat. Your chance of pairing on the turn or river is only 24 percent, so unless he's a weak player, you must check and fold.

FACT

Another advantage of isolating with a top hand is that by thinning the field, you deny drawing hands the proper pot odds to call.

The second example is going all-in with a big bet in no-limit or pot-limit—the quintessential isolation play. If you have lowly pocket deuces and can get it heads-up, you're actually a slight favorite against all other hands except higher pairs—even A-K! If you had to play limit through four betting rounds, however, the A-K would kill the deuces, because all the overcards would either get them beat outright or prevent them calling all the way.

Take the third example. You have pocket nines. Unless you want to just limp in and hope for trips against a large field, you know your only chance is to get it heads-up, so you bet it up preflop. Of course, a favorable flop, like 8-6-2, would give you an overpair. But heads-up, unless the flop is scary (like A-K-J, and so on), you can count on your opponent missing the flop. Then you bet him out. But since at least one overcard will flop 69 percent of the time (when you don't flop a set), with *multiple* opponents, someone's going to pair up and beat you.

Setting a Trap

In no-limit poker, trapping is king. It's all about waiting for someone to go all-in against your hidden monster hand, playing some cards others might not expect, and buying pots with big bets while praying that this time, you aren't betting into the nuts. Take the last hand of the 2003 World Series of Poker. Chris Moneymaker called a preflop bet from Sam Farha with 5-4 offsuit, a horrible heads-up hand. The flop came J-5-4. Chris had hit a miracle: pairing his hole cards, a 49-to-1 shot. And it couldn't have come at a worse time for Sam. With J-10 offsuit, he had top pair, huge in heads-up. Chris checked, Sam bet, Chris raised, Sam went all-in, and of course, so did Chris. End of tournament. Chris had two cards Sam could not have expected, despite the "anything goes" nature of high-stakes heads-up play. He set the trap by checking his two pair. A more classic trap would have been if Chris had pocket aces, kings, or queens, limped, and just checked and called until Sam went all-in.

Slow-Playing: Risks and Reward

In limit poker, your traps aren't as deadly, but they are no less essential because your opponents must know you are capable of setting them. Trapping, more often called "slow-playing" in limit, brings an element of unpredictability to your game that keeps foes guessing. When a player bets little or nothing on his strong hand to disguise its strength, hoping to make other players overvalue their hands and pay him off handsomely, he is slow-playing. When you check your big hand, you're just begging someone to try to buy the pot. Then it's check-raise time! It is quite simply a method of maximizing profit on a great hand—but with greater profit comes with greater risk.

One of the first strategy points to look for when analyzing adversaries is this: who slow-plays high pairs early, and who never does. Not only is this identification important to your bankroll, but it also is a clue to their overall playing style.

Slow-Playing the Big Pairs

Getting a wired pair (pocket pair) of either aces or kings is a 110-to-1 shot, so you want to make sure you make hay when you get 'em. This means that *sometimes* you will slow-play early. You don't want *everyone* to fold if you bet preflop. You'd like to thin the field to two or three foes. With more than three, there is too much risk of someone hitting a crazy flop. One opponent might just fold if he misses the flop, but with two or three, someone could catch a pair or a draw and he'll pay you off.

As always, the nature of the game (loose, average, or tight) and your table image determine your strategy. In a loose game where multiple players are in every pot, you bet big pairs preflop from any position. In a tight game, you check in early position, and you raise in middle and late positions if there are already callers. In an average game, you know your players, and you bet to ensure two or three callers (no more) and try to disguise your hand. You don't want them to *know* you have aces until the moment when you want them all to fold, usually after the flop if there is a flush draw or scare cards, or after the turn if the flop is ragged. But the last thing you want to do is to give free cards to a draw after the flop. If you're in early position, you want to check-raise the flop. If you're in late position, bet or raise. A check-raise is usually the cue for everyone to fold—you choose the time. If you've got a live one chasing, then milk him.

Be aware of your image! If you're viewed as tight, your bets will be more likely to thin the field or fold everyone. If you're seen as loose, then you can bet, raise, and even reraise with the big pairs preflop, and still get some action.

If others know you will slow-play big pairs, it adds a whole new dimension to your play. Your bets throughout a hand will get more respect, and so will your bluffs. You have them thinking, "Did he slow-play aces again?" But remember, you don't slow-play often. You pick your spots.

ALERT!

Big John's Tips: A "big pair" means aces or kings here, not queens or below. With queens, there is a 41-percent chance of an overcard hitting the flop, and that spells trouble if you slow-played. With kings, a dreaded ace will flop only 23 percent of the time. If that's still too scary, then only slow-play aces, and bet strong on the rest.

Here's a big note of caution to keep in mind. Limit poker is still about thinning the field and betting your leading hands. Resist the home-game "strategy" of always going for the big score, unless you're a mortal lock. With trapping, you always are weighing the payoff versus the risk of letting others stay in the hand. If you flop a 49-1 shot, like Moneymaker, you want to get paid off. But you don't want to let a 5-4 hand in cheaply, because you'll want to shoot yourself when a crazy flop puts a big loss on you.

Chapter 10

Bluffing: Poker's Treacherous Heart

When you use aggressive betting to isolate opponents, you are in poker paradise because you are being honest. You need not worry about disguising your hand or giving anything away. It's all out there in black and white. In a game of deception, you are telling the truth: "I have the best hand. Fold." You have them beat, and you want them out. It is so simple when you don't need your poker face. But most poker is not so easy.

What Is Bluffing?

Poker becomes difficult when you do not want foes to know your cards. Knowing what you're holding allows them to make correct decisions. And it follows that if they don't know your hand, they will make mistakes. So you take steps, through misdirection, to keep the true nature of your cards secret—by acting contrary to your hand. If you have one of those hard-to-get great hands, sometimes you'll hide that fact to get paid off by weaker holdings. So you might check. And if you have a weak hand, you certainly want to be feared, to get as many free cards as possible while you pray your trash will turn to gold. You might try things as basic as acting super-interested in the hand, having chips ready to throw in, or even betting on a cheap street so others check to you later.

But the ultimate misdirection play is bluffing, and even non-players know what *that* play is: a gutsy, crazy, stomach-churning move where some fool bets a whole bunch of chips—on nothing! He *must* convince others he has them beat through his courage, his betting, and his manner because if someone calls, he loses it all. But if everyone folds, he wins the pot—on a *stone-cold bluff.*

QUESTION?

What is a poker face?
A poker face is the countenance every player "puts on" to conceal his emotions, his thoughts, and his cards during a poker hand, but it is not a *robotic mask.* A good poker face is natural, relaxed, and reveals nothing, even if the player makes a royal flush—or misses one.

Misdirecting Other Players

Bluffing is a move that resonates throughout the game, and sometimes games to come, but it is no easy trick. In fact, it goes so against the grain that many players just can't bring themselves to try it, and those are the players doomed forever to mediocrity. You bluff by risking money, sometimes lots of it. There's no way around that. But it is a move that every poker player must make, whether it is successful or not. What non-bluffers don't realize is that bluffing can be profitable even when it fails, because it sticks in the minds of your opponents like glue.

Poker is the only game where the best hand doesn't always win—that is why it is called a "psychological" game, and why "people" players usually beat "mathematical" players. (Top pros, of course, have both sets of skills.) Your hand is as good as your determination to back it up. If you know what makes your opponents tick, you can figure what they're holding and use their actions to read their thoughts and predict their responses. Then you can choose the optimal time to bluff. If the bluff is successful, your opponents will drop their cards like hot potatoes, and you will take the pot with a worse hand. If the bluff is unsuccessful, your foes are on notice that you will try anything—and could do it again.

There Is Nothing to Fear but Fear Itself

If you can bluff without flinching, you are on the road to winning, so if the money means less to you than it does to your tablemates, you have a huge advantage. If you can accept the risk and know which opponents are fearful, you can take control. And pick up pots by bluffing.

When there's serious money on the line, your hand starts to shrink like the cup on a winning putt at the Masters. So does your opponent's, when you put *him* to the test. So it goes without saying that bluffs will rarely be successful if your opponents are in their safety zones. Just as with isolation, the stakes must matter. You cannot bluff in a low-limit game where players throw money in to keep someone honest, or someone "sheriffs" the pot. These are amateur games where you cannot use your skills, so make sure you play stakes where losses will sting.

Strategy is simple in low, loose games. You bluff early until you are called, then rarely bluff again. Both the frequency and the importance of the bluff increases as the stakes increase, all the way up to the ultimate— no-limit poker.

ESSENTIAL

High-stakes player Rick Bennet writes in *King of a Small World*, "Everyone, in life and poker, has good points and bad points. One of my good ones is that I don't give a **** about money when I'm playing. That part of my brain is missing."

The Benefits of the Bluff

Bluffing is the essence of poker; in fact, the name comes from the French word pocher, which means "to bluff," and the German word pochen, "to boast." Without the twin threats of bluffing and monetary loss, the game is incredibly boring. It is so important that even in games where it is very difficult to bluff successfully, bluffing remains one of the most profitable moves in poker. Why? Because without bluffing, you are an open book.

Unpredictability

Remember that guy in your home game who only bets with the nuts and hasn't bluffed since the '80s? Bluffing makes you unpredictable and disguises your future hands. If others know you bluff and will risk money on less than the best hand, they will pay you off when you get those nut hands. You know how frustrating it is to get that monster and win nothing. If that happens frequently, you're just not bluffing enough, so *advertise* that you bluff. When you get caught, make sure everyone knows it. Announce that you have nothing: "Good call! I was on a total bluff!" Show your hand. The money you paid for this "ad campaign" will return big dividends, because it will help "sell" your big hands later.

> And note what many poker writers have forgotten over time: The game is all about bluffing and knowing who is bluffable. Bluffing, misrepresenting, and buying pots you didn't "deserve" was at the core of the game from its inception. Without the element of bluff, the game is predictable, humdrum, and simplistic.

Bluffing gives you that elusive "second way" to win a hand. You don't have to hold the best cards to grab the pot. But unless you're against the world's weakest players and just running them over, you aren't going to bluff all the time. You bluff until you are caught, then pick your spots. You know they will start calling you more once they know you try to buy pots. When they get in the calling mode, shift gears and start playing top hands. After beating their brains out with top hands, they'll start folding again. At that point, you can start bluffing again. Pretty soon they won't know if they're coming or going—they will be guessing, and usually guessing wrong. You're just slapping them silly. You're Moe. They're Curly. They're just sitting back reacting to you, and after awhile—nyuck, nyuck, nyuck—they'll become fearful, conservative, and predictable. They'll be flinching before you've even bet, hiding in their shells and only coming out with obvious top hands, to which you quickly fold.

The Worst Case

Compare this to what happens if you do *not* bluff. First, since opponents know you will never bet on a hand you do not believe in, they soon will cop to what hands you like. If you play some questionable cards, they will take advantage of that. If you only play top hands, they will quickly fold when you bet—except when someone else has a monster hand, in which case he will beat your brains in. To say you are predictable would be an understatement. Since you never bluff, you won't get called on the river unless someone has you beat. You can't figure out why you never win the big pots.

> Famous poker author and player David Spanier summed it up in *Total Poker:* "Bluff is the essence of poker, yet it is hard to catch on the wing. It can be conceived, at its finest, in the fleeting glimpse of an opportunity, instinctively; or it can be slow and premeditated. It is lurking in every single hand of the game. Has he or hasn't he got what he says he's got?"

It all boils down to this: Opponents must believe that your bets do not always mean what they say. That is how you get action on your good hands. But it is a fine line you must walk. You know you must be able to drive people out and thin the field on some hands. Remember, your bets must be respected, so you can use them like a hammer when you need to bet drawing hands out of the pot, isolate, or get it heads-up (and yes, bluff successfully). Think "shock and awe" here. Therefore, you can't be constantly bluffing or playing foolishly. No one respects a bad player, no matter how aggressive he is. Foes should just have a subtle awareness that "this person will bluff" somewhere in the backs of their minds. This leads to questionable calls, guessing, and confusion. Knowing *when* to bluff will keep you balanced on that tight-rope.

It is imperative that you be aware of how your opponents view you as the game progresses hand to hand. If you're seen as the "bluffer," then shift into conservative mode without seeming to. If they see you as "cautious," then that's the time to "be visible" as you bet it up with marginal hands and steal some pots. Their perception of you is mutable, and you *must* stay aware of how you are viewed. Your decisions are often dictated by this perception.

Aggressive Play

Since you will bluff until you are caught, you will be caught. Once discovered with your hand in the cookie jar, your opponents will call you more often. That's a given. But how do you reconcile bluffing, which encourages future calls, with your desire to have your bets respected, so you can protect your tenuous leads and force people to fold when you don't have a lock?

The answer is to be aggressive from the start in the hands you have carefully chosen to play—bluffing or not. Plain and simple, your opponents must know that it will cost them dearly to call you. If you are in a hand, you will be betting. Sometimes you may not have it, but sometimes you will. Either way, they are going to have to invest some serious money to find out. *You* are willing to pay the price—all the way to the river. If you've figured your opponents correctly, *they* will not be.

What if you are played back at, and someone has put *you* to the test? Here is where knowing your players will save you. What hand is he representing? Does he have it? Does the way he has played the hand support it? Has he caught on to your aggressive style and is now trying to take the play away from you with trash, or is he a rock who finally has a hand? Your people skills here will tell you whether to raise back—even with nothing—or to back off. Remember, there's no shame in folding. Losing a little skirmish is okay, as long as you win the big battles.

Control, Intimidation, and Confusion

If you are aggressive *and* winning, others will back off. It's control. You can see and feel it happening. Someone might even whisper in your ear, "They're afraid of you." That's intimidation. The bad players will just be confused, the better ones will go into a shell until they figure you out, and the rocks will get "rockier"—just waiting for those monster hands that never come.

Now you have two decisions. First is finding the proper moment to shift gears into a more conservative style, and second is determining whether they think you are aggressive in a calculated, intelligent way, or just a "maniac." If it's the former, they will sit and wait for good cards. Someone may make a run at you to test you, but you'll be ready for that. If they think you're a maniac making a lot of loose bets on average hands, the better players may challenge you and try to isolate you. Put yourself in your enemies' shoes: How do they see you? Caution—a maniac will be caught "betting on the come" much more often than someone who practices more selective aggression.

QUESTION?

What is a "maniac"?
In poker, a maniac is a loose, aggressive player who wreaks havoc in a game by making a lot of bets with questionable cards. Because his aggressiveness is not selective and he doesn't know when to back off, he loses a lot of chips to rocks who trap him with strong hands.

An Aggressive Move

Being aggressive is more than just making a bunch of bets. Others must view the bets as powerful. Remember that arcade game where gophers pop their heads up out of their holes and you have to smash them back down with a mallet? Think of your foes as those gophers. If you're facing someone who's popped his head up, bet him back down. Raising the raiser will quickly tell you what you're facing, and isolate. And check-raising, of course, is saying in no uncertain terms, "I have a monster hand."

Many new players will make the following play. They flop a top hand, like a set, and then check to the preflop bettor. They plan to check-raise when he bets. This often works, but you've told the bettor you have a monster. He'll now fold, or see the turn and fold. But if you *bet into the bettor*—bet first—he now very well might raise you (as long as you haven't given away that you're unbeatable). Then you can either raise back, or just call him and suck more money out of him on the turn. If it's more action you're seeking, betting into the bettor is usually the more professional play.

When to Bluff

Since bluffing means betting your cold cash on nothing, timing is everything. Mathematical players might tell you a bluff is recommended when pot odds warrant it. If your odds are 1 in 4 of being successful with your $20 bluff, but there is a $100 pot, you're getting 5-1 on your money. That's 5-1 on a 3-1 shot! It's a profitable play, if your assessment is correct. That, of course, is the tough part: predicting if those with better hands will call. You're getting into the nebulous region of reading players now, and if you can start figuring this kind of thing correctly, you're on the way to becoming great. Here are a few factors to consider when deciding when to bluff:

- The size of the pot. After the pot grows past a certain point, the pot odds are so great for a caller that he's not going to just let you walk off with it.
- The number of players in the hand. The more players, the greater the chance that someone is going to have a hand good enough to call, or even call just for the heck of it.

- The action to you. Obviously, if someone has bet, there's a pretty good chance that if you bluff, he'll call your bet. If anyone has called before you, get out of there.
- The personality of the players against you. There are some who just will not let someone take a pot uncontested and would rather waste chips than risk being bluffed out.
- Did everyone show weakness? If the whole table has checked, you almost are forced to bluff, if only to protect your future winning hands, especially on the river.
- What hands have you put people on? During the hand, you figured players for certain cards. Did they hit? How many have you beat? Are their hands good enough to call?
- Are the remaining opponents conservative? If so, they won't be calling unless they have something. What hands have you put them on? Did any of them bet during the hand?
- Is one of your remaining opponents loose or on tilt? If so, what was his past performance on the river? Does he check-raise? Does he call on the river "just in case"?
- Do you sense defeat? Do you feel weakness from the rest of the field? Do they look like they're already thinking about the next hand? Are they holding their cards, ready to muck?
- Has a scare card just hit the board? Has a card just shown up that you know will scare your foes, like pairing your door card in Stud, or an ace or third flush card in Hold'em?
- What is your history in the hand? Have you shown any strength? Have you just checked along, or acted like it was your pot? Do they fear you now, or will your bluff be "out of the blue?"
- What are the sizes of the stacks against you? Those with huge stacks (big winners) and those down to almost nothing (big losers) are often more inclined to call than others.
- How are you perceived? Are you the table bluffer, or are you solid? What hand have they put you on? Have you been called in a similar spot? Can you see them folding to you?

- Have your bets been getting called lately, especially on the river? If everyone has been folding, you have not been bluffing enough. This is the ideal time to start doing it.
- Do you have psychological dominance over your opponent? If so, you will be less likely to be called. Your aggressive (but not foolish) playing style fosters this advantage.

ALERT!

There are situations where a bluff just has no chance or is not financially sound. Don't try it when your bets are not respected at the table and you're always getting called, or when someone is on tilt and calling everyone down in the vain hope of a win. Also, if you're known as a bluffer or loose player, bluffing isn't likely to work well.

You can see how important it is during a hand to pay attention to betting patterns, expressions, and tells to set up a bluff early if you sense weakness. Always be figuring what your opponents have. Unless you have a line on their holdings, it's difficult to calculate if your bluff has a chance. Of course, if anyone has a line on your style, or if you cannot bet your bluff in exactly the same manner as you would a genuine hand, then your bluff will fail. In general, the larger the pot, the harder it is to bluff successfully. The lower the stakes, the harder it is to pull it off. And, believe it or not, the *less* savvy your opponents, the harder it is to bluff them out.

The "Semi-Bluff" Is a Moneymaker

This isn't no-limit poker, where you can push in thousands of dollars and know you won't be called unless your opponent has a monster hand or is a world-class expert with an incredible read on you. No, you're playing limit poker, and limit takes some finesse. In limit, the move called the "semi-bluff" is a powerful tool. A semi-bluff is betting when you are behind in the hand, but you have outs. You can win if you hit your hand, but you can also win because your opponents may put you on a made hand, and they may fold to your river bet even if you don't hit. Here are some examples.

You have raised the blinds preflop with A-Q and got three callers. The flop comes 10-8-5. You bet it, and two people call. You don't believe they paired up, but if they did, you still have two overcards. You're going to figure them for a straight draw or overcards not as high as yours. Although you have only a 24-percent chance to make a pair, you have control of the hand. Unless the turn is a king or a jack (and sometimes even then), you will bet the turn and drive them out. If someone is still around, you'll fire another bullet on the river.

In the above example, if your ace and queen were both spades, and the ten and the eight were both spades, you now have fifteen outs, or a 54-percent chance of hitting by the river. Just bet like you have something, all the way. If you don't make it, you might win with a final bet on the river. Betting with an overcard (or underpair) along with a straight or flush draw is a very sound semi-bluff.

ESSENTIAL

In addition to its other benefits, a semi-bluff can sometimes be "pot-odds correct"! If you have more callers (say, five) than your odds of hitting a nut draw (such as 4-1), your bet is mathematically right on.

Another Semi-Bluff

You call a preflop raise in late position with 10-9 suited. The flop is J-8-5 rainbow. There are two checks and a bet to you. You raise it. The two checks fold, and the raiser calls. He has at most jacks, maybe eights, but more likely just an ace and decent kicker. If he has A-J, you figure, he would've reraised. With eight outs to the nut straight, the odds are more than 2-to-1 against you, but by taking control, you might win anyway. If he just has overcards, he has to hit one of his six outs or fold to your aggression. You'll bet it right out if he checks the turn, and the large turn bet might get him to fold right there. If he bets, you'll probably fold. If you think he's just feeling you out, this is an advanced play. Is he that good? You could reraise him to find out, but if he calls, you can be sure he'll call the river as well, so you're cooked if you don't hit. If he reraises, you're done. If he only calls your turn bet, you'll fire another shot at the river, whether you hit the straight or not.

The beauty is you have outs—it's not just a bluff and a prayer. Do you see how you'd be in even better position psychologically if you had raised preflop? That's why they say, "If you're going in, go in raising!" With semi-bluffs, think in your mind that you've already made a hand, and bet accordingly, with confidence and power. You're representing a made hand.

What Hand Does He Think You Have?

Always keep in mind how you are perceived and what hand your opponent is putting *you* on. After all, he's not a potted plant over there. In the last example, what hand could you have that could scare him out? You want him to think A-J or a set, which would beat his K-J, Q-J, J-10, or A-8. Bluffing is rarely effective if you can't *represent* something. Ideally, you want to represent a specific card. Opponents need something tangible to fear. The bet has to make sense and be logical and plausible. It's hard to fear a flop like 8-7-3. What could you have? But if the flop is Q-Q-8, they will fear a queen. If you bet right out, they might believe you, depending on how you would play if you actually had it. Do you see how playing "made" hands coyly can backfire? If you always bet your hands, then when you bluff here, they will think you could have trips. But if you would always check the queens to trap (check-raise) someone, then you can't bluff, because your normal play would be a "check" here! And if you check and someone else bets, you must fold.

For a bluff to work, what you represent has to conform to the betting pattern during the hand—therefore, you rarely just suddenly decide to throw in a bluff bet on the river. You must be thinking ahead, setting it up. If the bet pattern doesn't compute, someone's going to smell a rat and call.

This is an aggressive way of playing drawing hands. The other way of playing draws is to get in as cheaply as humanly possible, since most times you won't make it. Semi-bluffing gives you another way to win for all those times, and it takes care of the problem of "setting up" your bluff during the hand because you'll bet all the way. Vary your play from one strategy to the other to keep 'em guessing.

ALERT!

There's a saying in Hold'em about when a scary high pair flops, as with J-J-9: "It isn't the person who bets who has trips, it's the person who calls." Beware of the quiet ones in this situation. This is a rare time when a check-raise bluff might work—just be careful if you're called. You might be facing a real hand!

Who to Bluff

Everyone's been there. There are scare cards all over the board, you're betting like crazy, having correctly figured that no one hit. You only have an ace and a draw, but with the scary board there's no way anyone's going to stay with you. The good players have long since folded, but some guy keeps making weak calls, and on the river he sees your last bet. The last card gave him a low pair—he wins! You can't believe it! You're even tempered, but really, you have to ask him what he figured you for. He doesn't know. What was he going for? Doesn't really know that either.

You can't get mad because this is the perfect opponent. He has no clue. But this brings up an important point about bluffing: You can't bluff a monkey! You just can't. You cannot represent a hand to someone who doesn't think about your hand, only his own. With someone who just puts in chips because he feels like it, you're just going to have to beat him with good hands, which he will pay off handsomely. Forget trying to bluff him. Many have gone broke trying.

Now, players who can think logically and analyze a hand, they are another story. Good players—they can be bluffed. Sounds strange, but it's true. They can also catch on when you are bluffing if you're not careful. Unlike bad players, who don't fold enough, good players can even fold winning hands. It happens, and that's okay. No one can call all the time. That's weak. Sometimes, in tennis, a shot will be just "too good." There's no defense for it. No need to chase the shot. Some bets in poker are like that, too—just "too good." It's the bet in the perfect spot, and it can't be called. If someone has bluffed, good for him. Only a fool is a "calling station" who pays off hand after hand just to keep from being bluffed once in a while.

You calculate how your foe will analyze the hand, and if your betting matches the hand he puts you on, and that hand is probable and would beat him, he's going to fold. But you must be facing someone who can think intelligently about a hand, and *you* must have a reputation as a solid player—not too loose, and not a flake. So ask yourself, "Who's paying attention?"

Bluffing may sound risky, but put yourself in your opponent's shoes. When you bet early and strongly, he figures he's going to have to call all the way to the river to find out if you're bluffing. But you're in a much better spot: You can call if off at any time. Since you can fold after firing just one shot, you have much less at risk than he does.

Your Risk

It's a general rule of poker not to risk a lot to win a little. For example, it's a foolish move in no-limit to put in a ton of chips just to win the blinds. Sooner or later, someone's going to have a hand and take you down. But it is perfectly correct to bluff at the blinds in limit poker. It's a high-percentage play that will win the pot immediately or after the flop if you bet then. And if someone wants to bluff at a tiny pot, and you're not sure whether to call, just give it to him.

Bluffing and Position

Running a bluff in late position after others have checked is expected, but doing it from early position can sometimes work because it's so gutsy. If everyone has checked (or at least not raised) on the turn and a weak card hits the river, try betting right out from early position. Good players know you're not going to bet early unless you really have something because there are so many to act after you, so they might overvalue your hand. You just might buy the pot. In a weak hand, the first person to bet often wins.

Should You Call a Possible Bluff?

The math players have a simple formula for calling. If the pot odds are greater than the chance he's bluffing, then call. For example, if the pot is $50 and the bet is $10, you're getting 5-to-1 on your money. But the player almost never bluffs. You figure it's 10-1 against him bluffing here. So you'll lose $100 and win $50 in eleven tries, for a net loss of $50. But if he's a known bluffer, you might figure he'll bluff once out of five times he's faced with this situation. In this case, you lose $40 but win $50 in five tries by calling, for a gain of $10. A good bet. Knowing your players will put you a step ahead of the math guys when it comes to calling bluffs.

The courage to "bet on nothing" comes from understanding the game, while fear comes from the unknown. The more you play, the more comfortable you will become, and the confidence to run killer bluffs will follow.

Chapter 11

Control Who You Are, Control the Game

Poker is a game of deception. That is a given. But it's not just the cards that must be hidden; you must also hide you. After all, the person throwing raises at you has plans and schemes, and his personality, his emotions—who he is—permeate every move he makes. But while you're figuring out what makes him tick, he's going to be staring right back at you. Have you thought about what he's picking up from you, and how you can use it?

What Is Table Image?

The way you are viewed while you battle for chips is called your table image. Since poker is a psychological game, you can be sure the good players will be watching your every move, without seeming to be. They will probe your head like a surgeon in search of a weakness. If you are looking back, they will try to use that. If you aren't, they will use that too. The bad players won't notice anything unless you hit them over the head with it; the good players are your main concern. They are the ones who can beat you up, and, counterintuitive as it might at first seem, they are also the ones who can be manipulated by a controlled use of your table image.

If you are to win, your image cannot give away your real personality or playing style, so it follows that your persona—like most things in poker—must be deceptive. From the moment you sit down, you should mold your image to be the way *you* want it. You choose the image that will win you the most money in a particular game, and then develop it. You present the face that *you* wish your foes to see. If you have to act, then go win an Oscar! If anyone catches on, just as with aggressive play, change gears.

Remember, you do not have to play like your real personality. Each poker game is an opportunity to re-create yourself. If you've got the guts, you can be anyone you want to be. You don't know these people, but even if you do, it doesn't matter. You don't care about what they think of you personally—all you care about is that they buy what you're selling. And besides, you won't see most of them again, anyway. You create a persona that sends a message—either subtle or overt, depending on the competition—and use it as long as it works. If it's not working, change it.

The most important image considerations are these:

- Be aware of the "vibe" you are projecting at the table.
- Manipulate that vibe for sound strategic purposes.
- Be aware of how your opponents will react to that vibe.

If you know how others will respond, then, to an extent, you are controlling their play. You can use those responses to make your foes predictable—and then make good plays of your own. This is just another way to keep opponents crossed up and guessing.

Many players believe personality is the key (or at least the first big clue) to discerning how someone plays. And with many people, it is a good indicator. There's an old poker proverb that says, "Know how a man plays poker, and you will know the man." Most of your opponents have just turned it around: "Know the man, and you will know how he plays poker."

What follows are some basic personality types many good players watch for when evaluating new blood. Closely observe the game you plan to join. You will have to decide when it is to your advantage to show your true colors when you sit down, and when it's better to represent an alter ego.

The Timid Type

The nonaggressive person gives himself away by not greeting players in a confident way when he sits down, not looking people in the eye, talking softly or not at all, betting in a "staccato" (not smooth) manner, mumbling when spoken to, not sticking up for himself, being run out of pots, hesitating, not betting his good hands strongly, calling all the way down on losing hands, checking and calling too much, not raising enough, not taking control of hands, not winning his first hand, and not bluffing in obvious bluffing situations—like stealing blinds or betting on the river when everyone's checked. With some shy types, this loose, passive play is replaced by play that is tight and passive, what is known as "weak-tight," where he or she folds all but "sure thing" starting hands and rarely bets.

Of course, it's easy to feel timid sitting down against nine strangers out to take your money, but you have to be strong—unless you plan to use the timid image to your advantage.

When you sit in a game for the first time, the minds of your opponents are blank slates upon which you can write the story of who are, along with your playing style. You can be anyone you wish and can manipulate them at will. Be aware of what you are writing on their chalkboards.

Why You Hide It if You Are Laid Back

You don't want to be challenged by bluffers and players trying to run you over or buy pots at your expense. It's hard enough without constantly being put to a decision. So use some phony bluster to hide that you are new and unsure or that your natural bent is to play tight and quietly wait for good hands. Bet it up early, take a few chances, slam some bets down, semi-bluff, and speak strongly and confidently. Hey, slap some guys on the back if you have to. Know the game and the rules—don't ask questions. Learn to shuffle your chips like the pros. *Make your first impression the opposite of how you intend to play.* Most people never go beyond first impressions when sizing up a new player.

The Deception Factor

To your foes, timid equals scared, and scared means "tight." That's why you should hide your quiet nature with macho posturing if you need to hunker down, such as in a real loose game. While others are thinking you are just one of the gamblers, you take pots by playing better hands and folding more. If you've always wanted to be an actor, here is the perfect stage. Acting, like poker, is rooted in deception. So study those loud, loose players to pick up mannerisms you can employ when conservative is your strategy. And if tight is the only way you can play comfortably, it is all the more important to hide that fact.

However, you do not have to play tight just because you have a retiring nature. Find a conservative game, and go be the aggressor. And if you plan to be aggressive, it isn't a bad idea to have them peg you for being tight, so—lucky you—you can just be yourself for a while after you sit down.

If you have qualities that keep you from winning, hide them. If you are not forceful enough, create a "new you." If you can't talk the talk, then work on a playing style that is more aggressive. Changing your core personality (even for a few hours) is easier said than done, sure, but the poker table is the perfect place to begin.

The Bully Type

Bully types are the same at the table as they are in life. Loud, boisterous talkers, they chat up the waitress ("sweetheart"), tip big, schmooze the dealer, play aggressively, bluff, bet it up, three-bet, try to take control, play the "rush," introduce themselves, and talk smack. Some of them can take over a table through words alone and can really put others off their games.

These aggressive players are dangerous, except the ones who overdo it and turn into ego-driven maniacs who play too loose, don't realize when to back off, and get themselves trapped by rocks with premium cards. Most players observing a boisterous personality think "loose," and loose usually means easy money.

If this is your personality, it will be hard to hide it, but if you are against quality opponents, you will do yourself a favor by acting tight and even a little timid at first. Then, when you start betting, your bets will be respected. You'll be able to rake a lot of pots that you would be called down on if others thought you were just a loud-mouthed yahoo full of hot air.

If you're a bully type, and you find you're called too often or are bluffing off too many chips, you must rein yourself in. Bullies can lose more chips in an hour than a drunken roulette player. It may not be your nature to be tight, but against top players you will have to try. Find a middle ground. You can't just ram and jam all the time. Find a slower gear— your wallet will love you for it.

When to Hide That You're Aggressive

If you're heading for a game that's tight, you will want to play looser, so start out imitating the rocks. Fold a lot, and make sure they notice. Fold to others' bets, and talk about it. Even lie about what you folded— and have it be some sure-winning hand that even the rocks would have called with. Then when you bring out your "A" game and start taking over, the rocks won't think you're full of it. They'll give your raises respect—at least for a while.

If you're in a wild game, you will want to be tighter than the field, even if every particle of your being is crying out to reraise these maniacs. So go in ramming for a loose first impression, then tighten up without letting them realize it. Still talk your macho game here, just don't play it!

That's Acting!

Becoming a good actor at the table has multiple benefits:

- Acting will help keep your feelings submerged and under control so they cannot be used against you.
- Acting allows you to disguise the value of your hand to maximize profits.
- Acting allows you adopt a persona that will win for you and to change it from game to game.
- Acting keeps opponents from knowing the real you. The less they know, the fewer weapons they have.

The above four factors are so important that alone, any of them be the difference between winning and losing. Don't you wish you had been in that high school play?

The Thinker

Intellectual types are mathematical players if they've read the books. And if they haven't, the thinkers will still always be studying and analyzing. They are methodical, unimaginative, and boring. They wear glasses, khaki pants, dress shirts, golf shirts, and nice watches, and they look professional and yuppie-ish. They're the ones who will bring up some current-events topic. They are engineers, teachers, computer guys, accountants, and other professorial types who would smoke a pipe at the table if they could.

What distinguishes these players is that they are always looking around, trying to pick up tells, and analyzing. These are positive traits, to be sure, but thinkers are way too obvious about it. Good players can do all these things without seeming to. Pros can watch you without lifting an eye from their cards.

When a thinker is at the table, he is a target for false tells and manipulation. The sharks know he is watching. They have an audience, unlike most of the time, when they are not sure if an opponent is smart enough to be ensnared by a move. They know what the thinker is looking for, and they can use that. The good players will make "obvious bluffs" with good hands, and they'll deploy transparent tells the thinker is sure to see to trap him next time.

How to Hide That You're a Thinker

To keep others from playing with your head, use deception. Be more of a good ol' boy and less of a professor. Thinkers are expected to play only top starting hands, so take some chances early. Some thinkers can hold their own with good technical play, but computer wizards who think they can roll into town for a convention and play with the big boys are in for a rude awakening. If you are attending a convention, don't tell anyone—and don't look the part. This is one time you should dress down and act like the locals if you are serious about winning.

What are "tight," "loose," "aggressive," and "passive"?
Briefly, tight means playing few hands (often too few), while loose means playing too many. Aggressive usually connotes betting frequently. Passive means not betting one's good hands strongly enough.

QUESTION?

Acting Dumb

If you're not the smartest person in the world, first, ask yourself why you're playing for money. The fact is, there aren't many dim bulbs playing poker anywhere but in $2–$4 games and at the kitchen table. So acting dumb when you are smart, as some locals do, is an iffy proposition. They wear John Deere hats and ragged clothes, don't shave, ask dumb questions, talk like yahoos, and appear to be just throwing chips around without thinking.

But the act is transparent. For one thing, after one or two good moves, it'll be obvious they know what they're doing. And the intensity can't be disguised. It is obvious they are playing to win—every hand. Acting stupid just doesn't work in poker. Intelligence has an energy to it that cannot be hidden.

ALERT!

Big John's principle of misdirection: If you're only betting quality hands, you want opponents to think you're always bluffing, so they call. If you're often trying to steal a pot, you want them to think you're only playing top hands, so they fold.

Tourists and Top Players

Nothing makes the casino locals salivate like the sight of tourists. In fact, to the regulars, being called a "tourist" is a serious insult. After days of living off each other's chum, the local sharks can smell fresh blood with the deadly acuity of their finned brethren. Were it not for tourists pumping money into the game, the locals would starve, because that bigger fish—the House—would eventually devour them with the rake.

Unless your game is killer, you don't want to be pegged as a tourist. Though it is not always true, regulars believe tourists are poor players. So they target the visitors in the game and try moves they wouldn't try on other locals who've seen it all before.

Skilled or not, a player new to the game is literally a fish out of water. He doesn't know if the person betting into him bluffs every other hand, or just once a year. So he must fold some hands. Either he plays a reasonable number of hands and is always put to the test, or he tightens up so much he becomes predictable and gets nibbled to death. It's a tough go when you're the only prey.

If you're really skilled, of course, you might just make a little cash acting like a tourist, but "dumbing down your look" while still playing skillfully is an acting job worthy of De Niro. You'd better have a lot of miles on you before you try that, because acting dumb makes you a target and is generally an unsound strategy.

Tourist Traps

Here are some "tourist" characteristics to avoid unless you want to be shark meat. First, don't look the part: no farmer hats from your hometown, outfits you would only wear on vacation, Hawaiian shirts, shorts, high socks, or T-shirts from your local auto parts store. Next, don't act the part. No fancy umbrella cocktails. Don't ask "Where are you from?" or having your spouse come by to say she's going to the pool or the Forum Shops, then talking about what shows she wants to see and wishing you good luck. At that point, you'll need it.

If you are a new face, many opponents will automatically assume you are from out of town, and they will thus assume you play poorly. As top pro D. R. Sherer writes, "They have little respect for their fellow players. They seem to believe that anyone who does not play as they do is of lesser intelligence." That arrogance is their weakness. Use it. Find the prevailing strategy at your table (usually some rock-like approach learned from some ancient book), and then start playing with their heads. Let them think you're loose or passive, and then disappoint them.

If you want to fit in and act like a low-limit local, just observe for awhile. It's pretty standard. Dress drably, never smile, whisper when you talk, and act like you're working, not playing.

How Not to Tip People Off You're a Rookie

Avoid these dead giveaways if you don't want anyone to know you're new to the game: carrying chips from a lower-limit table to a higher-limit game, reading the rules posted on the wall, asking questions, betting (and acting) in a manner that is not smooth and clean, too much inconsistency in your actions, too much slow-playing, too much chatter, not understanding the blinds, acting unsure, not sticking up for yourself, not being ready for raises or being run at, being intimidated, being too tight or too loose, not being able to get away from a hand, thinking everyone's bluffing you, not being able to "shuffle" chips, or acting uncomfortable.

Manipulate Your Image to Suit the Game

Since you will usually play against your image in order to sow the maximum confusion in the minds of the enemy, try these image plays:

- In a tight game, you will want to play looser, so create a tight image.
- In a loose game, you will want to play tighter, so use a loose image.

- If you are a very good player facing all locals, if you act like a tourist, they may not suspect your moves.
- If you are sitting with weak players, act like they do. Your skills will take over soon enough.
- If you are a "tourist," don't act like it unless you are really skilled and can take the heat.
- If you are a tourist sitting in with locals, your persona should depend on whether they are loose or tight.
- If you are a local sitting with tourists, be friendly and don't act like you're just there to grind it out.

Remember, a shy person doesn't have to play weak, and a wild man can play under control. A woman can face down a man. You just need the courage to cross that psychological barrier that exists only in your mind.

FACT

Many games will be comprised of players of all stripes—loose, tight, and "just right," and both aggressive and passive. But when people have played together for a long time (such as a tableful of locals), they tend to play very much alike.

Facing Very Good Players

If you must try your hand against good opponents, they will likely be more tight than loose, so a tight demeanor might work better. Then your bets will get more respect. But you will quickly notice that these players are not too tight or too loose, but "just right." And they will be more experienced at discerning table image—real and fake—than you. They will also be betting their good hands aggressively. You will not know when they are bluffing. They will be very aware of how much is in the pot.

Acting like a tourist is probable suicide against these guys, but if you do, some may try to run you out or bluff, so you can pick up chips when you put the nuts on them. For the more sober-minded, acting like a pro with pros is wiser. It'll take some study to master that. You won't make much headway, but at least you won't be picked on.

Take caution: When you are against good players, they will be looking at the hands you show down as much as anything else to decide your style. So if you are showing down just top hands, they will think you are solid (a good player) or tight (a cautious rock). You can then play a little looser.

On the other hand, if you've been called trying to ram-and-jam a hand through and ended up losing, and you've had to turn up some questionable cards more than once, they will view you as loose, so you must now play tighter (only premium hands)—while still projecting a ram-and-jam personality. From then on, your loose image will get your top hands called.

You have changed gears without appearing to and used your table image to mask your change in style. Well done!

Chapter 12

Tells: The Subtle Roadmap to Riches

In the last chapter you learned to manipulate opponents by using your table image. Now you are ready for another profitable endeavor: discovering who your foes really are, and, more importantly, what cards they are holding. You perform this lucrative magic through the surreptitious science of tells. Recognizing and reading clues about what a player holds are key to your game.

What Are Tells?

A tell is the unintentional giveaway of a player's personality, playing style, or hand. It may lurk in anything someone does or does not do. It can be as overt and deliberate as slamming chips on the table or as faint and involuntary as the dilation of a pupil. If you were playing against robots, the machines would have no tells. It is a person's humanity that betrays him—his emotions give him up like a sneeze in the dark. If someone is practiced enough to control those emotions when he hits a flush on the river, good for him—but then the act of suppressing them will leave a trail.

Tells can be facial expressions, revealing mannerisms, body language, gestures, movements, speech patterns, a break in routine, conscious acts meant to mislead, or unconscious bodily responses to stress. The tells are out there—they differ only in subtlety. A few may be obvious. With some, it will take hours of observation and repetition to find a pattern. Others you may never spot. But you must observe and analyze. Otherwise you are no better than that robot, and since poker is a "people game," not a "card game," you know a machine could never, ever win big consistently. The machine has no tells, but it cannot spot them, either. And if you are superior to your adversaries at spotting tells (and hiding your own), you are on the path to victory.

The higher the stakes, the more your people skills come into play—like detecting tells that will save you bets or allow you to bluff. Higher limits breed tells, but the better-quality players you will face in that rarified air will be more adept at hiding them.

Tells Reveal Deception

To discover tells, you become a human lie detector. As with the machine, you must establish what is normal behavior for your subject. Lie-detector operators ask simple questions with a known "true" answer, such as "What is your name?" Since poker is a game of deception, it will not be easy to find your foe in a natural, unguarded moment, but it can be done. Watch him when he's not in a hand. Engage him in conversation, and observe his demeanor. Watch how he acts during play when he is telling the truth: betting it up when he has a big hand, for example, or acting as if he missed a draw and following that with a "true" action—folding.

Next, try to pick up when he is being deceptive. How does his demeanor change when he has a great hand, good hand, bad hand, or bluffing hand? To be successful, a player can't give away his cards or let someone know when he's got the nuts, so he often acts weak to get a bigger payoff. And he never wants his enemies to know when he's weak, or they will bet him out of a hand he so dearly wants to play, so he will act strong.

ALERT!

If you think you've discovered a tell, never let that player just muck his hand if he has called on the river and been beaten. Ask to see his hand, and remember how he played it, his mannerisms and how he looked during the hand. Without seeing the cards, you cannot be sure that you have found a genuine tell.

This deception, which at its core is "fibbing without words," creates tension that reaches its zenith during a big bluff on the river or an all-in bet in no-limit. But any deception, in a way, can be considered a bluff—a lie. The subterfuge creates changes that can be measured by the lie detector, or you. (The one exception to this would be a semi-bluff, where a player does not have the best hand but is comfortable with his play, because he still has outs and is getting sufficient odds from the pot.)

What good poker players realize is that the struggle to hide deception creates internal conflict that manifests itself in involuntary responses in the body, which are sometimes observable. Detecting them is part of your winning strategy. You also must discover deliberate attempts to mislead you. Tells are the key that unlocks these doors of deception.

Unconscious Tells

"Unconscious" or "reflex" tells are not deliberate. Like a dog wagging his tail when he's happy, your opponents may not be aware of them at all. And if they are, they may be powerless to stop those telltale responses and only mildly successful at hiding them.

Some involuntary tells include the following:

- Sweating. Obviously a sign of nervousness.
- Sudden leg shaking. Another nervous signal.
- Trembling hands. Not always a nervous sign.
- Sudden dilation of pupils. He likes what he sees.
- Throbbing jugular. His (or her) heart is racing.
- Sitting at attention. Why is he doing this now?
- Not breathing. Why isn't she? She's not dead.
- Croaky voice. He can barely get a word out.
- Why so quiet? The table "talker" is abruptly silent.

When you see an opponent exhibit one of these tells, your work is just beginning. Since some of these are a sign of tension, not trickery, you have the same problem as the lie-detector operator. Is the "lying" response the result of nerves, or actual deception?

To answer this question, you must study your opponents—when you're in a hand *and* after you've folded. For example, with the sweating type, ask yourself if he always sweats or if it just happens at certain times. Then see if it's apparent when he's bluffing or on a draw, as opposed to when he's got the nuts. If it's one or the other, and it's repeated, you may have a usable tell.

FACT

Sigmund Freud believed in tells: "He who has eyes to see and ears to hear may convince himself that no mortal can keep a secret. If his lips are silent, he chatters with his fingertips; betrayal oozes out of him at every pore."

Some players will be just as nervous when they have a monster hand and are praying someone will call as when they are on a stone bluff. This is why you verify tells before you spend money on them. Hey, some rookie players are nervous all the time.

You can avoid nervousness after making a big bet by being "one" with your decision. The tough part is over—the time leading up to your action. Regardless of the outcome, have faith that you made the correct play. Be serene and don't look back.

Shake It Up Baby!

Speaking of "oozing out," how about leg shaking? You've seen it. Someone's leg starts bobbing up and down like a jackhammer so hard you can feel the floor shake. Other times you'll only notice it if you're sitting in the next seat. You know you have found a tell here. Something triggered this response—it's not random. But is it just nervous energy? Is it a big hand, or a chance at a big hand? Or a bluff? Watch and see.

How about those trembling hands? The rails are full of birds who went broke betting into a senior citizen who made a bet in a shaky manner. Hey, maybe his hands always shake! The average player thinks a player is shaking because he's bluffing, but usually the opposite is true. It's more likely a player of any age is shaking because he finally has a winning hand. When the "shaker" lays the nuts on him, it's off to the buffet for the player who thought he had found a tell but who in fact only jumped to conclusions.

They Can't Help It

It's a known fact that the pupils in a person's eyes will momentarily dilate when she sees something she likes—a perfect third hole card on the river in Stud, for example. Of course, who's close enough to see that sort of thing? Still, it's no coincidence poker players wear sunglasses, as well as hats, and not just to cut the glare from the overhead lights. Hats also cover those telltale forehead muscles. And the glasses? They hide the expressive muscles around the eyes, and the eyes that dart every which way with minds of their own. As Amarillo Slim says, "A man's eyes show 90 percent of what he's thinking."

QUESTION?

What is the "rail"?
The "rail" is the velvet rope or railing that separates the people watching a game from those actually playing poker. The watchers are called *rail-birds,* a pathetic lot reduced to plaintively asking for money to get back in action as players walk by to go to the bathroom.

The throbbing jugular vein on the left side of a person's neck is more visible than dilating pupils, so feel free to wear high-necked shirts. Take a look in the mirror to see if yours varies in intensity. How noticeable is it? As with the pupils, it's not easy to spot, especially from the other end of the table. Unlike pupils, the pulsing could mean nervousness as much as a bluff.

Some Reliable Tells

Players usually slouch all over the place in those uncomfortable chairs. The later the hour, the lower they go. This goes double for tall people. But when you notice a player suddenly sitting up straight, watch yourself. He usually has a hand. This one's easy to spot—a tall person sitting bolt upright is not only unusual, but he will tower about a foot over everyone else. He might as well just turn his cards over—it's that obvious.

Watch for posture that says "I'm interested" right from the get-go. Good posture, leaning into the table, or a sudden posture shift are all indicators of strength.

You'll have to pay attention to see this one, but how about the guy or gal who bets and doesn't take a breath? It's obvious something's going on here. Is she bluffing, or hoping for a call because she's a lock? This one is almost always a bluff, but again, study the players for verification. If you've put your opponent on a hand during earlier streets, your decision will be easier when that big river bet or raise punches you in the grill, because you can compare the river card to what you believe your opponent is holding.

Those on a total bluff have steeled themselves for the jitters and stare-downs, so they often appear calm—so calm they can hardly breathe, their bodies are rigid, and their faces are made of stone! It's unnatural—and a probable bluff.

If you can engage players in conversation before you make a tough decision, you'll be surprised at how difficult it is for them to talk if they are stressed. Sometimes the words come out as a hoarse croak, as if they have stage fright or have been called to the principal's office. Generally, the throaty rasp of a dry mouth indicates a bluff more than a monster. Those who can talk naturally here are truly a step ahead.

The question you must ask is, "Is it natural to be acting so natural in this spot?" Perhaps acting natural is unnatural. How would a normal person act? And how has this player acted in the past in a similar situation? Is this the kind of person who might be nervous because he might not get his nut hand paid off? Or will he only be nervous when he's bluffing?

Hard-core federal prisoners used to "play the dozens" to pass the time in the joint. They'd slam each other with the most vile, disgusting, and horrifying insults, what is today called "talking smack." The first one to get mad lost the game. Remember that the next time someone is using words to try to put you off your game. Don't fall for it.

Think about this if you're ever in a no-limit tournament and someone's just made an all-in bet that could bust you, and he or she is staring you down like a statue. If you can get the bettor to talk, who knows what information might come spilling out—not in the words, but in the way they are said. Logic says a person with a cinch hand will be more at ease. So if the serenity doesn't "ring true," it means a bluff. The same goes for some of these stone-like "poker faces" you see in crucial situations. They are such expressionless masks that you know something's up.

Words Will Sometimes Hurt You

Talking is absolutely one of the biggest giveaways in poker. Only the most experienced of players can babble away without giving something up, and then only if talking is his strategy. There are players who can talk others out of their game—get them so off-stride, distracted, and frustrated that they practically go on tilt. (Paul Newman in *The Sting* is a classic example!) There are others who deliberately bait people, criticize someone's play, or even bring up religion or politics to annoy others to the point that they cannot concentrate. Try remembering tells while some yo-yo is criticizing your pet presidential candidate!

But those who can talk a good game without revealing something are few—so many words coming out, and each one a potential clue! Pay attention. It may seem like an endless stream of nonsense, but the blather is loaded with hidden meaning. It is difficult for a nonstop talker to look at his hand without giving something away in his inflection or with a hesitation. Betting is doubly hard. If he gets a hand, he'll momentarily be on overload as he decides what to do. Listen for the hesitation, even a momentary stutter. The better the hand, the greater the hesitation.

ALERT!

The old expression "Loose lips sink ships" is certainly true in poker. You can give it all away to an astute listener through subtle, uncontrollable changes in tempo, tone, pitch, or even content. And since shutting up is the deadest giveaway of all, talkers need to keep talking—which can be pretty tough if they've pushed all their chips into the pot. For "normal" players, the more you talk, the more you give away. Practice talking under pressure, in case you go all-in and someone asks you a question.

It's obvious when a talker is suddenly very interested in a hand— it's like the crickets who've been chirping all summer, but then one day . . . *silence*! The talker has shut up! That means he's either got a monster hand or on a stone-cold bluff.

Is Your Opponent Bluffing?

To a pro, bluffing is just a normal part of doing business. He's comfortable with it. But to the average player, bluffing is lying, and the way you spot a bluffer is similar to how you would spot a liar. Remember, the bluffer doesn't want to lie. The bluff is stressful. The lie is inherently wrong. He is conflicted and wants it to end quickly.

Look for these tells at your next game:

- Talking rapidly. Or urging you to "hurry up" and make a decision. The bluffer wants to get it over with.
- Being too friendly. Laughing. The bluffer wants to be your pal. He wouldn't lie, now, would he?
- Folding arms, crossing legs. Truth experts say this is a way of going into a shell, keeping the fib secret.

- Hands over the mouth or around the face. This "hides" the untruth, especially if he's been asked if he has a hand, and he's said yes.
- Head movement. When asked if he's bluffing, he says "no," but nods his head "yes" at the same time. A dead giveaway.
- Licking the lips, swallowing excessively, yawning, touching the nose. All classic signs of lying.

But make sure a yawn means more than someone just being tired! Remember that famous scene in *Rounders*, where Matt Damon discovers John Malkovich's tell? The way John held that Oreo up to his ear and twisted it just a certain way, then ate it? That was a tell unique to a specific player. If you find a tell like this, resist the urge to tell the person about it just to show off. A pot here or there, or even a bet saved now and then on the river, are the difference between winning and losing.

These tells could be anything. At the 2003 World Series of Poker, someone told Chris Moneymaker that he flared his nostrils when he bluffed. You might have a friend who bets with a different hand or puts his cigarette down when he has the nuts, or who talks more confidently, or keeps his hands on top of his cards only when he likes them. Some players bet with larger denomination chips when they have a great hand. The telltale signs could be anything from pulling on an ear to guzzling beer too fast, or taking an extra swallow. A tell might be anything at all.

Chapter 13
Tell(s) Me More!

As you put your opponents under your mental microscope to find the hidden meanings in their transparent tells, your more dangerous foes may not only be examining you—they could use your heightened interest to manipulate and direct you into a bog of quicksand instead of the lost city of gold.

A Bluffing-Tell Quandary

There is a tell that has become so well-known it has taken on a life of its own, and it illustrates the type of double- and triple-think that takes place among well-read players. The scenario revolves around the classic desire of players to appear strong when weak, and weak when strong, and it concerns those who are staring at you—hard—especially if they've put in a big bet and you're considering calling. The intense gaze was either supposed to make you whither and fold, or figure that the bettor could not make such lengthy eye contact if he was bluffing.

And there certainly is some truth to that. Many liars (bluffers) cannot look someone in the eye. It is often a legitimate tell (except among practiced poker players). Therefore, if the bettor was giving you the stare-down, it must follow that he had the good hand he was representing. So you fold. Right?

Not so fast. If he is aware of that thinking, then he will stare you down through an effort of will. He has nothing (weak), but is representing strength with intimidating eye contact, daring you to call. Here is where top player/author/lecturer Mike Caro comes in. His groundbreaking *Book of Tells*, published in 1984, is still the definitive work on the subject. In it, he states, "Players staring at you are usually less of a threat than players staring away."

FACT

In a pivotal hand of the 2003 World Series of Poker final table, eventual winner Chris Moneymaker bluffed out seasoned pro Sam Farha, who ignored two obvious tells: first, Chris stared him down after his all-in bet, and second, Chris put his hand over his mouth—a classic sign of deception.

Players staring away are nonconfrontational, passive—"not a problem." They are representing weakness, the thinking goes, and therefore they are strong, for rarely would someone deliberately represent weakness if he was in fact weak. Players staring at you want you to feel strength and back off. Someone with a very good hand wouldn't want you to back off, so he must be weak.

Now, two decades later, the "staring-at-you-means-weak" tell has been so publicized that many are back to staring at you with big hands again. They stare at you, you think they're weak, you call or raise, and—wham!—they put the nuts on you. Go figure!

Clues to Playing Style

If you've read Caro's *Book of Tells,* be aware that over the past twenty years, some of the tells described in the book have become common knowledge, so it's not unusual for players to do the opposite to cross you up. Here's a case in point. Caro talks about how players "shuffling" their hole cards—after getting their final card in Stud, for example—is often an indicator that they need "help" to make a hand. Today, players will shuffle these cards when they already have a made hand just to fool you.

But there remain some very reliable tells offering clues to how someone plays. For example, a neat dresser is more apt to play tight. Someone who keeps his chips in ultra-neat, twenty-chip stacks—even going so far as to line up the markings on the side—is almost always a tight player with a plan. People with money jammed haphazardly in their pockets are loose and prone to gamble. Those who reach in their wallets like a Florida octogenarian dipping into her change purse in the grocery line will be too worried about money to play a lot of hands.

Your basic strategy against the tight ones, of course, is to play fewer hands, bluff more, and realize that if they are in they have some kind of hand. Against the loose players, you play more hands but bluff less, as they are more prone to calling. It is harder to spot tells on top players for many reasons, not the least of which is that they are at peace with their play, win or lose. They are confident they have done the right thing, even if it's a stone-cold bluff, so they will not appear nervous, unlike an inexperienced player just taking a flyer.

Study the Players to Dig Up Deceit

Experts have their bodies under control and are skilled at appearing natural. You won't find them sweating, shaking, or croaking. Sure, it's unnatural to be perfectly calm in a pressure situation, but top players can sublimate the tension, and they are used to the mental conflict of deception. The stress will manifest itself, but in ways too subtle for most to notice.

At the same time, the experts will be deliberately deceptive to steal a pot that is rightfully yours. But all is not lost. Their moves require action, and within every action hides a tell. Subtle, perhaps, but still there. You uncover the deceit by smoking out what he wants you to believe and what action he really wants you to perform, and then doing the opposite.

If you don't think pros put out false tells, check this out from Phil Hellmuth's Web site: "When I put my chips into the pot, I bet them with my favorite 'bluffing tell.' I tried to make Erik (Seidel) think I was bluffing with my hand motions, facial expressions, the way I put in the chips, and the way I stacked the chips before I bet."

Make a List, Check It Twice

A major weapon is a mental rundown of who the deceptive players are at your table. Observe the game closely. Ask to see called hands. Some folks will never represent a hand they don't really have. It's just too much trouble. This might cost them some bets, but for them, to be free of mental conflict is worth it. Then there are those who are rarely deceptive. They'll run a play once or twice in position. And, of course, there are the dangerous players—those who are a threat to steal on every hand. If you give them an inch, they'll take the pot.

When you have a tough call, look at the player. If he's on the deceptive list, of course you should call more often, especially if there's been something about the betting pattern that isn't "quite right."

Hold'em Illustration

Say you have Q-J in Hold'em. You and three others see the flop without a raise, which is Q-10-7 rainbow. Two players check to you, you bet, and the player behind you raises. The two checkers fold. What do you do? Here's where your list is a lifesaver. If the raiser is a tight player, you know full well he has at least a queen, and he probably wouldn't play a queen with a lower kicker than yours. The fact that there was no preflop raise and he was on the button is your only hope. If there had been a preflop raise, you would be 100-percent certain the rock has a better hand than you. (See the value of raising preflop in late position?) You could reraise, and then if he raised you back (unlikely for a rock), you fold. But if he calls, then what do you do? You risk a check-raise on the turn or a sure bet if you check. Best option is to either fold right now, or check and call him all the way to the river to see if you are beaten. But wait! When he raised you, he did it with authority. You know from playing with him for five hours that he only does this when he has a real hand. Is this the one time all night he's crossing you up? Don't bet on it! Fold with confidence.

QUESTION?

What kind of expression should you have at the table?
The best poker face appears confident, natural, and doesn't give anything away when the cards hit. Show the countenance of a warrior: strong, smart, and ready, and ruled by neither anger nor passivity.

There's a big difference if the raiser is on your "loose" list. Then you reraise him for sure. At best, he has a queen with a worse kicker than you, or a draw. He's a guy who would automatically raise preflop on the button into three limpers with almost anything. You figure him for an ace or second or third pair, perhaps J-10, K-7, or A-7.

There's one caution, and here is where your tell-reading comes in. Did he slow-play a real hand (A-Q, K-Q, aces, kings, queens, tens) on the button? The only thing that will save you in this situation is if you know this player! The moral is this: The odds can give you the probability that you're beat, but with a tell, you can be certain.

Your Opponents' Unguarded Moments

Players give away their hands most often in the instant they see cards for the first time and when they must take some overt action, such as betting.

Watch your opponents' eyes, faces, hands, and bodies at these crucial moments:

- The first time they look at their hole cards. Recall their reactions to different hands.
- When they look at their last hole card (Stud). Watch others, not your own hand.
- When the flop is turned over. Look at others, not the cards. You can peek later.
- When the turn is exposed, then the river—especially the critical final card.

Once you have noted players' responses to the cards, compare them to the final hands turned over on the river. Caution: Try to hide that you're watching! And as for yourself, train yourself not to react. Use the same expression, the same routine, the same body language, and the same "vibe," no matter what your hand is.

There's Nowhere to Hide When You Bet

It's easy to be still and quiet sitting in your chair, but when you must act, the whole world is watching. The most overt act in poker is betting, and it is imperative you give nothing away here. Remember to bet in a smooth, controlled, consistent, confident manner. You're not at a final table on the World Poker Tour, so don't take a ton of time. Don't bet too strongly or too meekly. Practice handling your chips so you know what you're doing. The more consistent you are, the fewer tells. Remember to bet with your whole body, not just your hands, so make sure your eyes, facial expression, and body language all back up the bet. As detailed in Chapter 8, you want the bet to convey strength. Most importantly, you want to have a set routine and to bet the same way every time. If you say "bet" or "raise" verbally, then your voice must be identical from bet to bet, hand to hand.

Look for the opposite of these things in your foes: a break in their routine, inconsistencies in the way they have a bet a hand, inconsistencies in the "emotional message." These are all tells. It's probably the old trick again of pretending to be strong when they are weak or weak when strong.

How to Spot a Bettor's Pants on Fire

Someone hiding the nuts or running a bluff must bet. Watch for a break in routine, such as betting faster or slower than normal, slamming chips down harder or softer than usual, betting with a different hand, counting the chips differently, betting high-denomination chips instead of a stack of lower, saying "raise" when he usually just puts the chips in, putting the chips out in a different spot, and being less smooth.

FACT

After reading *Penny Ante* by Edward Allen (1992), it's easy to understand why someone might have trouble maintaining a poker face while betting: "The pure sensuality of the betting moment. . . . It is a neurological jolt made up of greed, lust, and excitement mixed together with a strong dose of fear."

Inconsistency means something isn't quite right with the way a foe played his hand. For example, if there's Q-J-10 on board and he's representing A-K in the hole, why didn't he bet it preflop like he always has before? Inconsistencies in emotional message you grasp on an almost subliminal level. If you've ever seen someone smile without seeming happy (a phony smile), you get it. Somehow, a player's gestures don't seem to link up with the strong message inherent in the bet. Something seems weak. The body language, the face—lying eyes, perhaps. There's nothing behind it; she didn't really believe in the bet. It's a lazy lie, a bluff by someone not comfortable with lying and who deep down doesn't want to do it. The internal turmoil, the unfamiliar ground, throws the *timing* of the bet off. Everything just "feels" wrong.

Handling the Cards: Information Overload

A player's cards are his beloved children, yet he must part with them so soon. But while he has them, you should watch those precious jewels closely because the attention (or lack thereof) he lavishes on them can be very telling. What does he do when he first gets his hole cards? No matter how he hides it, there will be a reaction. Is his heart racing?

Or is he ready to fold? You cannot always see it, but you can usually feel it.

If you look left, some players in preflop Hold'em will be holding their two cards in their hand, ready to muck. What a great tell! More players you don't have to worry about. Still others, only slightly less obvious, remove their poker faces and don't try to disguise their imminent departure.

Watch Players Looking at Their Cards

Unless you're under the gun preflop, first watch the other players look at their hole cards. Don't peek at your own until you have to. Then look around before you commit yourself to the pot. Observe who's already decided to see the flop. Better players aren't obvious, but after they've taken that first peek, they always do something with the cards. It's common to pull them back toward their chips if it's a good hand. Placing some chips or a marker on top is a good indicator as well, because most players are too lazy to go through all that trouble if they are going to fold right away.

ALERT!

Don't be a preflop monkey who gives away if he's going to fold. Treat your hole cards exactly the same whether you have a great, mediocre, or trash hand. Place them in front of you as you observe others look at their hands, then, when the action is coming to you, look at your hand and either muck it or put a chip on it.

Better players, however, sometimes will "play games" by putting the marker on there—then fold anyway. Or if they are in the blind, they use the marker to represent strength and discourage raises, so they can get in cheaply. But if it's a good hand, you can be sure the player will protect it somehow: wrap his hands around it, put chips on it, something, at least until others have ceased flipping their cards into the muck.

Avoid Looking at Hole Cards During a Hand

You shouldn't have to look at your hole cards. Memorize them. You don't necessarily have to recall suits, unless you're suited, but if you can't even remember your cards, you really have no business playing. If you have to return to your cards, it is a tell. It means you think you have something.

You can be sure your good opponents know their hole cards, so if you see one looking at or "analyzing" his hand, it is a move. He knows what he has. Now it's up to you to decide what he's up to. Watch for reaction whenever anyone goes back to his or her hand—it's a free second chance to pick up a tell.

QUESTION?

Should I watch the dealer put down the flop?
No. When the dealer is turning up the flop, don't watch the cards; watch players' *reactions* to the cards. You can look later. In Stud, watch for tells as players receive up cards.

There is one time when even some good players check their hole cards in Hold'em. It's when three of a suit hit the board, and people scramble to see if they have a card of that suit in case a fourth one hits. If someone bets after taking a peek, you can rest easy that he does not have a made flush. If he had two suited cards, he would have known it, and wouldn't have had to peek.

False Tells

In David Mamet's great film *House of Games,* a tough backroom player sets up his victim by twisting his ring when he's bluffing. After he knows his quarry has picked up on the tell, the pro switches up and takes the money. He twisted the ring—and had the nuts. It was no tell at all—it was a trap. All that was necessary was for it to get noticed.

Smooth, confident, and calculating under pressure, the pro knows he can't do much against a bad player but show him good hands and wait for mistakes. But against thinking players, he'll set traps and use false tells, and they'll be a lot subtler and more complex than just grabbing some chips and acting like he's going to bet so you think he's strong, when in fact he just wants you to check because he is weak and wants a free card.

Chapter 14

Your Opponents: It's a Jungle out There!

Modern gladiators don't duel with swords—they duel with dollars. The blows can be just as cruel, but that doesn't keep a true warrior from battle. You bet on yourself and stride confidently into the arena. But before you do, it's a good idea to know who you're fighting.

The Four Classic Styles of Play

There are four distinct types of casino players, and your strategy against each will be markedly different. You will fall into one of these categories as well—more or less—but you will outplay your foes, first by changing your style of play during a game and adapting your style to the specific players you're facing; and second, by disguising which type you are at any given moment by playing "against" your personality, as described in Chapter 11, and by giving verbal and visual cues that identify you as a different type than you really are. Of course, you'll be on the alert for other savvy players doing the same. The four types are discussed here, in order from weakest to strongest.

"Loose" and "tight" refer to how many hands a person plays and how long he or she stays in the hand. "Passive" and "aggressive" describe how strongly a person bets with a hand, and how often someone will bluff, semi-bluff, or push an advantage, even a small one.

The Loose-Passive Player

Loose-passive is the weakest way to play. Loose-passive types play too many hands, which means they are second-best (or worse) starting out. They stick with the hands too long, so they often just call all the way, where they are again second-best. They always believe someone is trying to bluff them, and a lot of people have gone broke trying to, because loose-passives will always call if they've stayed to the river. This is the type who will "keep you honest." Known as "calling stations," they come to play, and it pains them to fold a hand. In fact, they will keep calling if there is even the remotest chance of hitting a hand. They don't understand (or don't want to understand) outs, odds, and pot odds.

This is the type that always seems to be putting a bad beat on you, but in reality, this is the player who is feeding you the most chips. Sure, he'll hit a longshot draw once in a while, but that's good, because he'll be less inclined to change his style. Whatever you do, don't criticize his play, and if he beats you, just say "Nice hand"—like you mean it! Calling stations are common in low-limit, and if you have a few loose-passives in a game, it will be hard for you to lose. More than a few, and you should never leave the game. Don't sleep, don't eat, don't even go to the bath-room until you have their money.

Loose-passives will play almost anything in almost any position. If they have 9-5 offsuit, it's, "Hey, I could make a straight!" Any two suited cards, and it's "Hey, I could make a flush."

Loose-passives are constantly getting burned by having the ignorant (low) end of a straight or a jack-high flush when someone else has ace-high. Or the flop is 8-7-6 when they have that 9-5, and they think they have a lock. Then a better player turns over 10-9 suited.

FACT

Phil Hellmuth uses animals to characterize the four playing styles. Loose-passive players are elephants, tight-passive types are mice, loose-aggressive players are jackals, and tight-aggressive types are lions. The lion, of course, is the desirable type.

The problem with the "passive" part of their play is that when they finally get in the lead, they don't bet it. They're real liberal when it comes to contributing to the pot, but not when it comes to pushing a slight edge. They don't isolate, buy pots, and won't use their passive image to steal a blind. If they bet, you know they've got a real hand, so that's your cue to fold like your cards are on fire.

The Tight-Passive Player

Of all the player types, tight-passives are held in the most contempt. Also known as "weak-tight," they play like their last meal is on the line. These "rocks" will wait and wait for a good starting hand, but they rarely bet it when they get one. These often-older players can remember back to when they had kings cracked or the times when A-K lost for them, so they often won't raise with these hands preflop. They've learned their lesson, by cracky! And queens? Forget it! What if an ace flops?!

Tight-passives have an idea of position but not of isolation. They will get angry when you raise their blinds—or raise at all—and if *they* raise, they expect you to fold. In Stud, they will raise the maximum on third street with an ace showing, but if you call, you'll get a dirty look. Their idea of odds is a sure thing—having a 2-to-1 edge isn't enough for a bet.

Tight-passives often check on the river with the best hand if they don't have the nuts, and they play as if they expect their opponent to have the best possible hand.

ALERT!

Each type of player wants you to play just like them. "Rocks think you should only win pots with the big cards . . . but they're wrong. You're supposed to win pots with any cards you can."
—D. R. Sherer, writing in *No Fold'em Hold'em*

With such a tight image, a bluff from a tight-passive would be powerful, but they rarely try it—the money is just too precious. When these players bet, you can be sure they have something. If they raise, they've got the nuts! If a rock is in the hand past the flop, there's a reason—and it won't be a draw. These players can be driven from pots, but be careful. Many of them are stubborn. If one is in with his premium starting hand, he will very often call you down. Their feeling is that you should respect their tight image and give them the pot when they're in it. If you are going to bluff, make sure there's a scary flop and you have been betting your hand like you have what you are representing. Remember, they fear the worst, so bet like you have it.

The Loose-Aggressive Player

Loose-aggressives are the wild men (or women) of poker. They single-handedly can change the nature of an entire game. Constantly putting everyone to the test, they put the "A" in aggression. Unfortunately for them, and fortunately for you, their aggression is extreme—not controlled. They are not selective, and they don't back off soon enough when they encounter strength.

These loose players are the serial daters of poker; they've never met a hand they didn't fall in love with. Called "maniacs," they can drive good players crazy, because good players won't call even a crazy man with just anything. And their aggressiveness takes away many of the good players' moves.

Like the loose-passives, they play too many hands, and they see a lot of flops in Hold'em and fourth and fifth streets in Stud. But unlike the elephants, maniacs will bet their hands. And bet them big. It seems like they are always bluffing and "betting on the come." Even when you realize they are pushing some hands that aren't all that good, you will have to risk some serious money to beat them.

QUESTION?

Do cardrooms use shills and proposition players to start games?
Yes. *Shills* play with casino money and are called on to start new tables or keep games going when players are scarce. *Props* are good players paid an hourly wage by a cardroom to fill empty seats on demand. Props use their own money and keep their winnings. Here's a tip to remember: House players cannot check-raise. And if you ask, floorpeople must tell you who the House players are. Most are very tight-aggressive.

If the maniacs are catching cards, they can win a bundle. They control the game, and they sure know how to build a pot. But sooner or later, they have to pay the piper. You can only go in with second-best hands so often before folks get the stones to call you down. You can lose a lot of chips in a great big hurry trying to ram through speculative hands, like four-flushes, four-straights, and Q-9 suited. When they start getting beat, they go on tilt, yell at the dealer, and their money will fly around like it's raining hundred-dollar bills.

Curiously, it isn't always the better players who take the maniacs' money. It's the rocks and calling stations! They keep calling and calling, and soon the maniac is no more, because without chips to bet with, Puff the Magic Dragon must silently slip into his cave.

The Tight-Aggressive Player

Compared to the other three types, tight-aggressive players are experts. They are selective about their starting hands and will vary those hands according to position. They play fewer hands than the maniacs and calling stations, but more than the rocks. But the big difference between experts and rocks is that when experts enter a hand, they go in betting or raising. Their philosophy is, "If it's good enough to stay in with, it's good enough to raise with." Expert players protect their hands, bet them, and push the lead—however slight—and they know when to back off. They don't keep trying to bluff out players who aren't going anywhere. They pay attention to their opponents and adjust their play accordingly. They will change their image and shift gears, and they won't get rattled.

Unlike the calling stations and maniacs, experts don't just play their own hands. Their strategy is based on what they think their opponents have. They are aggressive, but unlike the loose-aggressives, they are selective. Experts aren't relentlessly driving at pots, so their bets maintain respect.

The Game Itself Has a Personality

It isn't just the players who will fit (more or less) into one of these four categories—the games themselves will also. You can think of the game you're in as loose-passive, loose-aggressive, tight-passive, or tight-aggressive. You make this judgment mainly by the amount of betting and raising that's going on, the quality of the hands being played, and how many see the flop. Then you adjust accordingly, using the same general strategy you would use against a player of the specific type.

Here is a quick rule of thumb: Against the loose players, you call more but bluff less. Against the tight types, you call less but bluff more.

You'd be surprised how often this simple strategy works, and it works because of a sort of "poker peer pressure" among players who are "regulars" and play against each other often. You will find that most people who play together a lot play alike. It's amazing. In some L.A.-area cardrooms, eight out of ten players are loose. In Vegas and Reno, the ratio is reversed. This little nugget can help you tremendously when you are on unfamiliar turf: Know one player, know them all.

Strategy Against the Four Types

If you followed the sections on loose and tight games, bluffing, tells, and table image, you should have a pretty good idea about how to attack the four kinds of players. If you can ace this quiz on strategy, you're on your way!

1. Which types should you try to bluff?
2. Which ones should you try to isolate?
3. Which players would you like sitting on your right, acting before you?
4. Who should you not slow-play against?
5. Which type would you expect to try to bluff you?
6. Which one should you bluff if there is a ragged flop?
7. Who should you fear if three suited cards flop, or three to a straight (9-8-6)?
8. Which type would you most like to bring home to mother?

Answers

1. You bluff the tight players (experts and rocks), because the loose ones are more likely to call. Rocks don't like risk, and good players can lay down a hand, as long as your bluff makes sense and you haven't tipped it with a tell.
2. Isolate against the players who are more likely to have weak hands. These are the loose players, namely, maniacs and calling stations.
3. You want maniacs and experts on your right, because they can cost you money. If a maniac has raised, as he often will, you can reraise and isolate him. If an expert bets, you can fold cheaply. But if you must act before these players, you must fold hands that can't stand a raise.
4. Never slow-play against loose players. There's no reason to—maniacs and calling stations won't fold, and the maniac might raise! But if you have a monster and don't want to scare the cautious rock or tip off the expert that you have a hand, then slow-play. Just remember that giving free cards can be risky.
5. The ones who will bluff you are the two least likely to get away with it—the expert and the maniac. The maniac gets caught because he does it too often, the expert because you expect him to try something.
6. The rock. You know he only plays high cards, so he'll have missed the flop. He won't risk calling you all the way to the river (with his ace) just to see if you're bluffing, unless he has (maybe) A-K. Maniacs and calling stations may have paired one of the dubious cards they play, and they will probably call anyway, so it's not worth the bet—and the expert will know what you are up to.

7. The maniac and the calling station, of course, because they will play any two suited cards, and yes, even hands such as 10-7 or 7-5.
8. Bring home the maniac if your mom is a biker; the rock if your mother is an accountant; the calling station if your mom just likes to eat chocolates and watch television; and the expert if your mom appreciates good poker.

So, how well did you do? Take this quiz again until you get every question right.

What Does It Mean When They Bet?

When a calling station or a rock bets, be afraid—very afraid. The calling station has the nuts (or what he thinks is the nuts), and the rock has one of the premium hands he waits all day for. If the maniac bets—well, he always bets, doesn't he? When he doesn't bet—that's when you need to worry. Either he's taking a hand off to catch his breath, or he might actually have a real hand this time. If the expert bets, he probably has something, but more likely he's just betting because you didn't.

ALERT!

A raise from a rock or calling station should mean an immediate fold, and while one from an expert is to be feared, be alert for position bets and bluffs, especially if others appear weak. A bet from a maniac usually means nothing—he will only rarely hit his hand.

There's a strategy point regarding experts, especially those who have dropped down from higher limits. When you evaluate this person, remember that he is used to folding a lot of hands after a bet, because the high-limit games are tighter. So he will be susceptible to a bluff. He's used to laying a hand down—the exception being the high-limit player who is playing too loose after he drops down due to the smaller stakes. In this case, he will surely lose.

And here's an interesting dilemma when it comes to maniacs. If you are in a short-handed game, he will be tough to beat, as his wide-open play is tailor-made for four players or fewer, when you must play more (and weaker) hands and take some chances to keep the blinds and antes from killing you. If you are short-handed with this type, your best course is to find another table. He will either force you to toss some winning hands or call him all the way to the river with your unpaired ace, hoping for the best.

If there is an expert at your table, stay out of his way until you are sure you have a better starting hand than he does, then bet it strongly into him, and don't let up. Don't enter a hand where he has bet or raised and you are only able to call. Bet powerfully to get respect. Win your first hand against him at all costs.

A Cast of Characters

There's a key question that few players ever think to ask, and it is this: What motivates the person sitting next to you? Who are these people, really? Why are they in the casino, on this day, at this time? Fun, or conquest? Diversion, or desperation? Vacation, or vocation? Why aren't they home? Don't be afraid to make a little conversation to flesh out these human beings surrounding you.

Here are a few of the more predictable poker beings, and, in general, what to expect from them:

- Older men playing low-limit games in the morning or afternoon to supplement their Social Security. That's right, they play real tight and protect their bankroll.
- "Kids" in their twenties. They haven't played long enough to get it, and use scared money. Sometimes they're online players trying out real poker. They're too tight or too aggressive.
- Players with a boyfriend or girlfriend sitting behind them. Only a fool brings a significant other to a poker game. It's totally boring for him or her, and it hurts your play.
- Loud good ol' boys. They're too busy back-slapping, yapping, talking about home, gabbing on the cell phone, and calling the cocktail waitress to concentrate on the game.

- Dealers. When they go off-duty, many gambling halls let them take their tip money and sit in. A questionable practice, but lucrative—for you! Despite their hours watching, most dealers can't play.
- Guys in suits. He's obviously come right from work: What does that tell you? Unlike years ago, "suits" aren't necessarily losers. But they're not big winners, either.
- Women. Females are still rare in poker, so they get on the list as a "type." If you see a woman playing at, say, three in the morning, you must give her credit for knowing something. Be careful.
- Older women. They're tight, yes, but they will not be bluffed. Keep in mind that they had the courage to learn the game at a time when poker-playing was scandalous for a female.
- Macho men. You know the type—loud, blustery, and controlling. They bet a lot, but their Achilles heel is they feel it is emasculating to fold. They will not risk being bluffed out, so they pay off your big hands.

If you see people who quietly watch everything, rarely laugh, push for a fast pace, and act "impatiently patient"—like some internal clock is ticking—these are players concerned about their "hourly rate." That's how much they expect to make per hour—from you! If they're good, they can outwait you. When you get frustrated and start playing poorer hands, that's when they get you. You don't want many of these types at your table.

Is the Perfect Poker Player *Female?*

Poker is still very much a man's game. In any cardroom or tournament, 80 to 90 percent of the players will be male. But more women are trying their hand every day. If you are female, realize that you will be thought of as a "woman player" until you prove yourself, because women players have a reputation in low- and medium-limit games as being very tight and unimaginative. If you are female and skilled, you have a tremendous advantage, because most players will underestimate you. Many male players will assume you can be intimidated and will try to run over you, in which case you call their obvious bluffs.

It is an anomaly in these days when the sky's the limit for women that the majority of female players are older. They had to have learned at a time when poker was considered "unladylike," and "the fair sex" was all but banned from the tables. It is also a mystery why more women don't take up the game during these more enlightened times. After all, when you think about it, the game is perfectly suited for a woman. A woman can control a man and a relationship without lifting a finger. All she needs are her subtle manipulative skills, her shrewdness, and most importantly, a good poker face and the ability to "read" her mate with an "intuition" most men can only dream of having. When you think about it, the perfect poker player might be a woman, because she's grown up using poker skills every day. You know how men always complain that they "don't understand women"? Well, you never hear a woman say she doesn't understand men. Women understand men all too well. If they ever brought this insight to the table, the poker world would be turned upside down.

If you are a woman and want to know how a particular (male) opponent plays, just ask! He'll usually be happy to expound at length on this or any other topic as long as you act impressed. You'd be amazed at what tough-as-nails players will give away to a woman who feeds their egos. Just don't try this on another woman—she'll know what you're up to.

Women should use whatever it takes to get the money, whether it be playing "like a man" or using femme-fatale feminine charm. Guys, your best bet is to not underestimate the women and to play man-tough against them.

Remember, it's a jungle out there, full of lions, jackals, elephants, mice, maniacs, human beings of all persuasions, and that most dangerous beast of all: the expert poker player. You know that little voice in your head that alerts you to danger? That's your jungle sense. It makes your hair stand on end when you're being watched and warns you when someone's sneaking up behind you. Use this sixth sense to survive around the green felt, and you will be the most feared creature in the jungle.

Chapter 15

Texas Hold'em: The Pros' Game

Texas Hold'em has evolved from an obscure fifty-year-old community-card variation called Hold Me Darling to the most popular poker game in the world. Beloved by serious players, television and online exposure have spawned millions of new converts to this deceptively simple game. If you learn to play Hold'em correctly, these new players will be fattening your wallet real soon.

Why Hold'em Is Hot

For most players, Hold'em is simply more fun. While you enter the hand holding only two cards, you get your next three after just one (small-bet) round. That's five cards for the price of one betting round! To see your sixth card it's just one more small bet. In Stud, you must wade through two small-bet rounds to see five cards, and to see sixth street you must call big bets. As Doyle Brunson writes in *Doyle Brunson's Super System*, "Hold'em has more variety to it than any other form of poker. And more complexity. It has something for everybody . . . the mathematicians and psychologists . . . the 'loose-gooses' and the 'hard-rocks.'"

Here are some other good things about Hold'em:

- It goes twice as fast as Stud, so it's great for solid players who fold a lot.
- More hands per hour is good for pros who feel they have an edge.
- There is no memorizing of cards, so you can concentrate on strategy.
- More players (ten) means more participants and bigger pots.
- Your position stays constant throughout a hand, a big advantage.
- Hands are easier to fold in Hold'em when nothing materializes.

Most of all, good players feel they can win more money with less risk at this game.

The Effect of Shared Cards

Community cards turn Hold'em into a controlled burn. For one thing, you usually know "where you are at" in a hand. It is easier to predict opponents' holdings, you always know what the nut hand is, and hands are more competitive since 71 percent of your cards are shared with others. Because the hands are closer in value, the pots are bigger, and your player-reading skills become paramount.

ALERT!

Big John's Tips: Hold'em is much more complicated than it appears, and it is filled with subtlety and nuances that can cost you money. Play tight and cautiously at first.

If you are in the lead, it is much harder for someone to draw out on you than in Stud, where he or she is sitting with a mittful of who knows what. In Hold'em, you are not playing in a vacuum. Your hand is forever linked to your opponents' hands. When the river card hits, it is shared—and visible.

The Power: High Cards and Kickers

Good Hold'em play is based on the simplest of principles: High cards beat low cards. Hold'em is a game of being in the lead and betting strongly, so you want that power in the hole. Hold'em is not a game to be chasing pair versus pair because if you improve, your opponent will often improve also, due to the community-card nature of the game. If you don't consistently start with higher cards than your foes, you will not win. So you don't want to be chasing with drawing hands like 8-7 unless you can get in cheaply and have a large field to pay you off should you "get lucky" and hit. And as the hand progresses, you don't stay with the draw unless you're going for the nuts. In this case, you either have the pot odds to stay or have a reasonable chance at winning on a bluff when you miss. The good news is you will usually know if you are drawing at the nuts and can fold cheaply on the flop if you don't improve.

But draws should be the exception. Unless you are in a "no fold'em Hold'em" game, in which almost everyone stays in, drawing hands are not the primary way to win at this game. You win by playing high cards with high kickers and, because you know so much about your opponents' hands, you use what they don't have against them.

Hand Domination

Besides the rare monster pocket pairs (aces, kings, queens), starting hands like A-K and A-Q have the power. You ask, "Aren't these drawing hands, since you don't even have a pair?" Well, they are not drawing hands in that they are the highest hand *right now*. Since it is 16-1 against someone being dealt a pocket pair, you figure your high ace is tops. Sure, in a ten-person game, *someone* will get a pair every other hand, but unless it is aces, kings, or queens, that pair just isn't that strong if it's not heads-up, because odds are there will be at least one overcard on the flop. And the chance of someone being dealt a pair of aces, kings, or queens is slim: about 73-1.

Yes, you'll pair your hole card on the flop just three out of ten tries, but you can say the same about your opponents. Except for flopping "nothing," pairing a hole card is still the most frequent occurrence on the flop. All other results are freaks. If you hit, you know you have top pair with top kicker (with your ace-face hand). If you all miss, you're still high, and since you've bet preflop, you still control the hand. You can predict if your opponent has missed by knowing your players. The only bad result is if he pairs and you don't, and in that case you will likely have overcards. Unless your foe hits a longshot flop like two pair or trips or a straight-flush draw, other possibilities favor the high cards.

What you seek most with your high card/high kicker like A-J is for some sap to play A-8 or A-6 suited. This is called a dominated hand, and it is a big money loser. If you have A-K, the A-x has only three outs—pairing his "x" card (of which there are three remaining in the deck). With no improvement, your king kicker beats him, and an ace on board traps him. If the flop is A-9-5, he must pair his kicker to win—just a 12-percent shot with two cards to come—and even then you could pair your king. Being suited does not help. Two suited cards will make a flush just 6 percent of the time, and a third of those are runner-runner (made on the turn and the river). A dominated hand like A-x to A-K is a costly 4-to-1 dog from square one. Winning players avoid dominated hands.

Table 15-1 Odds of Being Dealt Hold'em Starting Hands					
Any pair	16-1	6%	Suited connectors	27-1	4%
Aces	220-1	.5%	1 or more aces	6-1	15%
Kings	220-1	.5%	A pair or an ace	4-1	20%
Aces or kings	110-1	.9%	Two suited cards	3-1	24%
Aces/kings/queens	73-1	1.4%	Unsuited connectors	7.5-1	12%
A-K (any)	82-1	1.2%	A top-ten hand	22-1	4%
A-K suited	331-1	.3%	A top-twenty hand	9-1	10%

There are exactly 1,326 possible starting hands in Hold'em. When you factor in the four suits, there are six ways of making a pair and sixteen ways of making any other hand. Since offsuit hands are the same, there are actually only 169 distinctly different hands: seventy-eight suited hands, seventy-eight unsuited hands, and thirteen pairs.

The top twenty moneymaking hands are generally considered to be aces, kings, queens, jacks, A-Ks, tens, A-K, A-Qs, K-Qs, A-Js, A-10s, A-Q, nines, K-Js, K-Q, K-10s, A-9s, A-J, eights, and Q-Js ("s" means suited).

Where Are the Aces?

Aces are your best friend in Hold'em, and you'll be dealt one 15 percent of the time (one out of seven hands). When you consider that your opponent has only a 6-percent chance of having a pocket pair, your ace seems even stronger. And even if someone does have a pair, you can still flop the *highest* pair. But be careful! You want your other friend guarding your back—a high kicker. Aces with low kickers are money-drainers. Realize that in a ten-handed game, if you have an ace, there is a 75-percent chance someone else out there has one, too. If you *don't* have an ace, there is an 84-percent chance of a bullet lurking out there. (In a five-handed game, if you have an ace, there is a 41-percent chance of someone else having one; if you don't, 51 percent of the time someone else will.) When an ace hits the board, you must take notice. And think about it. If an ace hits the flop, and you have an ace with a small kicker, can you call a bet?

E

ALERT!

Don't mistake ring-game limit Hold'em with the no-limit game you see on television on the World Poker Tour or World Series of Poker. The no-limit game is not as much about cards as it is about betting, reading players, and guts. No-limit strategies are the opposite pole from the limit game discussed in this book, so don't tackle no-limit until you've gotten some experience at limit and have digested a no-limit book or two.

Starting Hands: Choose Wisely!

Since second-best hands have a stubborn way of remaining second-best in Hold'em, your starting-hand selection is your most important decision. You want your raises to be feared in this game, so enter with good cards, and go in raising. Use selective aggression, not random wildness!

You know that there are only 169 starting hands in Hold'em, but unfortunately, it's not that simple. Most hands play differently depending on the situation, as follows:

- Position! Are you in the blinds, early, middle, or late?
- Type of game—loose, tight, or "medium"
- Number of players who have already called
- Number of players you believe will call after you
- Any raises so far? Any expected after you?
- The type of players in the game, and whether they're novice, pro, and so on
- Are the players already in the hand tight or loose?

With the exception of a pair of aces, any start hand in Hold'em can be folded preflop in the right situation. Examine the seven factors above before committing a penny to the pot, and always realize that a bad call early can cost you a lot more than just the preflop money—it can suck you into a very expensive quagmire.

Different Starting-Hand Philosophies

Knowing which hands to play—and not to play—is the difference between winning and losing, especially if you're new to the game. Before getting into some guidelines on how to proceed with different starting hands, here's a look at what some other experts are saying.

A Hyper-Aggressive Strategy

Some pros advise beginning players to raise and reraise strongly pre-flop with *all* pairs from aces down to sevens, as well as A-K and A-Q, in any position. The lack of positional consideration is a radical departure from most starting-hand strategies, and the emphasis is put on betting patterns and taking control. More skilled players can add the rest of the pocket pairs to their playable hands, as well as any suited ace and K-Q. Under this philosophy, you can make it two bets to go with these additional hands, call if it's two bets to you, but fold for three bets. Advanced players can cautiously add suited connectors as low as 6-5 or 5-4 with enough callers. You will have to decide if this will work in your game.

Position and Hand Value

The more sensible (and prevailing) starting-hand strategies use position to determine a hand's worth. In early position, only hands that can stand a raise are played. As the button nears, more hands are added because there is less chance of a raise from someone else. Playable early-position hands are aces, kings, queens, and any A-K or A-Q. In middle position, pairs down through eights are added, as well as A-J, A-10, A-9, K-Q, K-J, K-10, Q-J, and Q-10 (suited or unsuited). Late position adds the rest of the pairs, all suited aces, K-9, Q-9, J-10, and suited connectors down through 9-8.

> In Hold'em, to win, you must beat all the other hands. You need more than the best hand—you must have the best hand against all the other hands combined. This is the main reason it is almost always right to thin the field with the lead, and it's also why more players in the hand diminishes the value of pairs and increases the value of drawing hands. It's also all the more reason to be in with the best draw when chasing.

A more conservative philosophy gives some value to suited starting hands and advocates only playing pairs aces through jacks and A-K suited in early position. Tens, any A-K, and A-Q, A-J, and K-Q (all suited) are added as position improves, then nines, any A-Q, and J-10, Q-J, K-J, and A-10 (all suited). The remaining pairs, suited aces, suited connectors, and face-face offsuit hands can be added as you near the button, depending on game conditions and whether you can get in cheaply.

Nothing Is Written in Stone

Unfortunately, there is no hard-and-fast list of starting hands that will make this crucial decision easy. In their well-known book *Hold'em Poker for Advanced Players,* which favors a strict positional concept, authors David Sklansky and Mason Malmuth point out that "Starting hands actually move up and down the hand rankings depending on the circumstance. Because of this, it can be a mistake to rigidly adhere to the hand rankings." Good players adjust their starting hand play based not just on position but also on whether a pot has been raised and if the game is loose or tight, aggressive (much raising) or passive (little raising). So starting hand "rankings" should be only a guide. That said, let's look at starting hands in detail. (In the following discussions, a loose game means many players seeing the flop. A tight game means few seeing the flop. As always, strategies should be tempered by your table image.)

Which Hands Are Playable?

As you can see from Table 15-2, most starting hands in Hold'em won't be helped by the flop.

Table 15-2 How Starting Hands Fare on the Flop	
Pairing at least one hole card	32%
Pairing both hole cards	2%
Four-flush when suited	11%
Four-flush when not suited	2%
Flush with two suited cards	1%
Straight-flush draw with suited connectors	3.4%
Making a set with your pocket pair	11%
Making a full house with pocket pair	1%
Trips with no pocket pair	1.3%
Straight draw with connectors	26%

There are 19,600 ways to flop three cards when your hole cards are taken out of the deck. Odds of making quads (four of a kind) on the flop with your pocket pair? 407-to-1. Odds of a board pair on the flop? 16% (5-1). A straight flush with suited connectors? 5,000-1.

An early-position raise (making it two bets to go) is an effective way to thin the field. On the other hand, calling in early position builds a pot and encourages other callers with marginal hands.

There are two types of playable hands: powerful high hands that can win without improvement against a small field, and speculative drawing hands (like medium-suited connectors) that cry out for a larger field to get that big payday when they finally hit. Position will control whether you fold, call, or raise with most hands, drawing hands especially. Your lower pairs and connectors just cannot be played in early position because you do not know the size of the field, and most aren't worth calling a raise with. If you don't believe that, try limping in with pocket fives or 8-7 and then note your reaction when you are raised and are left facing one or two players, both of whom have better hands than you. You need a miracle flop, and you won't win much if you get it.

Playing High Pocket Pairs

Pocket aces are the best of the best. You are a huge favorite over any other single hand, and there is no chance of an overcard on the flop. Your objectives are to maximize your profit and keep others from drawing out on you. A fine line this is indeed, since to make money you must have callers, but callers increase your risk. This is the line you must find in every hand you play. Do you want callers here? Yes. Do you want the whole table to call? No, too many odd things can happen. With aces, your preflop strategy focuses on getting two or three callers—no more than four, where you could be an underdog to the field.

If you're in early position in a loose game, call, but reraise if you get the chance. If it's super-loose, raise right away because you'll get callers. In middle position, raise if there is at least one caller before you. Reraise if someone behind you raises. In late position, raise if you have at least one caller. Call if it's just you and the blinds.

If you're in early position in a tight game, call, but reraise if you are raised. In middle position, raise if you have a caller before you, and call if you have a raiser before you. In late position, raise if you have two or more callers or raisers in front of you, otherwise call. Don't get married to aces. While you never lay down pocket rockets preflop, later, if it's clear you are beat, fold 'em.

"I'd like to have a dollar for every time I have sat helplessly at the bridge table with a miserable collection of tickets, watching as the opponents chalked up huge scores. This need never happen to a poker player. When you have a terrible hand at poker you can just throw it away."
—Bridge champ Charles Goren

Pocket Kings

The Number Two hand is almost as powerful as aces. If you don't flop a set, you'll still face an ace on the flop only once every eight hands, so you can play kings like you do aces, except a little more strongly, because you don't want to let in drawing hands with aces, like A-x suited or an ace with a card five-or-under that would've folded for a raise. If hands with that dreaded ace are going to play, at least make them pay. You can be a little coy with kings in a tight game, but don't pull this move as often as with aces. Aces are really the only hand in lower-limit games where you can argue for a frequent slow-play. Kings and aces are the only (non-drawing) hands where you can feel comfortable enough to be thinking about maximizing profit preflop, rather than aggressively thinning the field.

Pocket Queens

A pair of ladies is the cutoff hand between thinking you have the pot already won and being nervous. You will face an overcard without a set one out of three hands. With aces and kings as your only overcards, you're in trouble when one hits, as these are the most likely cards your foes will play. So raise as early and as often as you can with queens.

ALERT!

Big John's Tips: "Solid" poker means playing a hand when you believe you have an edge, not waiting for pocket aces and kings.

The only time you wouldn't is if you feel like gambling a bit, or if you're on the button with no callers and want to let the blinds in cheap, hoping for a flop like J-9-6 when one of them has a jack or nine. Generally, queens do not want a large field.

Playing Medium and Low Pairs

Medium pairs are jacks through sevens. Though jacks may seem a lot stronger than sevens, they are really in the same boat. They may be the best hand preflop, but odds are they will face at least one overcard. These are the hands you would love to play heads-up or go all-in with in no-limit—after all, there are only three higher preflop hands than jacks—but in lower-limit they will tie your stomach up in knots.

In some games, you can play jacks and tens the same as queens, raising like mad, then betting on the flop and hoping everyone folds. With nines, eights, and sevens you can raise (or reraise) early to thin the field in a tight game, but if you already have callers in front of you, your best course is to just call, since it's obvious many will see the flop, where you will certainly face the dreaded overcard. These hands are not strong against a large field, unless a rare flop of all low cards hits. These five hands are also difficult to play in an aggressive game from early or middle position, since you don't want to be calling a lot of raises. Remember, you'll only make a set 11 percent of the time. The general rule for these hands goes as follows: Jam in a tight game, limp in a loose game. Multiple flop overcards mean fold.

Lower Pairs

Pairs sixes and below in low-limit are generally played for their set value. That is, if you don't flop a set, you're out of the hand. Since you're trying to get in cheap, you can't play them in early position because they are not worth a raise, and they are only worthwhile in middle position in a loose-passive game. If you're more aggressive, you can raise near the button if there's just a caller or two. You'll get the blinds out and win the pot on the flop if no one else hits. Only in the tightest games should you raise with these hands in early or middle position if you're first in, the idea being to get it heads-up, sow confusion, or buy the blinds. In most games, your philosophy should be to treat them as drawing hands: Limp in late with a large field and pray for a set or the high end of an open-end straight draw.

Fearing the Flop with Low and Medium Pairs

What are the chances that you will *dislike* the flop if you have a pocket pair? In other words, that you will not flop a set, and there will be at least one overcard on the flop? Here they are: kings, 12%; queens, 31%; jacks, 47%; tens, 60%; nines, 69%; eights, 77%; sevens, 82%; sixes, 85%; fives, 87%; fours, 88%; threes, 88%; and twos, 88%.

There's a reason the overcard is such a killer for lower pairs. If you are facing a higher pair, you usually have only two outs (the other two cards of the same value as your pair, to make trips). (If you have two overcards against a pair, you have six outs.) Compare the overcard to your opponents. Ask yourself, "Would they have played a hand with a nine?" The problem with the lower pairs is that you have to fold to most raises, even if you might still have the best hand.

ALERT!

If you have a pair of sevens, for example, and the flop is 10-9-8, this hand could cost you a lot of money. You have the low end of the straight draw, and that's trouble.

The Power Hands

A-K and A-Q (suited or unsuited) are hands you can raise and reraise with in any position. They are not meant to be slow-played, as you do not yet have a made hand. A-K need fear no hand except aces and kings. A-Q need fear no hand except pocket aces, kings, queens, and A-K. In a heads-up game, these hands are a coin-flip to win against any pair, but in actual play—when played aggressively—they blow away low and medium pairs. Those pairs have trouble calling both before and after the flop because the pair always has to be concerned with facing a higher pocket pair and, of course, flopped overcards.

Ace with Face Card

A-K and A-Q can be played the same. If you have A-Q, you should not worry that the person with the other preflop ace has a king kicker—it's just too rare. These are hands you play for their high-card value. If you pair on the flop, it's a cinch that you will have top pair and top kicker, which is your goal. You also sometimes have a straight possibility. The good news is it will be the nut straight. The bad news is it will always be an inside straight. But you don't play these hands for their straight value, and, if your cards are suited, you are not playing for the flush. You do not make flushes often enough for that even to enter your thinking. You play these hands the same suited or unsuited.

With A-K and A-Q, jam it preflop, and bet out again with most flops even if you miss. Maybe you can buy one. A-J is strong, but it's less powerful than A-K and A-Q. How aggressively you play it will depend on your personality and the game. A-10 is a borderline hand that can only be played strong in late position (or middle position if you're first in). There's a 75-percent chance that someone else has an ace, and if he or she has a higher kicker, you're a 4-to-1 dog. A-J and A-10 are hands that should be folded if there is a lot of raising.

Other Hands with an Ace

With A-x suited (any suited ace with a kicker below ten), your objective depends on the game, but remember: This is a drawing hand, not an ace (power) hand! In a loose game, you always play these hands, but get in as cheaply as possible because you'll only make a flush 4 percent of the time (not counting runner-runner). In a tight game, you fold in early position, and limp in middle position (fold to a raise). But sometimes you will raise in late position, setting up a bluff later into a small field after a ragged flop. You're looking for a four-flush, two pair, or to pair your "x" card on the flop. Pairing your ace might only make you second best. The small field in tight games makes your flush draws less attractive, so you only enter unraised pots. Generally, treat A-x suited as a speculative hand that needs a limp-in or large field to be playable. This is true unless you're in a weak game, where you can go in with ramming and jamming and buy pots on the flop or turn even if you miss.

Unsuited aces with kickers nine or lower are trap hands. Only play them in late position with few callers in front of you or in unraised pots, short-handed games, or to steal the blinds.

Suited Connectors—and More

High suited connectors K-Q, Q-J, and J-10 are tease hands. They look so good, but they don't always deliver. K-Q is a bona fide hand you can raise with in any position, but the other two are not as strong because if you just hit a pair, you could have kicker trouble. Your best bet is a straight draw, because the flush draw will not be to the nuts. With J-10, you can make an open-end straight draw three ways, and you can make the nut straight five ways. That said, with Q-J and J-10, you still want to see the flop as cheaply as possible, so against good players you must fold them in early position. Just limp in a loose game if you're in middle and late position, but raise in a tight game if you're first or second in.

Suited connectors below J-10 look pretty, but they are longshots, and they are weak since pairing a hole card usually doesn't help you. These are drawing hands looking for a cheap entry into a large field, so only play them in later position, when you are sure you won't be raised, or in "family pots." Don't ever play below 5-4 suited.

Unsuited Connectors

Besides A-K, K-Q is the only premium unsuited connector. It can be played from any position, but think hard before raising with it early. Q-J, J-10, and 10-9 are playable in middle or late position depending on the game, though not for more than one raise. High unsuited one-gap hands—K-J, Q-10, and J-9—are also playable late. Lower unsuited connectors and one-gappers are strictly for the button, "family pots," and in the blinds when you want to gamble.

Suited Kings

With suited kings, you are entering the realm of the loose players. These hands are money-losers, but for those who like to see flops, they are a good excuse. K-J and K-10 are okay middle-position hands, suited or unsuited, and if you raise, it won't be on the merit of the hand but for strategic purposes. You can limp late with any K-x suited only into a large field with no raises. Unsuited, don't play less than K-10.

Other Hands Are Garbage!

Other hands are trash, and you save big money by folding them. This includes the classic loser hand: any two suited cards. With the exception of limping with A-x and K-x (x is nine or below) into a large field, never play a hand just because it is suited. Unless a hand has been discussed above, just muck it! Another mistake is to play the top and bottom end of a straight, like K-9. If the board has Q-J-10, you will be killed by A-K—often. "Gap" hands like 10-8 and 8-6 are overrated. There is less chance of an open-end draw than with the connectors, and fewer of your draws will be to the nuts. Being able to fold hands in Hold'em is a big part of your edge. Better players play fewer hands.

Playing the Blinds

There are as many different philosophies of playing the blinds as there are players. Most low-limiters will always throw in the other half bet in the small blind, and automatically call one raise in the big blind. Better players don't throw in a cent if the hand doesn't deserve it. You do not have to "protect" your blinds, especially since you will be the first to act in the next round. If you don't at least have a hand you would play in late position, dump it, and if you have a borderline hand, make sure you won't be raised. Limping in for half a bet is often okay in the small blind, but don't call raises in the blinds without a genuine hand. Don't think it's correct to play garbage like 9-4, 7-3, and 4-2 just because it's a family pot or you're in the blind. The odds aren't there.

One thing is certain. If the flop is ragged, watch out for the blinds. With their random hands, they might have hit something! If you have let the blinds in cheaply, shame on you for now no hand is safe. Also, remain aware of which players will defend their big blind with any hand and which will defend only with reasonable cards.

Lastly, if your blind isn't raised, go ahead—play that trash! Now, on to the flop!

Chapter 16

Hold'em: The Flop, the Turn, and the River

In this game of incomplete information, nowhere are you groping in the dark more than with your first two cards in Hold'em. It may feel like you're making out with the town hottie, but when the lights are rudely snapped on by those three flop cards, you may suddenly find you've been kissing the family dog. It's decision time. You now have a real five-card poker hand. Is it time to drop that dog into the muck pile?

Was It Good for You?

The flop is the critical juncture of the hand, and compared to decisions here, other streets are easy. These three cards offer hope—too often false hope—but they also provide escape. It's still not too late to get away cheaply, but quicksand is sucking at your shoes—so tread carefully, and look for reasons to fold.

You have two calculations on the flop, and they must be made quickly—without staring at the board. The first is whether the flop helped you. The second is whether it helped one or more of your opponents. The good news is you will know the first, and you can predict the second by knowing the kind of cards your foes play in certain positions (and for how many bets), and remembering the wagering prior to the flop.

In return for boosting the pot, preflop bettors and raisers have given something up—anonymity. Hold'em is a funny game. Some players won't reraise with anything but pocket aces, while others love to build pots. Good players don't call preflop raises without a serious hand unless they are playing against total maniacs, in which case they *still* make sure they have something. Generally, it takes a better hand to call a bet than it does to make the initial wager. (Since the preflop aggressor—last raiser— controls the hand, you should almost always bet on the flop if you've raised preflop, even with nothing. If everyone has missed, you pick up the pot.) Thus, a bet from a preflop raiser might not mean anything, but bets from others do.

When the flop comes, you can compare it to what you think the pre- flop aggressors were betting on. This way, you can significantly narrow down what you're up against. If a ragged flop like 8-6-3 shows up, for a preflop bettor to now have a real hand, he or she would have to have started with a high pocket pair, a rare holding. An ace-face hand is much more probable. Ask yourself, "What hands would the preflop aggressor raise on?" If your foe only raises on powerhouses, you're now better off with a drawing hand if you have the odds to call than to go up against A-K or A-Q with your A-10. You can get away from drawing hands like Q-J, J-10, or A-x suited on the flop if they don't pan out—a quick exit is part of their value.

Your hand is only as good as the flop that goes with it. Even aces can be crushed by the wrong three cards. No matter how good your hole cards, they can be folded if there is a troublesome flop. The most common problem is overcards, whose presence often means you are facing a higher pair. The more opponents you're playing against, the more probable that pair. Study **TABLE 16-1** to know your chances of facing an overcard on the flop.

You Have	No Overcards	One Overcard	Two Overcards	Three Overcards	One or More Overcards
Table 16-1 Chance of Flopping Overcards in Hold'em					
1 or 2 kings	77%	21%	1%	.02%	23%
1 or 2 queens	59%	35%	6%	.3%	41%
1 or 2 jacks	43%	43%	13%	1%	57%
1 or 2 tens	31%	46%	21%	3%	69%
1 or 2 nines	21%	44%	29%	6%	79%
1 or 2 eights	13%	40%	37%	10%	87%
1 or 2 sevens	8%	33%	42%	17%	92%
1 or 2 sixes	4%	25%	46%	25%	96%
1 or 2 fives	2%	17%	45%	36%	98%
1 or 2 fours	.6%	9%	40%	50%	99%
1 or 2 threes	.1%	3.4%	29%	68%	99%
1 or 2 twos		.2%	12%	88%	100%

If you think someone has a higher pair than you on the flop, you are cooked unless you have the pot odds to play a four-flush, open-end straight, or gutshot (inside) straight with a hole card paired. All of these you'll make one out of three tries. Look at the depressing probability of improving your lower hand by the river when you face an overpair. If you have a pocket pair, chance is 8 percent; two overcards, 24 percent;

one overcard, 13 percent; one hole card paired, 20 percent; and with two undercards, forget it.

FACT

If the flop has missed you, it's probably hit someone else if you have multiple opponents, unless it's total rags. The more players seeing the flop, the more luck is involved in winning the hand, and the less skill.

So Many Flops, So Little Time

With more than 19,000 possible flops, it is impossible to discuss them all, but there are general patterns. Here are some observations on frequent flop types. Remember, the fewer the players, the more chance the flop has missed them. The more players, the more chance someone has hit. Be aware that the flop will only hit the typical hand one out of three times (not counting straight and flush draws). But if you include draws, high suited overcard hands like A-K and A-10 will hit the flop a whopping 52 percent of the time!

Unlike Stud with its commonplace two pair and trips, Hold'em is often won by a hand with just top pair on the board—that is, the flop is K-10-7 and you have a king in the hole with a high, bettable kicker (queen or ace, maybe jack). This is your bread-and-butter hand and you must bet it strong, so you cannot fear the worst-case scenarios on every flop. Flopping two pair, trips, and four-flushes are aberrations. Don't worry about aberrations in poker unless someone tells you in no uncertain terms that he has one.

Having top pair doesn't mean you are a shoo-in. Watch the board for combinations with cards that a lot of people play—like a bundle of cards ten and above. If you have multiple opponents, your high pair could be in trouble. Protect your hand aggressively here. If you are facing flush and/or straight draws on the flop, do everything you can to get them out. Don't give free cards: Make them call multiple bets, or fold. If you have top pair and top kicker and are raised, you're going to stay for the turn unless there's a raising war going on. After the turn, with the big bets coming, you will be forced to evaluate whether your top pair is worth taking to the river. If you are only called on the flop, you bet your top pair on the turn no matter what card comes off, even if it's an overcard.

Loose and Tight Players and the Flop

It's been stressed over and over: The primary detail to know is which of your opponents are loose and which are tight. What kind of cards are your opponents playing? This is everything on the flop. In some games, no one will play a hand with a card below ten. Others won't play a card below six, except with an ace, while others only will play six or under with a suited ace. In other games folks will play any suited or connected cards.

You must consider this when evaluating every flop. There is a huge difference between K-10-10 and K-5-5. In your game, do you have to worry about trip fives? Need you fear a flop of 6-5-4 or 4-3-2? If the flop is 9-8-6 and someone bets, is he or she the type to *ever* play 10-7 or 7-5? Now is the time to put players on hands using their tendencies, the preflop bet pattern, the flop, and the flop bets.

ALERT!

Decide early what your objective is with your hand. Is it a power hand, or a draw, or a prayer? Does it call for a large field, small field, or heads-up? Are you going to play as cheaply as possible, or push the action? Don't play a hand without a plan!

The Differing Texture of Flops

While you cannot play scared of longshot hands—someone who's flopped a set or two pair—you have to know when flops make those hands probable. Here is a list with some observations:

- Trips on the flop, such as J♣-J♠-J♥. You don't count on anyone having the case card, so pocket pairs have the strength with this flop.

- High pair/lower kicker, such as Q♠-Q♥-8♣. If the pair is ten or above, someone could have three of a kind, but with only two of the rank left, trips is not as probable as you fear—so having an eight is strong.
- High kicker/lower pair, such as K♦-6♣-6♠. Would the player who just bet into you play a hand with a six in it from his position? A king in the hole is more likely.
- Three to a straight flush, such as Q♥-J♥-10♥. This is the kind of hand that can crack aces and kings with straight and flush possibilities galore. A lower sequence like 8♥-7♥-6♥ is a little less scary.
- Three of a suit, such as Q♠-9♠-6♠. You need to decide right away if you are going to take your K♦-Q♣ or pocket kings to the river when someone bets. This is a great spot for someone to try to buy the pot, and you shouldn't always fear the flush, but if there is a bet and a raise to you, that's when you really need to know your players. Your best course usually is to fold. If you hold the A♠, that's a playable hand, as you have nine outs. (But if you think someone has a made flush, you only have seven outs!)
- Three in sequence, such as J♣-10♥-9♦. You don't fear straights as much as flushes in Hold'em, but three connected cards plays right into the hands of players who love connectors. The higher the row, the more chance of a straight, and someone for sure has a straight draw. For lower sequences like 6-5-4, you have to know your players to know if they would have stayed in with the cards to complete those straights.
- One-gap and two-gap straight hands, like 10♣-9♠-7♥ or 10♣-9♠-6♥. Again, the higher the cards, the more you have to fear. Someone has a draw here, but does he have the straight already made? With the first hand, a player needs J-8 or 8-6, for the second, only 8-7 will suffice. Here's where you evaluate your adversary's position and remember the preflop betting. There's a big difference between limping in on the blinds, which could happen with one of these hands, or calling a raise or two, which only a fool would do with these holdings. (Note that 8-7 is one of those connector hands that many low-limiters love to play.)

- Two flush cards, Q♥-9♥-5♣. This is a very common flop. If you have top pair, A-9, a pocket pair tens or higher, or were the preflop bettor, you must try to drive the flush draws out of the pot. If you can make it two bets to go, do so.
- Two straight cards, K♠-Q♥-7♣ or K♠-8♥-7♣. In Hold'em, almost every flop has some kind of straight draw. If you spend time fearing straights, you'll never play. You're more concerned with how high the cards are. The higher the cards, the greater the chances are that someone has a high pair, two pair, or an open-end straight draw. (You don't fear the gutshot—inside—straight draw.)

ALERT!

Big John's Tips: The more players there are in a hand, the less the power of the pocket pair and the greater the power of the drawing hands.

- Three high cards, such as A♠-K♥-10♦ or A♠-Q♥-J♣. This is a scary flop and is perfect for those who raised preflop. Often, this person will bet on the flop and everyone else will fold. If you raised preflop, you're obligated to bet into a small field or else give it up.
- Two high cards, such as A♠-K♥-5♣. This is also scary. Against a small field, you can bet even if you missed, especially if you raised preflop. Against a large field, you're done if you missed, unless you think that they're so afraid of your preflop raise that they'll figure you for A-K or A-Q and fold. Know your players.
- One high card, such as A♠-8♥-6♣ or Q♣-7♦-5♠. Once again, the pre-flop aggressor is in command. As for you, either you paired or you didn't. When he bets, do you want to pop him back to see if he's trying to steal, or would you rather just give it up and get on to the next hand?
- Rags, such as three cards below ten: 9♣-6♦-4♠. This flop favors those with pocket pairs. If you have those medium pocket pairs—like sevens, eights, tens, and jacks—this flop is an answer to your prayers!

Outs	2 cards to go	1 card to go	Comment
20	68%	44%	
19	65%	41%	
18	62%	39%	Open straight flush draw with 1 overcard
17	60%	37%	
16	57%	35%	
15	54%	33%	Straight-flush draw open-ended
14	51%	30%	Still better than 50-50
13	48%	28%	Open-ender with a pair
12	45%	26%	Four-flush with winning overcard
11	42%	24%	Four-straight with winning overcard
10	38%	22%	Flopped set, no full house on turn
9	35%	20%	Four-flush on the flop
8	32%	17%	Four-straight, open-ended
7	28%	15%	Inside straight with winning overcard
6	24%	13%	Need to pair either hole card
5	20%	11%	Paired a hole card, need to hit kicker
4	17%	9%	Inside straight; both hole cards paired
3	13%	7%	Need to pair a specific hole card
2	8%	4%	Pocket pair; need a set
1	4%	2%	Need a single specific card in the deck

Table 16-2   Odds of Making a Hand After the Flop

Note: Percentages are rounded up. All Hold'em players should know this chart.

Strategy and Tactics on the Flop

Much of your flop strategy is predicated on your having bet, raised, or reraised before the flop and taken control of the hand. Unless you are considered wild and loose, a preflop bet can be essential to winning post-flop. As has been stressed throughout this book, it is critical to be in a game where players will fold hands and where you can reduce the number of opponents. In limit, sometimes you are "limited" as to how much monetary pressure you can exert because there are only so many bets, and the amount of the bet is "limited." Still, it can be done, and it starts preflop. If you are going in, go in raising. If you are playing a drawing hand like A-x suited, suited connectors, or a medium or low pair, you have two choices. You can limp in and fold if you don't hit the flop, or you can raise and then bet the flop strongly whether you hit or not. This latter strategy is very effective against the right players, and if you don't buy the pot, at least you have sent out a "feeler" and know if you are beat. Like so many decisions on the flop, the strategy you choose depends largely on how many opponents you have and on whether they are loose or tight. But no matter how you play, realize above all that there's no shame in folding on the flop if you haven't hit anything.

Big John's Tips: With all the drawing hands in Hold'em, you don't want to give any free cards. If you believe you're tops on the flop, bet it up.

You Flop Nothing

Welcome to the club! You have nothing, but what of the others? Will they fold to a bet? Did you bet preflop? If so, maybe they're ready to muck. If the flop is ragged, your high ace might still be high. Bet it.

You Flop Top Pair

If the pair is high, you bet if you have a high kicker. If you have a *low* kicker, well, why are you in the hand? Guess you'll just have to bet—and pray. If the pair is medium or small, like if you have 8-7 and the flop is 8-4-2, you still bet, because you figure no one else has played the low cards. If you're in a loose game where everyone is seeing the flop, then you check, as someone likely has K-8, J-8, or something similar. If you face a raise and reraise, you might have to dump your hand as you may have two pair and/or a set against you. Beware of players who will bump it on just a draw.

You Flop Second or Third Pair

How high is the flop? There is a big difference between having third pair if the flop is A-K-J and if it is 8-6-5. Are your adversaries likely to have the higher pair? The smaller the field and the more ragged the flop, the more valuable second and third pair become. If you sense weakness, bet if you think you are the only one with a pair. This strategy makes you about a 3-1 favorite against two overcards. Knowing when to play second or third pair is one of the advanced skills in Hold'em that come only with time, and yes, second pair *is* better than third pair.

You Flop a Good Draw

If you have four to a high flush on the flop, or an open-end straight (the high end!), and two or more opponents (more is better), you will almost always have the pot odds to take the hand to the river. But you have some decisions. If you face a large field, one philosophy is to get in as cheaply as possible. After all, you'll only hit the hand one out of three tries, and bluffing will be difficult if you miss. On the other hand, with many opponents, you may want to build the pot if you're drawing at the nuts. Well, here's some food for thought. You're a 4-1 dog to hit your four-flush or open straight on the turn, but if you have five people calling, you make a "profit" on every bet.

FACT

All flops that do not include a pair or trips will have a straight draw except for K-8-3, K-8-2, K-7-2, and Q-7-2.

Against a small field, semi-bluff if you think your one, two, or three foes are capable of tossing their hands later. If you miss on the turn, you'll make your hand on the river only one out of five tries, but the semi-bluff gives you another way out. Any draw with fourteen or more outs, such as a nut flush draw with a pair or a straight-flush draw, should always be bet and raised strongly.

You Have a Longshot Draw

If your chances are slim but you have proper odds from the pot (and you can afford it), go for it! Inside straights are 5-1 with two cards to come and 10-1 on the river, while hitting runner-runner flush is 23-1 and unplayable. You only have two cards in the deck to make a set with your pocket pair, and three outs to pair your pocket ace (see **TABLE 16-2**), so fold these hands. There is one draw that is often overlooked: the pair with an inside straight. You have nine outs here, the same as with a four-flush. One note of caution: If you hit your inside straight, it often is *not* the nuts.

Should you call a bet with just A-K on the flop when you believe someone has paired a lower hole card? Rarely. The odds of getting an ace or king on the turn are 7-1 against. Then you will face a big bet if you want to see the river.

You Flop a Freak Hand

These are two pair, trips, straights, flushes, and higher. This is where experience comes in. You're obviously tops right now—and have already won the hand in most cases—so evaluate the chance of someone drawing out on you. The greater the chance, the more you should bet. With two pair and trips, you usually will bet and raise, as well as with the low end of straights and low flushes. With higher hands, you let them catch up a bit. If you're in a game where everyone calls and no one believes you, then of course you bet, bet, bet! If you're in a tight game, be more conservative. Be guided by how obvious your hand is. A flush is obvious, while a straight is usually much less so.

Knowing when to play "what they don't have," regardless of what you hold, is a fine art in Hold'em. When you believe the flop has missed your opponents, that's your cue to take over.

Overall, the flop is when you can get away from a starting hand that has let you down before the more expensive streets arrive. If you have two overcards to the high pair on the board, you might call one flop bet because it is still a small bet. That's not the case with the turn.

Getting a Free Card

This move is so well known that all Hold'em players need to be aware of it. When playing a draw such as a four-straight, four-flush, small pair with overcard kicker, or pair with a gutshot in late position, raise the bettor on the flop. On the next round, the field will often check to you, and you can then check as well, thus getting a free card on the more expensive turn. You've cut your losses on a draw that usually won't get there. An alternative play on the turn is to bet like you've got something. Since the others have now shown weakness, you might buy the pot there or on the river.

Playing on the Turn

In lower-limit games, many players will call a single "small" flop bet with marginal hands, but they will give it up when faced with a big bet on the turn. This is a turning point—the time of maximum financial pressure, where many pots are there for the taking. But many who bluff or semi-bluff on the flop will make the mistake of checking the turn, thinking that those who called on the flop have real hands. In fact, they frequently do not. They just didn't care as much about the small flop bet and would've folded on the turn if someone just kept the pressure on. Bet into weakness on the turn, but notice if someone's draw could've gotten there, such as when a third flush card hits. Don't fear the flush automatically, unless you have put someone on a flush draw before the turn. The more opponents, of course, the greater the chance someone has it.

You don't fear a third straight card as much as a third flush card on the turn, but the scariest card of all is a third high card. Since so many low-limit denizens play any two cards ten or above, a third high one threatens two pair or a straight or just plain trouble.

Other turn-card observations:

- If you have seen the turn on a draw, you usually will have the pot odds to see the river as well, provided you are not facing two bets or more. For two or more big bets with only one card to come, make sure the pot is big enough to take a stab at. You're more than a 4-1 dog with most draws at this point (as outlined in **TABLE 16-2**).

- If you bet preflop and on the flop, but you check the turn, they will put you on A-K or A-Q, or sometimes a flush draw if there was one on the flop. (A-K can sometimes win without improvement.)
- If you've made up your mind to call on the river, why not raise on the turn? It frequently won't cost you any more and gives you control of the hand. Then, on the river, you can bluff or get a free call.
- It can be scary if the board pairs on the turn. Here is where it really helps you to have put players on a hand. Is it plausible—given the betting pattern preflop and on the flop and knowing the players—for someone to have trips now?

Overall, the turn is a good time to fold, but it's also a time to use the higher limits to make your adversaries squirm.

Playing on the River

It's crunch time. The river. The end. The scene of brilliant moves and costly mistakes. This is where the elaborate plans, the hopes and dreams of you and your fellow card-holding human beings, come crashing down in ruins or join together like a successful space shuttle launch. And no one can tell you, except in the most general of terms, how to play here.

The Street of Dreams

In many ways, the river is the easiest street to play. You know your final hand, and if you are a solid player, you have a good idea of what others are holding. You know the flop, how the betting has gone, what the nut hand is. You know how much it will cost you.

If your only way of winning is a bluff, decide whether it has a chance. Don't waste your money if it doesn't, but don't be shy, either. In a weak pot, the first bettor often takes it. Judgment and experience come into play here. If you feel the odds against your bluff working are 5-1, but the pot is offering you 7-1, then it's worth a shot. And if you think someone might bluff you, say, one out of six times, but the pot is giving you 9-1, well, you should call.

The questions you ask on the river are pretty fundamental, but the answers are based on all the information you have collected during the hand. You should know the answers to questions like these: Do you have the best hand? Should you bluff? Are you being bluffed? Did anyone improve on the river?

If you've absorbed what's gone before in this book and gone out and played, you will have some internal stars to guide you. This is a good time to reread Chapter 4, especially the sections on pot odds, and the "When to Bluff" and "Should You Call a Possible Bluff?" sections of Chapter 10 (pages 120 and 127), as well as the one on semi-bluffing. But there is one certainty here: The river is no time to back off. Don't miss river bets! If there is a good chance you are best, make them pay.

Fearing River Cards

If you've been putting your opponents on hands, you know what cards you *don't* want to see on the river. You know the cards that will beat you. Don't just automatically give up if you miss. Everyone else may be in the same boat.

While aces always get your attention, you shouldn't panic over hands that are made on *both* turn and river. Most people don't hang around for runner-runner unless they are allowed to limp in on the flop. Were there flop bets? How many? Any bets preflop? You don't fear runner-runner suited cards (as in J♣-Q♥-7♠-6♣-3♣), a turn-river pair (J♣-Q♥-7♠-6♦-6♣), or two cards that make a three-card sequence on the board (J♣-Q♥-6♠-5♦-4♠). More scary than these late-developing hands are cards that would fit in with something a player could have been playing on the flop, such as a four-flush (J♣-Q♥-7♥-K♦-6♥).

QUESTION?

Should a turn-river pair ever scare you?
Yes, if it's a high card and someone bet it up on the turn, or if you have paired both hole cards and they are low—for example, you have 8-7 and the flop is A-8-7, with the turn and river 2-2. Anyone with an ace (or pocket pair above eight) now beats you.

Buying Pots at the Eleventh Hour

Stealing pots on the river when you've missed your hand is a dicey thing. If everyone has checked to you, you have to bet. If you're first and a blank hits the river, you might buy the pot by being first in. The more opponents (and the larger the pot), the harder this task is. The higher the limit, the easier it is. If the river card is a blank, the pot usually goes to the player in control. If no one's in control, evaluate your odds of a successful bluff. If the river is a good card—like a third flush card, ace, or high scare card—you can bluff if you sense weakness. It won't always work, but it doesn't have to work every time to be a moneymaker. While fancy plays like slow-playing, check-raising, and bluffing should be the exception rather than the rule, sometimes a river bluff is the only way you can win.

Keep the ancient proverb close to your heart: "Though I walk through the valley of the shadow of death, I will fear no river." Or that other saying of the grizzled old gamblers: "On the river, your odds are 50-50—either he's got it, or he don't!"

Chapter 17

Seven-Card Stud: A Hand of One's Own

Seven-Card Stud, known today simply as Stud, became a sensation in the 1950s and 1960s as games like Five-Card Stud and Draw waned and Hold'em had yet to explode. It remains hugely popular —especially on the East Coast and in Europe—and is spread in every casino with a poker room. Every complete poker player should know and understand Stud.

Stud and Hold'em: Like Night and Day

Seven-Card Stud is a game of memory, patience, and deception. Because you see four of your opponents' seven cards, two special skills are essential: first is remembering exposed cards, even after they have been removed from play, to correctly figure your drawing odds and pot odds; and second is the ability to put players on hands based on their board cards, history, and betting patterns.

You will recall that Stud uses an ante from each player, not blinds, and that there are two types of limits. A spread limit, such as $2–$10, allows players to bet anywhere between $2 and $10 at any time, as long as a raise is not less than a player's previous bet. In a structured (fixed-limit) game, such as $10–$20, the first two of Stud's *five* bets must be exactly $10, while the final three rounds would be at the higher limit ($20). Yes, the extra bet can make Stud more expensive than Hold'em, which has just four rounds. But at least you get to see three cards before you face a decision, instead of Hold'em's measly two.

If only *one person* remains in the hand, that person wins the pot, regardless of what hand he or she has. The winning hand does *not* have to be shown, even if someone asks to see it. This is the origin of the phrase: "You want to see it, you pay for it." It is usually to your advantage *not* to show your hand.

Most players underestimate the power of the ante. Antes add up. In a game with a large ante compared to the limits, you must be in there swinging. In a game with a small ante, you can be more patient and wait for better starting hands. (Casino antes generally run 20 to 25 percent of the minimum bet. Fifty percent of the minimum bet or more is a large ante.) Stud also uses a "bring-in" bet on the first round. After the first three cards are dealt, the player with the low *door card* must bring it in— bet a specified fraction of the minimum bet. Others may call, or, if they wish to raise, they can complete the bet to the minimum. (In $10–$20, for example, the bring-in might be $4, and to complete the bet, a player would raise it to $10.)

The main differences between Stud and Hold'em are these:

- You receive seven cards of your own. No community cards.
- Except for the first round, high hand on the board bets first.
- A maximum of eight can play Stud. Ten or more can play Hold'em.
- The river card is face down in Stud, face up in Hold'em.
- The final three bets in Stud are at the higher limit. In Hold'em, it's the last two.
- In Hold'em, you know the nut hand. In Stud, a player could have anything.
- Just because you hit your hand on the river doesn't mean others have missed.

Because the high hand on board changes, your position will change in Stud, but in Hold'em it is constant during a hand.

FACT

The Paradox of Stud: Because of the four up cards, there are fewer surprises, yet with three hole cards, your opponent could be showing the world's worst board and still be hiding four of a kind! No wonder they used to call Stud "Down the River!"

The Board-Card Bonanza

If you play Stud, you do so for one reason: because you want to use your opponents' board cards against them. The board is the key. Unlike Hold'em, opponents each have their own individual board, and they must act after each card. This is huge! There is no "flop" where players can see three cards all at once and then flee the scene. The cards are dealt one at a time, and each round is an opportunity to pick up tells, reactions, and clues. Players must bet, raise, fold, or check five times in Stud. And you're right there watching.

You know how in Hold'em you are always figuring odds based on forty-seven unseen cards after the flop? Well, in Stud, you are much better off, much closer to knowing your true odds, because you have exposed cards to figure into the equation. You must keep track of these cards and use them to your advantage. If you cannot remember folded cards and use the exposed cards to make your drawing odds more precise, you have no business playing Stud. Stud is about the board. You have traded the knowledge of what the stone-cold nut hand is for the wealth of clues provided by your foes' up cards.

Say you are dealt three spades and are wondering whether to play the hand. You know you are a 5-to-1 underdog to make the flush. But here comes your Stud advantage. There are seven other players, each showing a card. Stud is not a community-card game, but it is a *community* game, so you never evaluate your hand in a vacuum. You see seven other cards already—they are not "unseen." If you see no spades out, your odds have improved. If you notice three spades in others' hands, that's 30 percent of the remaining ten spades gone, so your odds are now 8-1, your flush is not "live," and you're gone too. Unless, that is, your door card is highest on board. Maybe your three spades are all ten or above. If you have the high board card, you have the power. You're still in there. Unlike Hold'em, you can see how you relate to the field, at least enough to put a bet out there. And when you bet, you have something to hang your hat on: a scare card! You're not just whistling "Dixie." You can represent something plausible, and while you may not have a bona fide monster, at least foes can see you have *something*—and have something to fear.

Since Stud is about boards, the scary board can control a hand. Its pervasive power sweeps over the table like an evil presence. If you have one, you must decide early whether you are going to bet it all the way as though you have something, or whether you're not going to bother and be doomed to check/call or fold when someone runs over you.

Starting Hands: The Crucial Decision

Even more than in Hold'em, your most important decision is which starting hands to play. The principles of avoiding draws against one opponent and tossing hands that are probably second-best apply to Stud more than ever. In casino or tournament Stud, you will be facing raises, and with five betting rounds, mediocre start hands can't stand the heat.

Rolled-Up Trips

Since you'll only be dealt trips once out of every 425 hands, job one is to keep from jumping out of your seat and singing "Hallelujah!" Here's where your practice at betting in a smooth, consistent manner comes in. Bet in the same way as you've made every other bet you've made in your poker life. Job two is maximizing your win. Loose and tight game strategies apply. In a tight game, you want to keep some players in, even if it means just calling the bring-in bet. In looser games, go ahead and bet. Think a moment. If you have an ace or king as your door card, would it look funny if you checked? Then you must bet. If you have a seven or below and you bet or raise, will they figure you for a high pocket pair and fold?

Evaluate your situation carefully to get maximum mileage from this monster hand, but be aware that high trips are much more powerful than low trips, so if you're in a loose game, you don't want the whole family calling. Realize that the median winning hand in an eight-person Stud game is medium trips, and bet accordingly. Jam on later streets depending on the threat level. Make the straight and flush draws pay dearly, but use more discretion against underpairs. When in doubt, bet it out.

QUESTION?

What are "live" cards?
Your cards are "live" if they have not appeared on board. If you are dealt (7-7)-A and no sevens or aces have appeared in your opponents' hands, your cards are live. If there is a seven or ace out there, your cards are not "live"—you have fewer outs.

High Pairs

Pairs jacks or higher are premium starting hands in Stud, but there is a big difference between a concealed (pocket) pair and an exposed (door card) pair. Because of their deceptive value, high pairs in the hole are huge. You can manipulate your foes like puppets because of a Stud truism: When you bet on third street with a medium or high card, players will believe you have paired your door card. Should you ever pair your door card on board, many will figure you for trips.

What message does your third-street raise convey? In Stud, you always must be cognizant of what others believe you are betting on. If you have bet, the odds are 2-to-1 that *if* you have a pair on three cards, you have paired your door card rather than having a pair in the hole. If you have a queen showing, they will figure you for queens. They won't figure you for a high concealed pair, and since they will never fear a drawing hand, no one will fear your raise if they have a pair higher than your door card. Thus concealed aces and kings are deceptive, monster hands.

ALERT!

The lower your starting pair, the lower the two pair you will likely make. Two pair is a common hand in Stud. With the average winning hand being three nines, low two pairs are losers. If you must play a low pair, make sure you have a kicker higher than the pair you are facing.

However, with high pairs, isolation remains key. You must protect them by thinning the field. With the exception of (sometimes) aces or kings in the hole, you want to jam the pot. You are still an underdog to a large field. In general, don't pussyfoot around. Jamming is the way to play Stud. Raise, raise, raise!

With the high pairs—and every other starting Stud hand—you must look before you bet, especially to your left! Clues are all over the board. Since you want to be starting with the best hand, your pair might already be second-best if you're facing overcards on third street. If you have jacks and you see an ace, king, and/or queen out there, someone already has you beat, or they will soon enough!

As in Hold'em, your high pair is only as good as the overcards against you, and so there's a gargantuan difference between aces and kings and jacks and tens. The odds against being dealt aces *or* kings on three cards are 38-to-1. Odds against getting *any* pair: 5-to-1.

It is a money-losing move in Stud to play a pair against a higher pair (suspected or on board). This is true unless your pair is a pocket pair, because when the hidden pair improves, you will be paid off big-time. But if your door-card pair improves, you will make little. It's just too easy to read. Solid players won't play a lower pair without overcards to the higher pair.

High Suited Connectors

Big suited cards in sequence, such as A♥-K♥-Q♥, K♥-Q♥-J♥, Q♥-J♥-10♥, or J♥-10♥-9♥ are strong in Stud, more for the high cards than the straight and flush possibilities. But if you receive a fourth straight or flush card to go with those high cards, you have a powerful hand. (The odds of making a flush with three cards to go, for example, is about even money.) Suited high cards with only one "gap" are almost as good, for example, A♦-K♦-J♦, K♦-J♦-10♦, A♦-Q♦-J♦, and so on. With these hands, you have ten cards that will make a four-flush, at least six more for a four-straight, and nine pairing cards. That means a lot of good things can happen on fourth street. Odds against being dealt three suited cards are 18-1. Just how good is this hand? Odds of improving to two pair or better with suited connectors are actually a little better than 50-50!

ALERT!

Big John's Tips: If on third street you hold connectors Q-J-10 or below, there are sixteen cards (all A, K, 9, and 8) in the deck that will give you a four-straight, half of them open-ended. However, with A-K-Q, only jacks and tens will help you, and any straight draw will be to an inside straight. The power of queen-high connectors and below comes from the straight possibilities. Ace-high and king-high sequences get their power from being high cards.

Pairs Ten and Below

Contrast the previous powerhouses to start hands with pairs 10 and below. Most of these latter hands are unplayable without a kicker that is an overcard to the board, and you certainly wouldn't call raises with these pairs unless the pair is hidden or is an overpair to the board. The only time you would bet them is if you were able to come in raising yourself, preferably with the pair hidden and a scary door card. Other than trips or pairing your kicker, not much good can happen with the low and medium pairs. You're a 2-to-1 underdog to an overpair from the get-go; and the odds go up to more than 3-1 to two overpairs.

Unsuited Connectors

High unsuited connectors (three cards in sequence ten and above) and one-gap high connectors are playable, but lower ones are not, unless you're first in the pot. The lower unsuited connectors (J♦-10♣-9♠ and below) are hampered by a small door card and lack of overcards. Without the additional power of the flush draw, these hands do not play well. Straights in general are overrated in Stud. You'll only hit the straight one out of six tries.

Lower suited connectors are little better than the low unsuited connectors, and they suffer from the same drawbacks. They should only be played for a limp-in if your cards are live, and they should be chucked if nothing materializes on fourth street. You can expect a card giving you a straight or flush draw about one out of three hands. As with any game, drawing hands are better in multiway pots. Fold on fourth street if you don't get help.

Any hands not discussed above are trash and should be folded unless you're trying to buy a pot. If you have an ace or king as a door card and it's to you, you will probably have to bet it whether you have the pair or not, to protect your future hands. Note that if you are playing a two-tiered betting system, you can sometimes get in cheaply on third and fourth streets with a marginal hand (like a hidden small pair or small suited connectors) that could pay big dividends if you hit. But muck it when the big bets come.

Fourth street is the street of decision for most drawing hands. If you have suited connectors and haven't hit an open-end straight or flush draw or a high pair, it's time to give it up if there's a raise.

Some Significant Stud Odds

Here are some Seven-Stud odds you should know. Study **TABLES 17-1** and **17-2** to get a feel for the game. There are 22,100 possible starting Stud hands.

Table 17-1 Odds Against Being Dealt a Specific Hand in First Three Cards	
Three of a kind	424-1
Pair of aces	76-1
Jacks, queens, or kings	25-1
Any pair	5-1
Three cards to a straight flush	85-1
Three to a (non-straight) flush	24-1
Three to a (non-flush) straight	5-1

If you have rolled-up trips, you will make a full house or four of a kind by the river 40 percent of the time. If you have trips with three cards to come, your odds are still almost 40 percent. With two cards to go, your chance is 33 percent (1 chance in 3), and with one card left the chance is 22 percent. With two pair and three cards to come, your odds are 3.5-1 against a full house; two cards to come, 5-1; one card, 10-1.

Table 17-2 Odds Against Making a Flush When You Hold These Hands	
Three of a suit, four cards to come	4.5-1
Three of a suit and one blank	8.5-1
Three of a suit and two blanks	23-1
Four of a suit, three cards to come	1.5-1
Four of a suit and one blank	1.75-1
Four of a suit and two blanks	4.25-1

Odds against making a straight by the river when you hold certain cards are as follows: open-end three-straight and a blank, 8-1; open-end three-straight and two blanks, 22-1; open-end four-straight (three cards to come), 1.5-1; open-end four-straight and a blank, 2-1; open-end four-straight and two blanks, 5-1; inside four-straight (three cards to come), 3-1; inside four-straight and a blank, 5-1; and inside four-straight and two blanks, 10-1.

If you are dealt a pair, you will make two pair 42 percent of the time by the river, and you'll make trips or better 20 percent of the time. If you are dealt three suited connectors, you will hit a straight, flush, or straight flush one out of three hands. With any three unrelated starting cards, you can expect to finish with two pair or better about 22 percent of the time.

Here are your best bets: three of a kind with two or more cards to come; a four-flush or open-ended four-straight with two or more cards to come; and an inside straight with three cards to come. If these great draws contain overcards, of course, you have a raising hand.

The Importance of "Live" Cards

The previous odds assume you have no knowledge of board cards. In actual practice, you will use the known cards to help figure "live" cards and your real odds. So, when is a hand not "live"? If you have a four-flush, and you see just one of your nine outs on board, that's live. Two is borderline—you usually won't call raises without overcards to the sus-pected pair betting into you. Three or more is not live—fold city. With an inside-straight draw, even one "out" gone means fold. With an open-end straight, one "out" on board is okay, but two or more means fold. If you have two pair and need to fill up, forget it if you see even one of your four outs in someone else's hand.

Take our first example. If you have four outs and thirty-six unseen cards, your odds are 8-1 against. But if just one of your four outs is on board, your odds are now 11-to-1. In the second example, you have nine outs to your four-flush and thirty-six unseen cards. Your odds are 3-to-1. But if your hand is not "live" (three flush cards are on board), you now have just six outs and a much worse 5-1 shot. When in doubt, use pot odds to guide you in a tough spot.

There is a big difference between seeing two of your flush cards on board on third street and two on board after sixth street. That's because by sixth street, many more cards will have been exposed. Every card you see that is not one of your outs improves your chance of making your hand. Here's our final example: Say that on fourth street, there are eight cards that will make your flush out of forty unseen cards, giving you 4-1 odds. By sixth street, you notice that there are just six of your suit left in the deck of thirty unseen cards, so your odds are still 4-1! They have not changed. If the bet is $10, there's more than $40 in the pot, and you're drawing to the nuts, you can call. Keep careful track of the board in Stud!

It may seem daunting when you realize you should remember all the exposed cards in Stud. But consider this: You really only have to remember the folded cards. The rest are sitting right there in front of you. It's easier than you think.

Seven-Stud Strategy and Shortcuts

Stud is the best game for picking up tells and patterns in your opponents. You're not just groping in the dark, as with Hold'em. Because cards are showing, you can make more than an educated guess about opponents' hands. You can observe actions, "vibes," and body language with particular hands, match bets to cards, and put that info in your memory bank. Ask to see the called hands at the end to compare the player's moves with his or her hole cards, and you're on your way.

The Door Card

The door card is your entryway into a player's hand and his mind. If he or she bets on third street, your first instinct is to suspect a door-card pair. You operate on this assumption (modified by your read on the player) until you find evidence to the contrary. If a player pairs his door card, you look for reasons to fold. Fear the trips. At the same time, use your foes' door-card fears to bluff when you pair your own door card.

Early on, opponents' door cards create some good raising opportunities if you have a pair. If all players have door cards below a queen and you have a pair of queens, you know—since the odds are 16-1 against someone having a pocket pair—that you have high hand. So you take advantage of the prime directive in Stud: RAISE! In the rare event someone raises back into your overcard, you can reraise or back off. Maybe you're facing pocket kings or aces, but it sure isn't likely! Here's where knowing your player saves you again.

QUESTION?

What happens in an eight-person Stud game if the dealer runs out of cards?
The dealer will put a face-up "spit" card in the center of the table. The spit card is a community card functioning as each player's seventh card. This is rare. (The spit card does not change the betting order.)

In real Stud (not no-fold Stud) you put out expendable "feeler bets" early to "know where you're at." (See section on "Send Out a Probe" on page 93 in Chapter 8.) For example, if you believe a player has made a position bet with the high door card, by all means, raise him and observe his reaction, especially if you have a lower pair. Using bets and raises to get a line on another player if you have a hand that might be best (or second best) is a solid Stud stratagem.

Playing on Later Streets

With the price doubling on fifth street, late-street play is crucial. This is decision time. If you stay for fifth street, you will probably be committed to stay to the river. Your play on fifth and sixth street will be dictated by live cards, kickers, and overcards. How you play on fifth street when you have a pair or two pair will determine whether you make money at this game. Hands below a pair, drawing hands where you use pot odds, and hands trips or higher play themselves, but two pair is the critical hand—because it is so often a loser. First, two pair is less than the average winning hand (trip nines), and second, it is rare that your hand will improve. Your fifth-street two pair will fill up by the river only one out of six tries, while trips will hit one out of three. Low two pairs have sucked more money out of poker players than the IRS! Trips are a far, far superior hand. If you have a low two pair facing a higher pair that may already be a higher two pair, you need *at least* one very live overcard to that pair to play.

Similarly, if you have a lone pair facing another pair or two pair, you want your pair to be an overpair, or at the very least have live, overcard kickers. There is no advantage in improving to a low two pair, as a low two pair is a loser. If you don't have a reasonable shot (your cards live, his not) at making a *higher* two pair or better, let it go. It is more profitable to face two lower pair with your lone pair, than a single higher pair.

QUESTION?

What is the difference between seeing and calling?
They are almost the same thing. After a player makes a bet, others, if they do not raise or fold, must "see" the bet by putting in the amount of the bet. The last player before the bettor "calls" the bet. Today, the terms are used almost interchangeably, with "seeing" losing favor. Once all nonfolding players have "seen" or "called" the bet, the betting round is over.

Some of the costliest mistakes in Stud are chasing with a low two pair or a low pair with low kickers or chasing when your cards are no longer live. Remember, your opponent can improve also. How live are *his* kickers and his pair? If you have a low or medium pair on fifth street, you'll improve by the river four out of ten tries, and on sixth street you'll hit about three out of ten, but your improvement won't win the pot if you have not paired a card that is an overcard to the likely two pair your opponent is holding.

If you hold a low two pair on fourth or fifth street, you have to jam it if there's any chance of getting people to fold. That's because someone with a higher pair can easily improve and beat you, while you are stuck with your trap hand.

Deception in Stud

Because so much of your soul is bared for all to see on the board, seek out the deceptive hands that can pay off big. Strong Stud hands are hidden hands that run counter to your board cards, and when you improve, it is not apparent. Pocket pairs are the best example, as well as flush draws that hide two pair (which can turn into a full house), and an ace in the hole with a door-card pair. In Stud, aggression is a big part of your early deception—and your foes'. If you bet a strong-looking board early, you may have to fire shells until the more expensive streets before others will finally give it up. In most cases, you will have to bet if you are high card on third street, or if you have the only board pair on fourth or fifth. But think before you do, since you may be hit with a testing raise. Evaluate the boards, and decide up front if you will reraise. If not, then realize that the hand is probably over for you unless you get lucky on the next street.

FACT

> If a player pairs his door card, trips are a strong possibility. However, if he pairs his fourth-street card, two pair is more probable.

If you have a strong draw that you know you will play all the way, play it strong, like you have a made hand. This could win you the pot sooner or later unless a foe has a very strong hand already made. Remember, with two hole cards, you could conceivably be rolled up. On the river, with three hole cards, you could have quads on any given hand!

Here's an example of deception defeated. If someone bets on fourth street with nothing showing, what is the reason for the bet? A slow-played pocket pair, or a paired-up hole card? What else could it be? You can always relate a player's action to his board and the up cards of others. The board allows you to narrow the possibilities—that is the beauty of Stud.

Be a Stud at Seven-Card Stud

Here are some concluding thoughts and a summary of Stud:

- Play live cards and use board cards to figure your odds. How "live" your cards are is the number-one factor in deciding whether to pursue a hand.
- Use the exposed cards to figure how live your opponents' cards are, not just your own.
- If there are two or more of your straight- or flush-draw cards already exposed on third street, don't pursue the draw.
- Avoid head-to-head battles with overpairs. If you have a high pair, such as queens, see how many aces and kings are out.

- Jam, jam, jam! Slow-playing in Stud can cost you some pots. Of course, know when to back off.
- Jam with top drawing hands. Sometimes you will take the pot without having to hit the draw.
- If a player has a pair showing on board higher than your pair, fold your hand—unless you have a very strong draw.
- Opponents can use their boards to misrepresent a hand, just as you can. Watch for these "board moves."
- Keep an eye on the math, and make sure you are getting a good overlay from the pot when you call.

It is an art form in Stud to always be aware of how other players view your hand. What message is your board conveying? Learn to manipulate that message to your advantage. Your bets and raises will be linked to your board and to your past history. Use it! The more powerful the board, the easier it is to bluff. Determine early who you can bluff and who you can steal antes from. With so many clues out there, bluffing, deception, isolation, and using table image become huge. Stud is a game where you can use *all* your poker skills.

Chapter 18

Online Poker: The Genie's out of the Bottle

Over the past few years, two phenomena have combined to push poker into the stratosphere and into your living room—Internet casinos and tournament poker. Can't find a game? Too tired to leave the house? It's no matter. Online card-rooms can have you in action at the click of a mouse. This new format has created thousands of new players and revolutionized the game, and for many, it is the wave of the future.

The Double-Edged Sword of Internet Poker

Online casinos rake in more than $4 billion (yes, billion) a year. More than 1,800 Internet sites offer slots and any table game you can imagine. Gamblers don't even have to leave home to get their fix. As for poker, you will find thousands of players in action from all over the world at a plethora of Web sites. At first glance, the Internet seems like a godsend for pressed-for-time or isolated poker aficionados. Of course, when it comes to gambling, when something seems too good to be true, it usually is.

Advantages of Online Casinos

Look at this formidable "plus" column. You can always find a game—without driving, or trying to organize your friends. Even if you live in Timbuktu, you can get a game. If you just have an hour or two, you can jump on your computer and be in action in minutes. If you are homebound, you can still play—with limits as low as a quarter. If the brick-and-mortar casinos won't deal your favorite game, like Draw or Five-Stud, some online rooms will. Most sites have a large variety of games and limits, day or night—including tournaments. If casino play is too slow for you, online play is twice as fast. If you like heads-up or short-handed play, you can find that, too. Changing tables is a snap, there's no smoke, and you can even play in multiple games at the same time—in your underwear!

FACT

Online poker is good for learning the basics. Most Web sites offer no-risk "play money" games for free, and in real-money games, you and a few pals can gather around the computer and discuss your hand before you act. That's one thing you'll never be able to do in a real-world cardroom.

Those who struggle in face-to-face games love it. No one can discover their tells, and strangers and superior players can't intimidate them. Those who play unorthodox poker or who find the casino crowd too critical feel right at home online. It's also much easier to be aggressive without tough players staring you down. Some people just like to be anonymous—and you don't have to tip the dealer! Besides not having to tip, some sites sweeten the financial pot by offering free tournaments ("freerolls") for those who have played enough hands, bad-beat jackpots, and deposit bonuses. The rake is usually less as well. Though most of the 1,800 cybercasinos don't offer poker, there are more than enough virtual rooms to choose from.

You're Not in Kansas Anymore

Not all the differences between online and brick-and-mortar games are good ones. For the undisciplined, the lure of a poker game in the next room of your house can be too much. The play is so fast—sixty or more hands per hour—that it becomes mesmerizing. The rake, blinds, and antes can eat you up quickly. Sitting at the computer late at night, hour after hour, tired and alone, it's so easy to keep seeing hand after hand, rather than get up and go to bed. It's tempting to play loose, to just click that mouse and call, card after card, or suddenly bluff off a lot of chips on a whim. In a casino, a bluff is a major move. Players will stare you down and look into your soul. Online, you just click the mouse and off go the chips. It's no surprise there is more bluffing online.

Money management can go up in cybersmoke along with discipline. After awhile, the chips don't seem real. They're just fuzzy images on a computer screen—until you get your credit-card bill. Then you realize it is all too real. You remember you haven't seen your kids for a while, your spouse is a stranger, and the only camaraderie you've had is a few typed lines from a wiseass computer nerd with no life.

It is way too simple to waste time and money online. Playing multiple games is foolish, and players who say they can do it effectively are kidding themselves. All they are doing is being raked and blinded twice as fast. And don't forget the very real problem of "mis-clicking"—hitting the "raise" or "call" button when you meant to hit "fold." That happens more than players will admit.

Online Strategy Changes

You won't find a lot of top players competing online for serious money. Why? Because many weapons in their poker arsenals are useless in cyberspace. Since so much of good poker is "playing the player, not playing the cards," you can see where Internet games could be a nightmare. How can you play the player when the player is invisible? Forget finding tells, discovering someone's personality, reading body language, betting motions, or any of the other myriad mannerisms that provide such a sumptuous buffet of information to the astute player. You won't see through opponents' tricky moves because you can't see them at all. And making moves of your own will be difficult. You won't be staring people down, hearing their voices change, or watching the way they protect their hole cards. Basically, online, you could be facing a Martian and not know it. However, strategy isn't totally nonexistent. Following are a few pointers.

If you are going to play online, play in short sessions and book some wins! Build up a bankroll—slowly. Don't be a zombie! Get in and get out with small victories. The wins will boost your confidence. Then you can play with "their" money for a while.

Find a Promising Table

This is much easier online because you can observe any table you wish for as long as you wish. You can take notes, get a feel for the players, and determine if the crowd's loose or tight. The sites even help you out. The games will be listed in their "lobbies," along with the number of seated players, waiting list, average pot size, and percentage of players seeing the flop (or fourth street in Stud).

Screen-Name Misdirection

Controlling your table image and using deception is problematic, but you can make a stab it at with your betting patterns and with your screen name. Using betting to manipulate isn't as effective online, so for the most part it's best to play in a straightforward manner. Acting real loose for a while so you can act tight later (or vice versa) is futile when you don't know if anyone is even paying attention and players change tables so often. Over time, if you play with the same characters for hours on end, you might get a line on someone. This is where you can exercise a big cyberadvantage: taking notes! You can scribble like a banshee, unlike in a casino, where you would be considered a nutcase. Some sites even provide a screen area to take notes on. Use it often! (Your note-taking will not be in vain because most sites will not allow players to change their screen names once they are established. Their only recourse is to close the account or to open multiple accounts.)

Your screen name, your state or country, and the figure you choose to represent you (on some sites) provide the bulk of your table image. They reveal valuable information (and misinformation!), so make sure you are delivering the impression you want others to see—usually a misleading one. Be aware that even states and countries have stereotypes associated with them. If you like role-playing, here's your chance! Don't be afraid to have fun with it. There are people who have "calling station" or the like as their screen name, when in fact they are total maniacs. An "old man" icon could in real life be a twenty-one-year-old biker with a nose ring. A hot-looking woman might really be a dirty old man. Watch for deliberately misleading screen names and icons (also called "avatars") and for those who are playing it straight. That goes double if someone asks you for a date!

"Chatting" Can Reveal a Lot

There is also a "chat" area where you can type messages to other players during the game. Often, this is where you will experience one of the negative aspects of cyberspace: anonymous cowards typing sarcastic insults and sexual innuendoes. These computer losers are rampant and would never have the guts to say this stuff to your face. But the good news is you can get a read on the personality and age of the "flamer," and you can use this information to "read" him or her.

FACT

You can track what's going on at the major online poker rooms at ✍www.pokerpulse.com. It lists the number of players in action at the different sites and what games are being spread.

Chatting can yield some valuable info. Like real-world conversation, you can sometimes get someone on your side, discover his or her personality and age, or get a line on how someone plays, how many games he or she is playing in, and how long your opponent has been at the table. Up all night? On tilt? And it never hurts to play dumb and ask for advice. It might not be right, but it will be revealing!

Here are some of the cutesy chatspeak abbreviations you will encounter in poker rooms:

bb	Big blind or bad beat
fh	Full house, or expletive used with the word "hand"
g1	Good one; a nice play
gc	Good cards, good catch, or good call
gg	Good game; a respectful farewell
gl2u	Good luck to you
nb	Nice bet or nice boat (full house)
nfh	Nice f****** hand; words of frustration
nh	Nice hand; sometimes facetious
nr	Nice river; usually facetious
str8	A straight
vnh	Very nice hand; usually sincere
wtg	Way to go
vvn	Very, very nice
utg	Under the gun
os	Offsuit
std	Suited
pp	Pocket pair
sb	Small blind

Pot Odds Become Huge Online

Although reading players is more difficult, you can still utilize your loose and tight game strategies and especially position play and pot odds. Pot odds calculations grow in value as your other skills lessen. A pot is a pot—online or not. Good position is good position. Play your quality starting hands, don't play too long, and let the pot be your guide. And if you think it will be less humiliating to go broke alone at home than in a casino, you might be in for a rude awakening.

Are There Tells Online?

Many online players insist that finding tells, noticing body language, table image, and "playing the player" is overrated. They say tells can be manipulated and that you can learn more by just following the money— that is, by studying the pattern of bets, checks, raises, and calls during a hand. But you can study the betting in brick-and-mortar rooms as well, along with everything else. And players can use their betting patterns to mislead, just as with false tells.

If you decide to play online, your chosen site will walk you through all the details of funding your account, and so on. But before you begin real-money play, go to the "play money" tables and practice using the software (the various buttons) so you can concentrate on the game and avoid costly mistakes when you finally dive in. E-mail the site with any questions.

Some online players believe that the speed at which players click their call, bet, or raise buttons can be a tell. You can discover some moves if you play with the same players long enough. For example, if someone hesitates a long time and then bets or raises, that usually means a strong hand. If someone hesitates and then checks, that means weak (the player wanted you to think he was considering a bet). If a player has clicked the automatic "check" or "check/fold" button, the decision will show up as an instantaneous action on your screen when it is his or her turn. This is revealing. You know he was ready to fold. On the other hand, when someone hits the bet or raise button quickly, does that mean a bluff, or does it indicate a strong hand? Here's where your notes come in handy. And like in the real world, acting at the same speed all the time can only do you good.

Gambling with Invisible Cards

The number-one, most important, absolutely essential question you must ask about Internet poker, since you are playing with make-believe cards against invisible players, is: Is it honest? In the gambling world, you really must keep your eyes open for scams and cheaters. When you're in a casino, you can use your jungle sense to "feel" when something's not right, when two players are in collusion or when the dealer spends too much time making eye contact with a particular player. The subtlest of moves, the smallest of edges, can be very large to a scam artist. It isn't common, but there are people who can cheat you right in front of your eyes without your even knowing it.

FACT

The first Internet poker casino, ✎*www.planetpoker.com*, started in August 1997 with play-money games. It spread its first cash games on January 1, 1998, and the rest, as they say, is history.

Contrast this to cyberspace, where you can't see anything other than computer-generated pictures, and this feeds right into the old gambling proverb: "Don't gamble with invisible dice." There's a story of a guy who gave a buddy three bucks to play a progressive slot machine on a trip to Vegas. The buddy came back $100,000 richer. The guy asked if it was his money that won. "No, the buddy replied, "Yours was the spin right before it hit. *My* money won 100 grand." The point is: How would the guy know if his buddy was telling the truth? He was essentially gambling with an invisible slot machine, for real money, and was only relying on his buddy to be honest. When there's that kind of cash involved, you quickly learn that no one's *that* good a friend or *that* honest.

What you're doing on the Internet is gambling with invisible cards against unseen players you assume are real. The "buddy" you have entrusted with your hard-earned pay doesn't know you or care about you, and he has only one goal—to make money—yet you expect him to be honest. In gambling, this is called being a sucker. The Internet is rampant with stories from players who feel they've been taken, either by opponents in collusion, the sites themselves, or both. There is no question that it happens. What is unknown is how prevalent it is. Because these Web sites are basically a license to print money, you know that greedy, unsavory characters looking for some kind of edge are being attracted to them like moths to a flame. Anyone with startup costs can open a Web site. And since these sites are poorly regulated and are located "offshore," who are you going to complain to? The government of Costa Rica?

Four Methods of Online Cheating

Of the four most feared ways to cheat online, "active" collusion between one or more players is the most familiar. It isn't much different than in a casino where two players "whipsaw" an unsuspecting rube with raise after raise, but the ruse is much more effective online. Here, the cheaters can discuss their hands by cell phone or even play on different computers in the same room! In a casino, this scam can get obvious, but online, where you can't look players in the eye, you're left wondering. Some sites have installed software to detect collusion, and the word is out that they are being diligent about it, but it's small consolation complaining to a site after you've been bet out of pot after pot or whipsawed into oblivion. If you are facing two, three, or more players who all know each other's cards, how can you possibly beat them consistently with your lone hand? This type of collusion is certainly easier and more effective online, but because of the computer record of hands, it is also easier to detect—after the fact. On the other hand, cyber play is so fast that by the time you realize what happened, many hands may have gone by.

"Passive" Collusion Between Players

This brand of cheating is subtler and harder to catch. Again, a number of players get an edge by sharing their cards—obviously a major advantage when figuring odds and deciding which starting hands to play.

This might not sound like much, but to a gambler, a small edge makes a big difference. Wouldn't you like to know what three of your opponents are holding?

Hackers

If a teenager can hack into the Pentagon, someone should be able to hack into a poker site, right? The sites say that their encryption software is as sophisticated as that of any online bank, and that only your computer is given information on your hole cards. So no nefarious nerd will be able to read your hidden hand by hacking a Web site. But ask yourself this: How safe is your home computer?

"All-in" Scamming

This is probably the most common abuse of the Internet system and has caused much controversy in the poker world. In the early days, when faced with a tough decision, some unethical players were just refusing to act, and thus were "timed out." A "timed out" player was treated as if he went "all-in" (ran out of chips) at the point he failed to act, the same as if his computer crashed or his service provider had a glitch and disconnected the player from the Internet. Remaining players built a side pot.

Today, most sites will "fold" the hand of anyone not acting. However, a player who disconnects himself from the Internet will still be put all-in, so the scam survives, but many cyber rooms *are* cracking down. Players suspecting abuse can e-mail site administrators, who can review the hand in question and other hands played by the perpetrator, looking for a pattern. In cases of abuse, they may bar the client from the site or even confiscate his chips and transfer them to victims.

ALERT! If your Internet connection is legitimately lost during a hand, you will still be put all-in (treated as if you've run out of chips), as long as you haven't used up your ration of "all-ins" for that day. Find out your site's policy on all-in protection before you play. Sometimes you must ask that they be reset.

Cheating by Sites?

The jury is still out on whether it's legal for you as a player to compete for money online, but the site owners aren't taking any chances. Their businesses are based in foreign countries, which reap a large tax windfall by giving them safe haven. The faceless cyber honchos answer to no one, and their computers totally control the action. So what would keep them from stealing you blind?

All you have to hang your hat on is a single tired argument. "The casino owners make so much money that they wouldn't risk killing the goose that's laying the golden eggs by cheating customers. They are making more than enough money *without* cheating." Does this extremely logical argument sound familiar? It should. It is the exact same argument you always heard back when the Mob owned the Las Vegas casinos. Everyone knew the Underworld ran them, and everyone knew mobsters were the most dishonest, brutal people on the planet. So why did anyone in his or her right mind gamble with them? Because normal, logical people believed it made no sense for them to cheat—not with that huge House edge making them millions. But they did cheat. All the time. In fact, they considered it a point of honor not to let a "sucker" out of the casino with any of "their" money—or any money at all. Were greedy mobsters winning tons and tons of money? Absolutely yes, but *there is never enough.*

"Murder, Inc.," was just maximizing its profits, like any corporation. Mobsters did what they could get away with, just like Enron, Worldcom, and their other corporate brethren. Even for billion-dollar corporations, there's never enough capital, the edge is never big enough, and you're only as good as your last quarterly report, which had better top the previous one. The Mob controlled Vegas under the noses of regulators, and Enron execs (and others) robbed people blind despite federal oversight. Thus, it is naïve to believe that gambling Web sites—which for practical purposes are unregulated—are *all* fair and honest, especially in view of the seedy characters attracted by gambling and easy money. If you were in their shoes, wouldn't you want to make as much as you possibly could before it all came crashing down?

You will meet some of the most honorable people in the world playing poker, but you will also encounter types who would steal their grandma's Social Security check if they could get away with it. Now, we're talking millions of dollars here . . . and someone's going to tell you what your cards are . . . from *Central America* . . . and you'll just have to take his word for it. Anyone who can devise worldwide poker software can easily create a way for that computer to take a little extra for the House and eventually break you.

Corporations exist to make profits, and they want every last nickel they can get their hands on, so don't think that just because organized crime sold its Vegas casinos to "legitimate businesses" that the "kinder, gentler" gambling halls are on your side. They want your money just as badly as the Mob did, and they have tricks of their own.

Don't Bet the Farm

If you are going to play online, you have to go in with both eyes open. You must be okay with the prospect of hanky-panky, be ready to report anything unusual, and be praying that your site is honest. Obviously, since you can't use most of your skills, you'd be foolish to compete for big bucks. But if you want to have fun with it, fine. Go for it. Play in a tournament now and then, try a new variation, or fool around with the lower-stakes crowd. But don't let it take over your life. Limit your hours online. Don't let your computer room become your opium den.

Out in Vegas, they say that video poker machines are the "crack cocaine" of compulsive gamblers. Those machines, which are everywhere from supermarkets to bars, will break a gambler faster than any other game. Pathetic souls spend every waking hour either staring into the machine, thinking about their next session, or scrounging money to play. *You* have a chance to be a good poker player, enjoying a *real* game with *real* people. Don't let online poker become *your* crack cocaine.

Chapter 19

Tournament Poker: Your Dream Come True?

For many, the tournament phenomenon represents the most extreme, cutting-edge brand of poker. The serious competition, do-or-die decisions, big prize money, and even television exposure have put the game and its players on the national map. But doing well in a tournament—large or small—takes a lot more than wishful thinking and an entry fee.

All or Nothing

Tournaments are adrenaline-fueled competitions using a fixed buy-in paid by anywhere from ten to over a thousand players. With the exception of the early stages of some "rebuy" events, you can't purchase more chips, so if you lose them all, you go home. Blinds and antes increase at regular intervals, ratcheting up the pressure. The tournament ends when one player (the winner) owns every chip.

Competing in a tournament is intense. The chance to play for prizes in the thousands or even millions of dollars against the best players in the world is intoxicating, especially because your losses are limited to your buy-in. On a smaller scale, you can have a blast in $25 or $50 buy-in events where you may have hours of fun for very little money. You can also try your hand at small buy-in "satellite" events, where the winner receives an entry into a major tournament. And satellites aren't only at tournament venues. They are also all over the Internet. One player even reached the final table of a World Poker Tour television event by investing just *a single dollar* online. And longshot Chris Moneymaker didn't win $2.5 million in the 2003 World Series of Poker by paying the $10,000 buy-in—he paid just $40 in an online satellite! It's no wonder there is an event somewhere every week and tournament entries are shattering records.

FACT

The beauty of tournament poker is that any player with a buy-in can take on the planet's top players. If you have the guts, you can make the pros put up or shut up, and prove that they are the fastest guns in the West.

But before you quit your day job and hit the tournament trail, realize that not only will you be facing serious professionals, but many of them play hundreds of tournaments a year—and still can go months without reaching a final table. You can play extremely well in a tournament and yet come up empty, because usually only the final 10 percent win money. So you could conceivably grind it out for an entire day or more, outplay 89 percent of the field, and still come up a loser. In a ring game, if you outplay 89 percent of your foes, you will do quite well. It can be very frustrating. If you are relying on tournaments to pay the rent, it will play with your head, especially because buy-ins for big events start at $500 and run up into the many thousands of dollars. World Poker Tour events cost $5,000 to $25,000. However, if you are a retired millionaire, knock yourself out.

It's About Survival

If you tackle tournaments, you can leave your ring-game strategy at home. Of course, you still use your skills. You still read opponents and put them on hands, but tournaments require a new way of thinking. Since you can't dig into your pocket for more cash, you must never lose all your chips. It follows that if you are ever going to risk your last chips, not only do you want the best of it, you want very much the best of it—especially if you are one of the better players. If possible, you don't want to risk elimination if there's a significant chance of an unpleasant "surprise." You have three goals, and you take them one at a time:

1. To finish in the money. You want some payoff for all that hard work.
2. To place in the top three. This is where the really big money is.
3. To win it all. For some, a first-place result is their only ambition.

Realize that just finishing in the money in a large event is a victory to build on, and because it's a "short-term" situation, you will need a little "luck." You will need to survive at least one bad beat and put a bad beat on someone else along the way.

QUESTION?

What are the four main factors controlling whether you play a particular hand in a tournament?
Consider how many chips you have relative to others at your table, strength of the hand, position, and opponents (who they are and whether any have already called).

Implications of the Survival Mentality

In tournament play, your chips are finite. There is no never-ending supply as big as your bankroll. So your stack of chips becomes as precious as a canteen of water to a parched soul hopelessly lost in the blistering heat of the Mojave Desert. And as this water supply is used up, the remaining droplets become even more precious, so much so that the last moist mouthful has a value beyond measure because once it's gone, there is no life. So that water must be preserved at all costs, since survival depends on it.

FACT

Benny Binion invented the poker tournament in 1970 when he got a bunch of the best road gamblers in the country together at the Horseshoe for the first "World Series," to settle once and for all who was best. A handful of players put up $10,000 each, and Johnny Moss came out on top. Today, the tournament format is used all over the world.

What does this mean to tournament play? Everything. Every decision to risk chips has far-reaching implications. And the fewer you have, the more valuable each one is. For you, yes, but your opponents are in the same desert. So you can use their fear in several ways. First, when you bet, you will be less likely to be called. Therefore, you can open with worse hands than usual. (Most of your opponents will *not* open with worse hands than usual, but watch closely for those who do.)

Second, if you *are* called, you can expect to be facing a better hand than normal. It generally takes a better hand to call than to bet in tournament poker. It follows that you don't really want to be called, nor do you want to just call the bets of others. You'd much prefer to be aggressive and win small pots uncontested. Third, you rarely want to be entering pots with two or more players already in. If you're going in, you always want the option of buying the pot right there.

Fourth, survival means you will often lay down some very good hands, especially early in the tournament. And in no-limit, you want to avoid early coin-flip situations (such as a pair versus two overcards), unless you are one of the weaker players or are short-stacked (have very few chips left compared to the other players). *Position is extremely important, pot odds are much less so.* You want a clear advantage before you risk your chips, not a drawing hand—no matter how big the pot. You're not thinking long term here; tournaments are a short-term scenario.

While they may be short-term odds-wise, these events can last all day and far into the night or even into several days. It follows that you need tremendous patience and stamina, in addition to your other poker skills. Going on tilt is not an option. You will be amazed at how some players who have been solid for hours just all of a sudden lose it late in a tourney and blow themselves out with some impatient, bonehead move. Discipline and serenity can move you into the money, even without good cards. Realize that you will be there a while.

ALERT!

Picture going all-in in no-limit with A-Q. This is a legitimate move if you're first in the pot. But do you want to call a big all-in bet with A-Q for all your chips? That is a much tougher decision.

What Kind of Tournament Is This?

Job one is finding out the payout, how many places are paid, rebuy policy, and when the tournament begins. With so many events being sold out these days, it pays to get there early! Sign up, and then check out and chat up the other entrants. Before devising strategy, you must be able to recognize the nature of the event. Some require great skill, while some take great luck. The key is how long the tournament will go. The longer it lasts, the bigger the edge for the better players, who have more time to use their skills. You can predict length by comparing the number of chips each player is given to the size of the initial blinds or antes and finding out how quickly the blinds/antes will be raised. If the blinds/antes are raised quickly (more often than every forty minutes), the event will be quicker—and chancier. If the blinds/antes are doubled at each level, that is a short tournament. If they only increase 50 percent or less, or if they are using a structure called "TEARS," that will be a longer event.

Play will start out fast in shorter events, so you cannot be as cautious. In longer events, you can be much more patient.

How does the House make money on tournaments?
Events are listed something like this: "$500 plus $50 No-Limit Hold'em." This means $500 goes to the prize pool, and $50 goes to the House. You will pay $550 when you sign up and are given a table and seat assignment. The House also makes money on all those players who hit the ring games after they bust out of the tournament.

Rebuys and Add-Ons

Rebuys allow busted-out players to buy their way back into a tourney. Most lower buy-in events and super satellites allow rebuys during the first three rounds if your chips fall below their initial level. At the end of the rebuy period, there is one last chance to up your stack, regardless of chip count, and that's called purchasing an "add-on." Most major events do not use rebuys or add-ons, but smaller events and most super satellites do. Rebuy tournaments favor those with deep pockets.

It is important that you decide in advance how much money you're willing to invest in the tournament. First, be aware that 95 percent of the field will buy the add-on, so you will have to as well. As for rebuys, you want to set limits. It is foolish to go into a low-buy-in competition and then spend so much on rebuys that you could've entered a more significant event. Rebuying over and over is just throwing good money after bad. There are cases in which a player rebought so many times that he had to finish in the money just to break even! That's just stupid. Your rebuy usually gives you an amount equal to your initial number of chips, but meanwhile, other players have doubled or tripled their stacks, so you are already an underdog. One or two rebuys and the add-on should be the max, and you should buy the add-on only if it doubles your stack or if you will own a below-average stack if you do not add on.

The idea is to invest as little as possible. Let your opponents inflate the prize pool, not you. And if you are going to rebuy, don't wait until after you've gone all-in and lost. Rebuy as soon as you are eligible, so you have some power. Then if you get a hand, you can make some money with it.

The real tournament doesn't begin until players can no longer buy chips—when "death" is final—so during the rebuy period, strategy isn't much different from a standard ring game.

You have two things to watch for during the rebuy period. First, maniacs will be wildly building pots to quickly double their stacks if they get lucky, or going broke and rebuying if they don't. Second, some players will be trying to create a table image as either extremely tight or extremely loose-aggressive. Watch out for these players later if they try to use this image to play against type, with the maniac only playing rock-solid hands, and the tight player bluffing and stealing pots. Many players are loose early and tight late, but the opposite strategy might actually make more sense.

FACT

"It is ten times worse to commit a mistake in a tournament as it is to make that same mistake in a cash game where you can reach in your pocket for more money."

—Longtime tournament superstar T. J. Cloutier

Chip Position and Stack Size

Playing chip position is one of the most important strategies in tournament poker. To survive, you must know how you stack up against the field and especially against the rest of your table. Find your position by dividing the number of remaining players into the total chips in the event, which will be posted. If you have more than this average, you're in the top half. If you're below the curve, you may have to loosen up a bit. Remember, winning small pots and stealing blinds and antes uncontested is a big part of tournament strategy, and you will find that players will not defend their blinds as often as in a ring game. Selective aggressiveness is rewarded—you need that second way to win (forcing others to fold) in every hand you're in. (The first way, of course, is having the best hand at the river.)

Now, how do you stack up against your table? In tournaments, the big chip stacks have an edge, and the small ones are sweating it out. A big stack can bust a small one at any time in no limit, but not vice versa. Small stacks must think twice about calling a big stack. Thus big stacks often can run over small stacks, but you can't be foolish with a big stack or you'll find yourself making those small stacks a lot bigger! A big stack gives you the comfort level to wait for premium hands and pick your spots to steal. Small stacks don't have that luxury. What you must avoid with a big stack is getting into big battles with other big stacks, especially late. Those big stacks can hurt you, so stay out of their way. Often, you can coast into the money if you don't get into a turf war with another giant. Don't get greedy. Let them come to you. Your goal is to get into the money, not win a certain number of pots. Winning one pot per level could be enough to get you to the final table.

"Tournament winners combine extremely good judgement with some lucky breaks. The trick is to survive long enough to put yourself in the position to get lucky."

—Top tournament player and author Tom McEvoy

If you have a small stack, keep a close eye on your chips. If you have less than four times the big blind in limit or six times in no-limit or pot-limit, that is a small stack. If you get in dire straits, loosen up to maintain enough chips to ensure yourself that second way to win. If you cannot make an all-in bet that is at least a little scary in no-limit, or be able to bet through to the river in limit, others will call you down or put you all-in long before you have that big hand you're praying for.

There will come a time with a small stack when you will just have to go for it, but keep an eye on the blinds. Once they pass, you will be free and clear for another seven hands. If you are on the bubble (near the money), look for players with fewer chips than you. Can you outlast them without risking your stack? Watch the clock! Will the blinds increase soon? Can you make it to the paying spots without playing a hand?

If you are a short stack and the money cutoff line is nearing, don't focus on your own table. Get up and check out other tables for tiny stacks. How many are as desperate as you? Will they have to go all-in on their blinds soon? How many need to bust out before you finish in the money? This information is often the difference between being paid and getting nothing.

Tournaments Change Speeds

If you are alert for a tournament's ebb and flow, you can pick up some pots. For example, early in a rebuy event, play is fast. Maniacs are trying to pick up pots by pushing draws and taking chances. This is a time to trap them with a better hand, but remember: A poker tournament is not going to be won early, but it can be lost there. A very cautious early strategy is not a bad way to go.

No-rebuy events usually start slower. Generally, the speed of play will be dictated by the size of the blinds in relation to the average stack. When the stacks are threatened, play speeds up, and desperate players will be betting some less-than-premium hands. Because of the changing nature of tournament play, you must be able to change gears to win and be adept at a variety of styles, not just one.

Some pros say there are three rebuy-tournament player types: experts; maniacs, whose early aggressive play causes trouble for experts; and rocks, whose severely conservative play eventually traps and kills the maniacs, but who are defeated by the skill of the experts in the end. After the maniacs and weak players are gone, play slows down (becomes more cautious) as competitors consolidate their chips and there are more big stacks. This is a time to be more aggressive, especially right after a blind/ante increase when players are intimidated by the higher limits. Play won't speed up again until some stacks grow short, the blinds threaten the average stack, or perhaps not until the final table.

In many of today's top no-rebuy events, there seems to be only two types, best characterized as wolves and shepherds. Wolves are skilled, aggressive players who nibble away and steal pots from shepherds, who cautiously guard their sheep (chips) all the way to the final table. By that time, the wolves will have devoured much of their flock, but at some risk. Shepherds won't have many sheep left. Though surrounded by predators, however, they've made it to the money.

ALERT!

Even in a limit tournament, at the final table you will often be playing what amounts to no-limit, because the stakes are so high that to bet all the way to the river, you will need to risk all your chips.

The Four Stages of a Tournament

The following summaries describe play in no-rebuy events, or rebuy events after the rebuy period is over. During the early stage, play good tight-aggressive poker—patient and cautious. Wait for a premium hand. Try to identify the maniacs, and study the players for later reference. Pay attention to who's loose or tight, who are veterans and who are rookies, and who will call versus who can lay down a hand.

Middle Stage

The middle stage begins when players settle down following the initial period of craziness, bust-outs, and nervousness and the blinds begin to have a little bite. Take advantage of the early large stacks who might be playing a little loose and throwing their weight around. Also, notice if any of the large stacks are playing the opposite way: too tight. Against short stacks, you can gamble more, but make sure it's heads-up so you're not at risk. Desperate players are forced to play weaker hands. If you're against a shortie, put him or her all-in. Don't leave the short stack with a few chips. It could come back to haunt you.

ESSENTIAL

If you and another player have called a small stack's all-in bet, there is often an unspoken agreement not to bet each other out of the pot. This ensures the best chance of busting out the smaller stack and moving closer to the money. So be reluctant to bet unless you feel you have a lock. Against multiple opponents, bet your hand.

The Late Stage

If you have a large stack, with position you can bully small stacks, tight players, and those who can lay a hand down, but if you can avoid confrontations with other large stacks, you often can coast to the final table. Pick your spots. If you're small, look at the other stacks, and decide if you can make it without winning any pots or blinds. If not, pick a spot and using your best "strong" tells, get it all in.

The Final Table

You could fill a book just with final-table tactics, but again, your strategy will depend on your stack in relation to others and to the blinds. Generally, play starts cautiously, but it soon gets aggressive as players bust out. If you are in no danger of being blinded off (having the blinds eat away your whole stack), you can be more careful. Try to trap the other big stacks, but don't confront them unless you're sure you have the best of it. Try not to double up a small stack by being foolish. You've come too far to lose patience. Remember that with fewer players, there will be more stealing. Against aggressive players, you want to play good cards. You don't need to make a stand if you own a large stack—not yet.

If you're the short stack, you have to gamble and play some hands, but don't be hasty. If it's crunch time, come in with a raise before you're down to just a few checks. You just want to isolate or buy the blinds/antes. You may have to go all-in on coin-flip hands like any pair, ace, or two face cards, and you want to do this before you get such a small stack that everyone can call you with impunity. The fewer the players, the more hands you will be forced to play.

QUESTION?

On the World Poker Tour, why does a player hesitate so long with a hand he knows he's going to fold?
He wants to make his opponent sweat and squirm. Since this is an unpleasant experience, the opponent will be less likely to raise this player next time, especially if he is bluffing. The player also wants his foe to think he had a decent hand, not trash.

One of the principles of tournament poker, best illustrated at final no-limit tables, is that it is dangerous to risk betting on a hand that can't stand a raise or an all-in raise over the top (unless you're trying to steal). Before you bet, you must always have in mind what your response will be if that happens. If you're uncertain, the hand is either unplayable or you should not open or raise with it (just call). You want a hand so good that you'll welcome a raise or so bad that folding is a no-brainer. Watch out for situations where you would be pot-committed, that is, where you have put so much of your stack in the pot that you must go all-in if you are raised. Thank God you have position!

What If You Are Outclassed?

If you're one of the better players, you try to avoid situations where luck is a major factor. But what if you are not? What if you're sitting at a final table surrounded by pros putting you to a decision on every card? Your best option is to minimize those decisions and maximize the luck factor. One way is to get all your chips in as quickly as possible. In no-limit, that's preflop. Go all-in, and let the pro sweat. Avoid situations where you have to call his bets, especially if you must do it on more than one street. He will know what you are holding and make your life miserable. Instead, bet it all and let him try to figure out if you've hit a hand. Most pros will be reluctant to risk their tournament lives on a coin-flip, so unless he has a monster hand or a really good read on you, you will take the pot. This assumes, of course, that you have a stack large enough to scare him. This strategy drives pros crazy.

FACT

Good tournament players are like good ring-game players. They're aggressive, they come in raising, they know where they stand in a hand, and their starting-hand play is not predictable.

If you use this all-in strategy, don't overdo it. Sooner or later, someone's going to call you with pocket aces, kings, or queens in Hold'em, or a hidden primo hand in Stud.

Getting It Heads-up All-In

Here's some food for thought: Your best-case scenario is to hold a pocket pair higher than another pair in Hold'em. That makes you a 4-to-1 (80 percent) favorite, and it's the same if you have an overpair against suited connectors.

If you hold two overcards against suited connectors, you'll win 58 percent of the hands. If the connectors are unsuited, you're up to 62 percent. If you have a pair against two overcards, you're about a 55-percent favorite. Except for the pair over pair, none of these advantages is enough to risk your life on, unless you're desperate. So when you go all-in, you just don't want to be called. And notice the soaring value of high cards over drawing cards. Hands that are 50-50 against a random hand are these: low pairs, 10-8, Q-6, J-7, and K-3.

ALERT!

Note this no-limit quandary: If you have A-K and you go all-in, you are a big underdog only if someone holds pocket aces or kings. You are a coin-flip versus any pair, but you still need to improve. If you have a pair (even deuces), you are a coin-flip against any other hand except a higher pair, against which you win only one hand out of five.

Tournament Tips

Try these strategy tips on for size:

- Winning a pot is more important than wringing a few extra bets out of someone. Take the sure thing.
- Don't go all-in against more than one player or if you believe you will have more than one caller.
- The players most likely to call an all-in bet are those with very large or extremely small ("desperate") stacks.
- Don't "get married" to a hand, no matter how good. If you're not desperate, don't take a big risk.
- When you're in cautious mode, try to see flops and fourth street in Stud cheaply in case your hand doesn't develop.

- Let others go to war. It's better for you to have one enemy with $50,000 than two with $25,000 apiece.
- Don't be afraid to go all-in in no-limit when you have top pair. You do not want the draws to get lucky.
- Heads-up, it's not about who has the best hand. It's about who doesn't have the worst hand.

Because a tournament is a short-term event, you will have to catch some cards to win, but don't be discouraged. Jack Strauss won the 1982 World Series of Poker after being down to his last chip! So don't throw in your final chips on a whim and a shrug. Fight to the end! Remember, like Jack, if you have "a chip and a chair," you're still in it.

One thing is certain: Online poker will continue to explode. The no-limit tournaments are hugely popular, and the online satellites for major real-world competitions are a big reason those events are setting records every year. The 2004 Big One had a prize pool of nearly $25 million, with $5 million going to the winner, Greg "Fossilman" Raymer—who won his entry in an online satellite. Both Raymer and 2003 champ Moneymaker won their $10,000 buy-ins at PokerStars.com. Amazingly, four of the nine finalists in the 2004 WSOP qualified at that Internet poker site. Thanks largely to the Internet, the 2004 field had 2,576 hopefuls—compared to 839 the previous year—including 100 women. The top five finishers all won more than $1 million! Two-hundred twenty-six players were awarded at least $10,000. Harrah's, which now owns the WSOP venue, the Horseshoe casino, expects the number of entrants to triple in 2005, and there is talk of raising the buy-in.

Tournament poker is a whole book in itself, but you won't learn tournament poker by reading. You're going to have to get out there and play. It's *that* different.

Chapter 20

Poker's Future, Your Future

You won't be able to turn around without hearing something new about poker this year. And if tournaments receive corporate sponsorship, watch out! That extra money in the prize pool will lure fortune hunters like Blackbeard's treasure. How do you fit into the game's burgeoning future? Will you grow along with it? And how do you stand in that full-time gamble that is your life?

Farewell to the Smoke-Filled Rooms?

The next card is unknowable, but the one sure thing about poker is that you'll be seeing much more of it on television. The soaring success of the World Poker Tour and World Series of Poker will breed imitators and entrepreneurs scrambling to get on the bandwagon. If corporate sponsors add money to tournament prize pools, they will create overlays that could mean money in your pocket.

How will an overlay help you? Look at this simplified example. Say you are one of a hundred players in a winner-take-all tournament, each paying a dollar to play. Your odds of winning are 99-to-1 if all competitors are equally skilled. But you know half the field has no chance, so your real odds are 49-1. Since your payoff is $99, you are being paid 99-1 on a 49-1 shot! Now let's say a corporate sponsor sweetens the pot and adds a hundred bucks. Now you are offered a $199 payoff for your dollar, when your real odds are just 49-1—a mammoth overlay that will guarantee a profit over time.

Another advance you might see—someday—is cameras on people playing online poker at home, so you can see the faces of opponents. Also expect definitive court rulings on whether playing Internet poker is legal in the United States and new legislation from Congress, one way or the other.

You have to hope that amid the high-tech innovation, television hype, and all-or-nothing tourneys that "real poker" will remain vibrant and thrive. There's a lot to be said for the rough, seamy charm of the smoke-filled rooms and the character of the road gamblers. Much will be lost if the game becomes a sterile exercise without the dangerous, nefarious edge that has sustained it since the time of the riverboat gamblers. Those back-room denizens who were poker's heart and soul for the past hundred years and those early winners of the World Series of Poker who risked going broke on a daily basis are deserving of every twenty-first-century poker player's respect and gratitude.

It doesn't take a prophet to realize that online poker will be huge in the coming years. One site, for example, went from just 300 players per day to more than 25,000 in the last two years. Here's what you can expect:

- Brick-and-mortar cardrooms will have to expand to meet the demand generated by television coverage and online games. Poker revenue jumped 30 percent in Atlantic City alone in the year 2003.
- Many online players are obviously teens and college kids. When they hit twenty-one, the brick-and-mortar casinos will be flooded with young bucks, who will be fish out of water at real poker.
- Because these teens were weaned on ultra-low-limit and play-money games, they will play way too loose, reversing the trend toward tight play of the past ten years.
- No-limit poker will get so popular online and on television that casinos will have to bring it back. No-limit tournaments will become an Internet (and brick-and-mortar) phenomenon.

The first million-dollar online tournament was held early in 2004. And that's only the beginning.

Your Lifelong Poker Game

The game of poker is growing and changing. This ensures its place in a new century—a century of instant gratification, short attention spans, and speed. But resist the temptation to believe Internet poker is real poker. Poker, at its core, remains a "people" game. Solid strategy fifty years ago is still solid strategy. So play with flesh-and-blood human beings. Make a conscious, active, deliberate effort to get out and play, to have a life, to make a friend at the table, maybe take a pro to dinner to hear his stories.

Do you have what it takes to grow with the game, to handle the ever-tougher competition? Reading this book is a start, as is going out there and diving into the fray and experiencing the rush of top-flight poker.

Winning the War

You know that every poker hand is a skirmish in a larger battle—the game you're in. But each game is part of an even larger picture: the war.

The war is your total poker experience. You win a game when you walk away with more money than you came with, but how do you win the war? If you decide that you will never play poker again, that for one reason or another you are through with it (for many, this won't be until they move on to that big casino in the sky), *and you're ahead,* then you are victorious. You have won the battle of poker and defeated your foes. You are quitting "winners."

But there is more to it than money. Poker would be a lonely pastime if money was all it was, as well as a waste of a lot of hours (unless you're earning a really good living at it). You are a winner at poker if it has been an enriching experience, if it has made you a better person, if you have met friends, acquaintances, and characters, gained knowledge, and stayed sharp and focused. If it has brought the thrill of competition and joy to your life, and if you have brought joy to others around the green felt (by some method other than by giving them your chips), then you are a winner.

"Every conscious act requires risk. Every conscious act requires decision. Put these two facts together and you realize that the secret to life is not to avoid gambling, but to gamble well."

—Author/lecturer/pro Mike Caro

The Long Trip Home with Empty Pockets

Not just empty pockets—you might carry a gaping hole where your heart used to be. That first tough loss: Everyone's been there. Full of hope, adrenaline pumping you sky-high, you finally hit your first game in a glitzy Vegas casino, a cavernous California cardroom, Atlantic City with the smell of saltwater in the air, an Indian casino in the boonies, or even a Florida "cruise to nowhere." But you end up getting killed, maybe even embarrassed. You're devastated—but don't let it sour you on the game, or yourself. Every top player has suffered a gut-wrenching loss that made him or her feel like throwing up on the plane from McCarran Airport. The long ride home is an acid test that will strip your soul bare and starkly expose exactly what you are made of.

Maintain Records to Keep Yourself Honest

Smart players keep three types of records:

- Wins and losses. Of course, you keep these so you can see exactly where you stand. It is too easy to deceive yourself when relying on memory. Track the type of game, stakes, venue, time at the table, and amount, with comments.
- Your calls. When you have a tough decision at the river and you call, keep track of whether you won or lost. You should win if you're in at the river. If you lose more than 25 percent, you call too much.
- The players. Keep a notebook of opponents with their tendencies, how they play hands, loose or tight, bluffs, tells, skill level—anything. Talk to your tablemates; they'll be happy to fill you in.

These records will help you when you are in a slump. But what if it's more than a slump? What if you are continually throwing the party and can't seem to break out of it?

If You Are Losing—A Lot

We have posed the question, "Why would you ever want to stop playing this great game?" To be honest, there are a few reasons why you would give it up: losing consistently over several years, not improving, and/or not enjoying yourself are the main ones. You don't play poker to lose, but you don't have to give up. You can fight it. You start by asking some tough questions. Chief among them is whether you are playing just to be in action. Do you totally understand the game? Are you playing with scared money? Are you overrating your skills? Are the other players too skilled? Does it seem like other players always know your hand?

Take a hard look at yourself. Do you really understand what a good hand is in this game? In various situations? Are you acting, or just reacting? Are you putting pressure on, or are you just passive? Can you put someone on a hand, or are you lost and just playing your own cards? Can you discern what a foe thinks you have, and when he bets, what he thinks of his own hand? Can you smoke out when someone is overvaluing a hand? Are you able to calculate your chances of improving to the winning hand?

Are you a predictable "book player"? Regulars can spot these types a mile away. It's a well-known secret among skilled players: They *want* you to read the poker books. As D. R. Sherer writes in *No Fold'em Hold'em*, "Just for the record, don't expect me to be following my own advice if you see me across the table in the next game you play." Book players are rigid. They rank patience too high on their list of priorities, and wait too long for premium hands. Worst of all, they only play their own cards, not their opponents' cards, their position, the game, and the situation. They are not the forceful table presence they need to be. *This* book, it is hoped, will move you beyond the "book player" level.

Big John's Tips: The most underestimated skill in poker is game selection; that is, who you are playing against. Some games will never be profitable. Play against people you can beat, or don't bother. You're wasting time and money.

How Not to Be a Loser

Here are some steps to turn it around:

- Ask other players for advice. Pay a pro if you have to.
- Vary your playing style. Get out of the rut.
- Try a new variation, venue, stakes, and/or players.
- Seek out a game with weaker players and loose action.
- Keep the expert, aggressive players on your right.
- Don't look for reasons to call. Look for reasons to fold.
- Don't play a hand unless you can bet aggressively.
- Be aggressive with good hands, not trash hands.
- Don't play second-best starting hands. They end second-best, too.
- Play the players. Are you analyzing and adjusting to your foes?
- Who's winning and losing in your game? It affects their play.
- In general, only bluff until you are caught, then tighten up.
- Cultivate a table image the opposite of the way you are playing.

- If you can't decide between a tight or wild image, choose wild.
- Don't call a bet on the river when you know you are beat.

Most of all, don't give up. You don't have to be an expert to win, just better than your opponents. Try some new things, like the strategies in this book, and tighten up until you find the problem, because playing too many starting hands and staying with them too long are the most serious mistakes in poker. In most cases, the best course is to just play straight-forwardly—fold with a bad hand, bet with a good hand. Don't overdo the fancy plays. If you get ahead, quit early and go home a winner. Last but not least, reread this book from time to time. There is no way you can grasp everything first time through, and some concepts will only become clear with experience.

When It's Time to Move Up

To maximize your profits, you take no prisoners when you have a winning hand. But the same goes for your game as a whole. When you've "got game," you make more money by going up in stakes. If you start out playing $4–$8 Hold'em or $2–$10 Stud—and you should not start lower—your goal is not to stay there. Your objective is to move up. If you are a winner and move from $4–$8 to $8–$16, you have doubled your stakes and your possible profit—if you can play the same style.

The question is whether you can adapt. You must be able to play with the same fearlessness and strength at the elevated level, because higher-limit players will try to intimidate you if they feel you're moving up. They know *they* can handle the pressure, but you'll have to prove that *you* can. You'll survive if you are in your safety zone and are convinced that a small bet is a small bet, and a big bet is a big bet, no matter what the stakes. It's all relative. It's play money at the table, remember?

You won't find as many "live ones" at higher limits, and you won't see as many obvious mistakes. But that doesn't mean these players are experts. They are beatable. Sometimes they just have more money behind them. Much of being a good higher-stakes player is just getting used to it.

Have Fun Around the Green Felt

As you gain experience and move up to fame and fortune, don't forget your second goal at the table: having fun. No matter how lucrative poker becomes, it is still a game first. Good players compete with joy in their hearts. Positive, upbeat people who take everything in stride seem to do better, almost as if they are attracting good fortune to them, and they certainly are more popular. And there is something to be said strategy-wise for making friends at the table.

Legend Johnny Moss on stakes: "I don't have much regard for money. Money's just paper to gamble with, and when I leave the table, I don't give it no nevermind."

Being Nice Pays Off

Those players on your immediate left can just murder you with raises. You want them to be your pals. But you don't want *any* enemies at the table. Why make yourself someone's target? Why make someone focus on you and be looking for ways to defeat you? Why give someone more motivation to stay sharp?

And if you are a consistent winner, you don't want the "losers" angry at you. You want them to get their money's worth, to have fun, to want to come back, even though they did not win. This is especially important for anyone making a living at poker. So don't criticize anyone's play or be contemptuous of someone inexperienced or less skilled.

Don't Quit Your Day Job!

No matter how successful you become, resist the urge to make poker a full-time job. This beautiful game is not meant to be an unimaginative daily grind. The world of the poker pro is not the glamorous existence you might envision. Most struggle to earn one big bet per hour, they play under pressure, and the majority are slowly going broke.

Many pros have lost the thrill of playing that attracted them to the game. You rarely see a smile, and winning brings them little joy, only a thought of which bill they will pay with that day's profit. Poker is a game, not a business. Why would you ever want to turn a beautiful game you love into a job you hate?

Cheating

Cheating isn't poker. If you are a poker player, you do not cheat. Cheating is for those who know they are losers. If someone is not as smart or as streetwise or as poker savvy as you, that does not mean they deserve to be cheated. If you win by cheating, you are not winning at poker, you are winning at dishonesty.

Those you would cheat are usually pretty good people. What kind of person, then, are you? The sad thing about cheats is that they think they are getting ahead, but you'll never find one who is happy, or with a big bankroll.

If you are playing outside a casino with people you barely know, any type of cheating is possible, but cheating is not epidemic in public card-rooms. Still, that doesn't mean you shouldn't keep both eyes open and your jungle sense working at all times.

Playing by "Feel"

To become a great player, you need to develop poker instincts, not just about when a game "isn't quite right," but also about what cards your opponents have and whether someone's being deceptive. You'll develop a "feel" for the game, situations, and opponents that is like a sixth sense. You'll just *know*.

Golf pros always teach stuff like, "The speed of the putt is so important. Use the right speed!" They think they are telling you something profound, but they are not. You are no closer to putting with the right speed than you were before he opened his mouth. There is only one way to achieve the right speed, and that's going out and practicing, learning how far to bring your arm back to hit the putt, and learning how the slope of the green affects the ball. This is "feel" and only comes with experience.

It is the same with poker. Serious poker, over time, becomes a matter of developing this poker "intuition."

Love the Game

Your two missions at the table are winning money and having fun. But they are really one. If you are having fun, you will probably be winning, and if you are winning, you will definitely be having fun. It all comes down to loving the game: If you don't love poker, you will not win.

The more skilled you become, the more money (and fun) will flow your way, because in poker, unlike golf, pool, and other sports, there is no handicap. Players of all levels compete one-on-one. No one's going to spot you strokes like in golf or a few balls as in pool, and there's no "minor league system" with A, AA, or AAA levels. No, poker players all think they're unbeatable, and you can use this overconfidence to win and achieve your goal of being "your own casino" with a built-in edge on every hand.

Then again, if you're facing the big boys, no one's going to spot you an ace or let you start with more chips. You have the same "chip and a chair" as big-bucks pros. You may be outclassed, but with what Nick the Greek called "the joyful acceptance of risk," you can go in there fighting, and, with a break or two, just might win.

ESSENTIAL

"A great poker player has to have really good instincts. He has to be able to feel out his opponent, try to outguess him, figure out what he's thinking . . . I don't sit down at the table with a strategy. Sometimes it's right to be aggressive. Sometimes it's right to wait patiently. Whatever the players are doing, I react to it. Like any other sport, you have to practice it. I've put in a lot of hours. I'm thinking about the game a lot. Because I do, I benefit from it."

—Tournament star Phil Ivey
at the 2003 World Series of Poker

Poker's future is as sky-high as the winner's chip stack at the World Series of Poker, and *you* can grow with this frontier pastime that is becoming a twenty-first-century phenomenon.

Remember, the more hands you play, the less deviation from the norm you can expect. This is why everyday players watch the odds so closely. They seek to minimize the deviation (luck) and make their long-term results predictable. But no matter how many hands they play, there is always the chance that at any given moment—or even over the long run—something "crazy" could happen. In theory, for example, you *could* flip a million heads or a million tails in a row. You could get pocket aces four times in a row, or win the lottery.

Or an online poker player named Chris Moneymaker who's never played in a real tournament could win $2.5 million in the 2003 World Series of Poker! Or *you* could! Good luck. No, good SKILL!!

Appendix A

Talk the Talk: Glossary of Poker Terms

action:
Gambling, as in "He loves to be in action." Also: A lot of betting, as in "The action was wild in that Omaha game." Also: It's your turn, as in "The action's on you."

add-on:
Additional chips that may be purchased at the end of the rebuy period of a poker tournament.

advertise:
Playing a certain way (such as loose or tight) early in a game, with the intention of playing the opposite way later. Also: A player making others aware he will bluff, to get his good hands called in the future.

all-in:
A player betting all his remaining chips. "I'm going all-in" or "I am all-in."

ante:
Money put into the pot by players before the cards are dealt.

backdoor:
Catching two cards in a row at the end of a hand to make a winner. Also: Making a hand a player was not originally going for.

bad beat:
To make a "sure thing" hand, only to be beaten by a longshot draw.

bankroll:
Money a player has to gamble with.

behind:
Someone who acts after you in a betting round. "I had a dangerous player sitting behind me."

behind the money:
Having the player or players with the most chips acting before you in a betting round.

belly buster:
An inside straight draw, as in 10-J-K-A.

Benjamin:
A hundred-dollar bill. (Named for Ben Franklin, whose portrait appears on it.)

best of it:
To have the odds with you.

bet:
Placing money in the pot after a new card is dealt and no one else has wagered.

big blind:
The larger of the two forced "blind bets" in community-card games, located two to the left of the button. The big blind is usually equivalent to the maximum single bet on the first round. "Big blind" refers to both the bet and the person making it.

big hand:
A really good hand.

The Big One:
The $10,000 buy-in no-limit Hold'em tournament at the World Series of Poker that is considered poker's world championship.

blank:
Community card that looks like it could not possibly help anyone's hand.

blind:
Money put in the pot by a player or players to the left of the button in community-card games prior to receiving cards. A forced, "blind" bet.

bluff:
A bet made representing a good hand, when in fact the player has a poor (or drawing) hand.

board:
The face-up cards on the table used by all players to make their hands in community-card games. Also: The face-up cards in a player's hand in a stud game.

boat:
A full house. Also called a "full boat."

brick-and-mortar casino:
A casino in a real, physical-world structure, as opposed to cyberspace. "Bobby is a good brick-and-mortar player, but not so good online."

bring-in:
Forced bet in stud games on the first round, often a percentage of the minimum bet. Other players may "complete the bet."

broadway:
An ace-high straight.

burn card:
The top card of the deck that is taken out of play before each round is dealt.

busted:
Broke. Also: To lose all one's chips and be out of a tournament. "I busted out." Also: A draw that did not get there; for instance, a busted flush.

button:
In a casino, the round plastic disc that denotes which player is the "dealer." The casino dealer gives cards to the player to the button's left first, the button last.

buy-in:
The amount of chips one must purchase to enter a poker game; or, in a cash game, the amount one must put on the table to be allowed into the game.

call:
To put the same amount in the pot as another player bet, thus remaining in the hand. "I call your bet."

calling down:
Calling someone all the way to the end of the hand, without raising.

calling station:
Weak player who calls other players too often and rarely raises.

cap:
To put in the last allowable bet in a round. "I capped the betting" or "I'll cap it."

case card:
The last card of a rank left in the deck. If three aces are on the board and a player receives the fourth one, he has been dealt the "case ace."

chasing:
Staying in a hand with lesser holdings than what an opponent has, hoping to make a winning hand.

check:
To not bet when it is a player's turn to act.

check-raise:
When a player checks, then raises someone who bet after that check.

checks:
Poker chips.

chop:
When two or more players divide the pot evenly, as in the case of a tie. Also: An agreement between the two blinds to not play the hand, and thus take back their blinds, if no players have called.

cold call:
To call multiple bets without having any chips invested in the pot.

community cards:
Cards on the "board" that are shared by all players in games such as Texas Hold'em and Omaha. All players can use the community cards to complete their hands.

connectors:
Two or more cards in sequence; for example, in Hold'em, having a jack and ten for hole cards.

cracked:
To lose a hand you were favored to win. "He caught a flush on the river and cracked my pocket aces."

crying call:
A very reluctant call of another player's bet.

counterfeit:
In Omaha Eight or Better, when the board pairs one of your low cards.

dealer's choice:
Game where the dealer has the option of choosing which poker variation will be played next.

dime:
One thousand dollars.

dog:
Same as underdog. A player not favored to win.

dominated:
To have someone's hand beat due to shared cards; e.g., in Hold'em, one person has A-8, another has K-8. The K-8 is dominated because the ace is higher than the king.

door card:
First face-up card in stud games.

double belly buster:
A double inside straight draw, giving a player eight outs; for instance, he has 10-8 and the board is Q-9-6-5.

down card:
An unexposed (face down) card in a player's hand.

draw:
A hand that needs additional cards to be of value. "I was on a flush draw," or "I was drawing to a straight." Also: A form of poker.

drawing dead:
Chasing a hand that even if completed, cannot win.

duck:
A deuce.

early position:
Having to act in the first third of players in a hand.

eight or better:
Refers to lowball games where a qualifying low must consist of five unpaired cards eight or below.

face down:
Cards that are unexposed and thus hidden. A player's hole cards are face down.

face up:
Exposed, so all players can see what the card is.

family pot:
Hand in which all players at a table are involved.

fast:
An aggressive style of play with a lot of betting and raising. "He played that hand fast."

favorite:
Player who has the best chance mathematically to win a hand.

fill up:
To make a full house. "I filled up."

fish:
A poor or novice player expected to be easy money.

flat call:
To call a bet with a strong hand, rather than raising. Smooth call.

floorperson:
Supervisory cardroom employee who also settles disputes.

flop:
The first three community cards exposed in Texas Hold'em. They are turned face up at the same time. Also, as a verb, to make a hand using just the flop: "I flopped a full house."

fold:
To drop out of (quit) a hand. Done by turning one's cards face down or saying "I fold," "I drop," or "I'm out."

four-flush:
Four cards to a flush, with one more needed to complete the hand.

free card:
When all players check during a betting round, the next card is considered "free," because no one had to put money into the pot.

freeroll:
Tournament where certain qualifying players can get in for free.

goose:
Unskilled player.

gutshot:
An inside straight draw.

heads-up:
Game where only two players remain.

HORSE:
Table that plays five poker games in rotation: Hold'em, Omaha Eight or Better, Razz, Seven-Card Stud, and Seven-Card Stud High-Low Split (Eight or better).

hole:
A player's unseen (face-down) cards. "I had an ace in the hole."

ignorant end:
The low end of a straight. If the flop is Q-J-10, and a player has 9-8 in the hole, he has the ignorant end of the straight.

implied odds:
What a player feels his actual payoff will be if he hits his hand relative to how much it will cost to play.

in front of:
Someone who acts before you in a betting round. "Two players called in front of me."

inside straight draw:
A straight draw with only one card that will complete the straight, such as 4-5-6-8.

isolation:
Betting, raising, or reraising to try to get heads-up with a weaker hand or weaker player.

joker:
Traditionally, a wild card. In modern parlance, a perfect card to complete a hand. "I hit the joker and won a huge pot."

kicker:
An unmatched card in a player's hand not used except in case of ties.

kill:
Variation of limit poker where if a player wins two pots in a row, the limits are doubled for the next hand. In a half-kill, the limits are raised 50 percent.

late position:
The final third of players to act in a game.

laydown:
To fold. "I saved some chips by making a good laydown."

limit:
The most that may be bet or raised at any one time.

limit poker:
Poker played with limits on the amount that may be bet, as opposed to no-limit, where any amount may be wagered.

limp:
To enter a pot by just calling, rather than betting or raising. "I limped in to the pot" or "I raised all the limpers."

live blind:
A blind that has the option to raise, even if no one has raised the initial blind "bet."

live card:
A card whose rank has not appeared on the board or in another hand. "I'm all-in, but at least my hole cards are live."

live one:
Player likely to bet wildly and lose a lot of money.

lock:
A hand that cannot be beaten.

lock it up:
What you tell the floorperson when you want the seat he's holding for you. You have now promised to take that seat.

longshot:
A poker hand that has little chance of being made, such as drawing to a hand with four outs or less. Also: Any event not expected to occur, such as a horse winning at 50-to-1 odds.

loose:
A style of play that entails playing a lot of hands, and often playing them too long.

lowball:
Style of poker where the worst hand wins.

maniac:
A wild, loose player who bets big with questionable cards to build pots.

middle position:
The middle third of players to act in a game.

monster:
A very, very good hand.

muck:
To throw away your hand in a game (fold). "I mucked my hand."

muck pile:
The haphazard collection of discards, folded hands, and unused cards in the center of the table.

multiway pot:
A hand with more than two players involved.

no-limit:
Poker game where the size of a player's bet is limited only by the amount of money he has on the table.

nuts:
The best possible hand given the cards in a particular game.

odds:
Chance that a specific event will occur. Expressed as a ratio (such as "3-to-1").

offsuit:
Two or more cards of different suits.

on the button:
To be last to act on every round in a community-card game.

open:
To be the first bettor in Draw, to open the betting. "I'll open for ten dollars."

open-ended:
A straight draw with "both ends open," like 4-5-6-7.

outs:
The number of cards left in the deck that will give you the hand you are seeking.

overcall:
To call a player's bet after someone else has already called the bet.

overcard:
A higher card. If a player has Q-J and the flop is 10-8-6, he has two overcards. If he has Q-J and the flop is A-9-8, one overcard hit the flop.

overlay:
Getting better than the correct odds on a bet.

overpair:
A higher pair than you can make. If you have Q-J and someone has kings, he has an overpair. If you have jacks and he has kings, he has an overpair.

over the top:
To reraise an opponent, especially in no-limit. "He came over the top for all his chips."

overs:
When there are some players in a casino game who wish to play a higher limit, they sometimes can play overs, wherein if these players are alone in a hand, the higher limits take effect.

paint:
A face card, that is, jacks, queens, and kings.

pat hand:
In Draw poker, a hand so good one does not have to draw cards.

pocket:
Your two hole (unseen) cards in Hold'em.

pocket pair:
Two cards of the same rank in the hole in Hold'em, such as two jacks or two kings.

position:
Where a player sits relative to the button. The player to the left of the button acts first, and play proceeds clockwise.

positional advantage:
When a player acts after another player in a hand.

position bet:
When a player bets (or raises) on the basis of positional advantage.

post:
To put an ante or a blind into the pot. "Please post your blind." Also: In some casinos, to put money up when you first sit down in a game, as an additional blind. "Do I have to post here?"

pot:
Chips and money—the sum of all antes, blinds, bets, calls and raises—put in the center of the table that players compete for.

pot-limit:
Poker game where a player may bet up to the size of the pot at the time he is making the bet.

pot odds:
The size of the pot relative to the cost of calling the bets needed to stay in the hand.

preflop:
Before the flop.

protect:
When a player bets and/or raises when he has the best hand to get others to fold. "He had to protect his pocket queens."

psychological player:
Poker player who relies mostly on "feel" and people skills—reading opponents and predicting what cards they hold—to win.

quads:
Four of a kind.

rabbit hunting:
Searching through the deck to discover "what might have happened" had a player stayed in a hand.

rag:
A weak card.

ragged flop:
When the first three community cards are weak and unconnected.

railbird:
Person who is standing behind a game, just watching. Often a player who has busted out of the game.

rainbow:
Cards of all different suits. "It was a rainbow flop."

raise:
Increasing the amount players must pay to stay in a hand, done by adding chips to another player's original bet.

rake:
Money taken out of every pot by the House. The House's take.

ram:
To bet and raise powerfully and often during a hand. Also: Ram and jam.

Razz:
Seven-Card Stud where the worst hand wins. 5-4-3-2-A is the perfect low.

read:
To figure out a player by studying his personality, mannerisms, expressions, and style of play. "I had a good read on him."

rebuy:
Buying more chips in a poker tournament when a player's stack falls below a certain level.

represent:
When a player bets and acts as if he has a particular hand. "She was representing a straight."

reraise:
To raise someone who has previously raised.

re-reraise:
To raise someone who has reraised. Thus if there was a bet, a raise, a reraise, and a re-reraise, it would cost a player four bets to stay in the hand.

ring game:
A standard non-tournament game.

river:

The fifth and final community card in Hold'em and Omaha. Dealt separately. Also: The last card dealt in any game.

rivered:

To make a hand on the river, as in "I rivered a queen to win the pot."

rock:

A tight, conservative player who only plays premium hands and takes few risks.

rolled up:

Three of a kind in the first three cards in Seven-Card Stud.

runner-runner:

Catching two perfect cards on the end to win. "I got runner-runner spades for the flush!"

running:

Two consecutive cards, usually the last two cards dealt in a game. "I caught two running hearts for the flush!"

rush:

Winning a higher-than-expected number of hands in a short time. A hot streak.

safety zone:

Area where a player feels comfortable and at ease with the stakes and limits. Comfort zone.

sandbagging:

Slow-playing a hand to induce an opponent to bet. Also: Check-raising.

satellite:

A mini-tournament, usually one table, where the prize is an entry fee into the main tournament.

scare card:

A card that seems to greatly benefit a player. "A scare card hit the turn."

scoop:
To win the entire pot in a split-pot game.

seat charge:
Fee collected from each player on the hour or half-hour in high-stakes casino poker games in lieu of a rake.

see:
To call someone's bet. "I'll see your ten dollars" or "I'll see that bet." Generally not used in today's poker slang.

set:
Three of kind in Hold'em consisting of a pair in a player's hand and a matching card on the board.

sheriff:
Someone who calls other players to make sure they aren't bluffing.

short-handed:
A game with four or fewer players.

short-stacked:
To have the fewest chips at the table, especially in a tournament.

showdown:
When, after all betting in a hand is completed, the players expose their hands and determine a winner.

short pair:
A pair below jacks in Draw (Jacks or Better) poker.

side game:
A standard ring (non-tournament) game. "I busted out of the tournament early, but I found a very profitable side game."

side pot:
After a player has gone all-in, others in the hand may continue to bet and raise, but their money is placed in a separate pot. The all-in player is not eligible to win the side pot.

slow:
A style of play with lots of checking and calling, and not much betting and raising.

slow-play:
Playing a top hand in a weak manner to disguise its strength. "He trapped me by slow-playing those three aces."

small blind:
Located to the left of the button, the smaller of the two forced "blind bets" in community-card games. Generally half the size of the big blind and placed in the pot before cards are dealt.

smooth call:
To call a bet with a very strong hand, rather than raising.

spit:
A community card placed face up in the center of the table. Often used in stud games when there are not sufficient cards left in the deck to complete all players' hands.

split pair:
In a stud game, having a pair with one card in the hole, the other on the board.

stack:
How many chips a player has.

stakes:
The amount of money being played for; also, the limits of the game.

standing pat:
Playing your original five cards in Draw poker; that is, not drawing any cards.

starting hand:
Cards dealt to a player before the first bet.

stealing:
Bluffing. "I'm not going to let you steal the pot."

steaming:
Same as tilt.

stone-cold bluff:
A bluff with a hand so weak that it has no chance of winning unless all other players fold.

straddle:
When the player to the left of the big blind puts in a raise before being dealt a hand. With a "live" straddle, he is last to act in the first round and may raise his own bet.

street:
A betting round. "She bet on fourth street" means she bet after the fourth card.

string bet:
Illegal move where a player puts chips in the pot, then returns to his stack for more, rather than betting in a continuous motion.

stud:
A group of games that use hole cards and face-up cards. There are no community cards. Also: Slang for Seven-Card Stud.

suck-out:
To outdraw someone on the river. "That guy is a real suck-out artist."

suited:
Two or more cards of the same suit.

suited connectors:
Two or more cards of the same suit in sequence. For instance, in Hold'em, hole cards that are the 10♥ and 9♥.

super satellite:
A multi-table tournament where the prizes are one or more entries into a major event.

swing:
The fluctuation sustained by a player's chip count during a given session. "It was a wild game. I had a huge swing today."

table image:
Someone's personality and playing style as perceived by other players.

table stakes:
Stakes wherein a player is limited to betting or calling with the chips and cash he has on the table. He cannot be bet out of a pot because he does not have enough capital.

taking a card off:
Just calling with the intention of seeing another card as cheaply as possible, then likely folding if the hand does not improve.

technical player:
A poker player who relies mostly on mathematical calculations to make decisions.

tell:
A mannerism, expression, action, or other unintentional clue that reveals a player's hand, personality, or strategy.

tight:
Conservative, cautious strategy; playing very few hands.

tilt:
When someone begins playing wildly due to emotional upset. "He suffered two bad beats, and went on tilt." Steaming.

toke:
Poker players' term for a tip.

top kicker:
Best possible kicker in a community-card game. If the Hold'em board is 8-7-2 and a player has A-8 in the pocket, he has the top pair with the top kicker.

top pair:
In a community-card game, when a player has paired a hole card with the highest card on the board.

trap:
To underplay a hand until other players bet, then punish them with raises.

trips:
Common term for three of a kind.

turn:
The fourth community card in Hold'em and Omaha, dealt separately.

underdog:
Player not favored to win a hand. Also called a "dog."

underpair:
A pair that is "under" the board in a community-card game. If the board is 9-8-7 and a player has pocket fives, he has an underpair.

under the gun:
Player who must act first. In community-card games, the player to the left of the big blind.

unsuited:
Two or more cards of different suits.

up card:
One of a player's face-up (exposed) cards in a stud game.

value bet:
When a player bets a hand that is not a sure thing, but feels that the bet, over time, will win more than it loses.

wheel:

A five-high straight, that is, 5-4-3-2-A. In most lowball games, the wheel is also the best low hand. Also called a "bicycle."

wild card:

A card that can become any card in the deck a player wishes.

wired:

To have a pair in the hole from the start. "I had aces wired."

WPT:

The World Poker Tour. A series of high buy-in Hold'em tournaments televised on the Travel channel, culminating with a $25,000 buy-in event at the Bellagio resort/casino in Vegas.

wrap:

In Omaha, four cards in sequence in the hole, such as 7-8-9-10.

WSOP:

The World Series of Poker. A string of big-money tournaments held at the Horseshoe casino in Las Vegas each spring.

Book 'Em!
Further Reading

7-Card Stud, by Roy West. Poker Plus Publications: Las Vegas, Nev., 1996, 2003.

24/7, by Andres Martinez. Villard Books/Random House: New York, 1999.

Against the Gods: The Remarkable Story of Risk, by Peter L. Bernstein. John Wiley & Sons: New York, 1998.

The Arm, by Clark Howard. Sherbourne Press Inc.: Los Angeles, 1967.

Beneath the Neon, by Michael "London" Haywood. Carlton Press: New York, 1984.

The Big Biazarro, by Leonard Wise. Doubleday & Co.: Garden City, N.Y., 1977.

Big Deal, by Anthony Holden. Viking/Penguin: New York, 1990.

The Biggest Game in Town, by A. Alvarez. Houghton Mifflin: Boston, 1983.

The Complete Book of Hold'em Poker, by Gary Carson. Lyle Stuart/ Kensington Publishing Group: New York, 2001.

Dostoevsky's Last Night, by Cristina Peri Rossi. Picador USA: New York, 1992.

Gambling Secrets of Nick the Greek, by Ted Thackrey Jr. Rand McNally & Co.: Chicago, 1968.

Getting the Best of It, by David Sklansky. Self-published, 1982, 1989.

The Green Felt Jungle, by Ed Reid and Ovid Demaris. Trident Press: New York, 1963.

How to Figure the Odds on Everything, by Darrell Huff. Dreyfus Publications Ltd.: New York, 1972.

Inside Las Vegas, by Mario Puzo. Grosset & Dunlap: New York, 1977.

Internet Poker, by Lou Krieger and Kathleen Keller. Watterson ConJelCo: Pittsburgh, Pa., 2003.

Johnny Moss: Champion of Champions, by Don Jenkins. JM Publishing: 1981.

King of a Small World, by Rick Bennet. Arcade Publishing: New York, 1995.

Knights of the Green Cloth, by Robert K. DeArment. University of Oklahoma Press: Norman, Okla., 1982.

Lady Las Vegas, by Susan Berman. A&E Network and TV Books: New York, 1996.

Loaded Dice, by John Soares. Taylor Publishing Co.: Dallas, Texas, 1985.

The Man With the $100,000 Breasts, by Michael Konik. Huntington Press: Las Vegas, Nev., 1999.

Mike Caro's The Book of Tells, by Mike Caro. Gambling Times Inc.: Hollywood, Calif., 1984.

Nick the Greek, King of the Gamblers, by Cy Rice. Funk & Wagnalls: New York, 1969.

No Fold'em Hold'em, by D. R. Sherer. Poker Plus Publications: Las Vegas, Nev., 1997.

The Odds, by Chad Millman. Public Affairs: New York, 2001.

Play Poker Like the Pros, by Phil Hellmuth Jr. HarperCollins Publishers, Inc.: New York, 2003.

Play Poker to Win, by Amarillo Slim Preston. Grosset & Dunlap: New York, 1973.

Poker! (Las Vegas Style), by Bill "Bulldog" Sykes. Bulldog Publishing: Las Vegas, Nev., 1992.

Poker Tournament Tips from the Pros, by Shane Smith. Cardoza Publishing: New York, 2003.

Psyching Out Vegas, by Marvin Karlins. Gambling Times Inc.: Hollywood, Calif., 1983.

The Quotable Gambler, edited by Paul Lyons. Lyons Press: New York, 1999.

Shut Up and Deal, by Jesse May. Anchor Books Doubleday: New York, 1998.

Doyle Brunson's Super System, by Doyle Brunson. B&G Publishing Co., Inc.: Las Vegas, Nev., 1978, 2002.

Tales Out of Tulsa, by Bobby Baldwin. Gambling Times Inc.: Hollywood, Calif., 1984.

Tap City, by Ron Abell. Little Brown & Co.: Boston, 1985.

Texas Bill's Winning a Living, by William T. Melms: Self-published, 1998.

The Theory of Poker, by David Sklansky. Two Plus Two Publishing: Las Vegas, Nev., 2002.

Total Poker, by David Spanier. Simon and Schuster: New York, 1977.

Winner's Guide to Texas Hold'em Poker, by Ken Warren. Cardoza Publishing: New York, 1996.

Zen and the Art of Poker, by Larry W. Phillips. Penguin Putnam, Inc.: New York, 1999.

Index

THE **EVERYTHING** SERIES!

BUSINESS

Everything® Business Planning Book
Everything® Coaching and Mentoring Book
Everything® Fundraising Book
Everything® Home-Based Business Book
Everything® Landlording Book
Everything® Leadership Book
Everything® Managing People Book
Everything® Negotiating Book
Everything® Online Business Book
Everything® Project Management Book
Everything® Robert's Rules Book, $7.95
Everything® Selling Book
Everything® Start Your Own Business Book
Everything® Time Management Book

COMPUTERS

Everything® Computer Book

COOKBOOKS

Everything® Barbecue Cookbook
Everything® Bartender's Book, $9.95
Everything® Chinese Cookbook
Everything® Chocolate Cookbook
Everything® Cookbook
Everything® Dessert Cookbook
Everything® Diabetes Cookbook
Everything® Fondue Cookbook
Everything® Grilling Cookbook
Everything® Holiday Cookbook
Everything® Indian Cookbook
Everything® Low-Carb Cookbook
Everything® Low-Fat High-Flavor Cookbook
Everything® Low-Salt Cookbook
Everything® Mediterranean Cookbook
Everything® Mexican Cookbook
Everything® One-Pot Cookbook
Everything® Pasta Cookbook
Everything® Quick Meals Cookbook
Everything® Slow Cooker Cookbook
Everything® Soup Cookbook

Everything® Thai Cookbook
Everything® Vegetarian Cookbook
Everything® Wine Book

HEALTH

Everything® Alzheimer's Book
Everything® Anti-Aging Book
Everything® Diabetes Book
Everything® Dieting Book
Everything® Hypnosis Book
Everything® Low Cholesterol Book
Everything® Massage Book
Everything® Menopause Book
Everything® Nutrition Book
Everything® Reflexology Book
Everything® Reiki Book
Everything® Stress Management Book
Everything® Vitamins, Minerals, and
     Nutritional Supplements Book

HISTORY

Everything® American Government Book
Everything® American History Book
Everything® Civil War Book
Everything® Irish History & Heritage Book
Everything® Mafia Book
Everything® Middle East Book

HOBBIES & GAMES

Everything® Bridge Book
Everything® Candlemaking Book
Everything® Card Games Book
Everything® Cartooning Book
Everything® Casino Gambling Book, 2nd Ed.
Everything® Chess Basics Book
Everything® Crossword and Puzzle Book
Everything® Crossword Challenge Book
Everything® Drawing Book
Everything® Digital Photography Book
Everything® Easy Crosswords Book
Everything® Family Tree Book

Everything® Games Book
Everything® Knitting Book
Everything® Magic Book
Everything® Motorcycle Book
Everything® Online Genealogy Book
Everything® Photography Book
Everything® Poker Strategy Book
Everything® Pool & Billiards Book
Everything® Quilting Book
Everything® Scrapbooking Book
Everything® Sewing Book
Everything® Soapmaking Book

HOME IMPROVEMENT

Everything® Feng Shui Book
Everything® Feng Shui Decluttering Book, $9.95
Everything® Fix-It Book
Everything® Homebuilding Book
Everything® Home Decorating Book
Everything® Landscaping Book
Everything® Lawn Care Book
Everything® Organize Your Home Book

EVERYTHING® *KIDS'* BOOKS

All titles are $6.95

Everything® Kids' Baseball Book, 3rd Ed.
Everything® Kids' Bible Trivia Book
Everything® Kids' Bugs Book
Everything® Kids' Christmas Puzzle
     & Activity Book
Everything® Kids' Cookbook
Everything® Kids' Halloween Puzzle
     & Activity Book
Everything® Kids' Hidden Pictures Book
     Everything® Kids' Joke Book
Everything® Kids' Knock Knock Book
Everything® Kids' Math Puzzles Book
Everything® Kids' Mazes Book
Everything® Kids' Money Book

All Everything® books are priced at $12.95 or $14.95, unless otherwise stated. Prices subject to change without notice.

Everything® Kids' Monsters Book
Everything® Kids' Nature Book
Everything® Kids' Puzzle Book
Everything® Kids' Riddles & Brain Teasers Book
Everything® Kids' Science Experiments Book
Everything® Kids' Soccer Book
Everything® Kids' Travel Activity Book

KIDS' STORY BOOKS

Everything® Bedtime Story Book
Everything® Bible Stories Book
Everything® Fairy Tales Book

LANGUAGE

Everything® Conversational Japanese Book
   (with CD), $19.95
Everything® Inglés Book
Everything® French Phrase Book, $9.95
Everything® Learning French Book
Everything® Learning German Book
Everything® Learning Italian Book
Everything® Learning Latin Book
Everything® Learning Spanish Book
Everything® Sign Language Book
Everything® Spanish Phrase Book, $9.95
Everything® Spanish Verb Book, $9.95

MUSIC

Everything® Drums Book (with CD), $19.95
Everything® Guitar Book
Everything® Home Recording Book
Everything® Playing Piano and Keyboards Book
Everything® Rock & Blues Guitar Book
   (with CD), $19.95
Everything® Songwriting Book

NEW AGE

Everything® Astrology Book
Everything® Dreams Book
Everything® Ghost Book
Everything® Love Signs Book, $9.95
Everything® Meditation Book
Everything® Numerology Book
Everything® Paganism Book
Everything® Palmistry Book
Everything® Psychic Book
Everything® Spells & Charms Book
Everything® Tarot Book
Everything® Wicca and Witchcraft Book

PARENTING

Everything® Baby Names Book
Everything® Baby Shower Book
Everything® Baby's First Food Book
Everything® Baby's First Year Book
Everything® Birthing Book
Everything® Breastfeeding Book
Everything® Father-to-Be Book
Everything® Get Ready for Baby Book
Everything® Getting Pregnant Book
Everything® Homeschooling Book
Everything® Parent's Guide to Children
   with Asperger's Syndrome
Everything® Parent's Guide to Children
   with Autism
Everything® Parent's Guide to Children
   with Dyslexia
Everything® Parent's Guide to Positive Discipline
Everything® Parent's Guide to Raising a
   Successful Child
Everything® Parenting a Teenager Book
Everything® Potty Training Book, $9.95
Everything® Pregnancy Book, 2nd Ed.
Everything® Pregnancy Fitness Book
Everything® Pregnancy Nutrition Book
Everything® Pregnancy Organizer, $15.00
Everything® Toddler Book
Everything® Tween Book

PERSONAL FINANCE

Everything® Budgeting Book
Everything® Get Out of Debt Book
Everything® Homebuying Book, 2nd Ed.
Everything® Homeselling Book
Everything® Investing Book
Everything® Online Business Book
Everything® Personal Finance Book
Everything® Personal Finance in Your
   20s & 30s Book
Everything® Real Estate Investing Book
Everything® Wills & Estate Planning Book

PETS

Everything® Cat Book
Everything® Dog Book
Everything® Dog Training and Tricks Book
Everything® Golden Retriever Book
Everything® Horse Book
Everything® Labrador Retriever Book
Everything® Poodle Book

Everything® Puppy Book
Everything® Rottweiler Book
Everything® Tropical Fish Book

REFERENCE

Everything® Car Care Book
Everything® Classical Mythology Book
Everything® Einstein Book
Everything® Etiquette Book
Everything® Great Thinkers Book
Everything® Philosophy Book
Everything® Psychology Book
Everything® Shakespeare Book
Everything® Toasts Book

RELIGION

Everything® Angels Book
Everything® Bible Book
Everything® Buddhism Book
Everything® Catholicism Book
Everything® Christianity Book
Everything® Jewish History & Heritage Book
Everything® Judaism Book
Everything® Koran Book
Everything® Prayer Book
Everything® Saints Book
Everything® Understanding Islam Book
Everything® World's Religions Book
Everything® Zen Book

SCHOOL & CAREERS

Everything® After College Book
Everything® Alternative Careers Book
Everything® College Survival Book
Everything® Cover Letter Book
Everything® Get-a-Job Book
Everything® Job Interview Book
Everything® New Teacher Book
Everything® Online Job Search Book
Everything® Personal Finance Book
Everything® Practice Interview Book
Everything® Resume Book, 2nd Ed.
Everything® Study Book

SELF-HELP/
RELATIONSHIPS

Everything® Dating Book
Everything® Divorce Book
Everything® Great Sex Book

All Everything® books are priced at $12.95 or $14.95, unless otherwise stated. Prices subject to change without notice.

Everything® Kama Sutra Book
Everything® Self-Esteem Book

SPORTS & FITNESS

Everything® Body Shaping Book
Everything® Fishing Book
Everything® Fly-Fishing Book
Everything® Golf Book
Everything® Golf Instruction Book
Everything® Knots Book
Everything® Pilates Book
Everything® Running Book
Everything® T'ai Chi and QiGong Book
Everything® Total Fitness Book
Everything® Weight Training Book
Everything® Yoga Book

TRAVEL

Everything® Family Guide to Hawaii
Everything® Family Guide to New York City, 2nd Ed.
Everything® Family Guide to Washington D.C., 2nd Ed.
Everything® Family Guide to the Walt Disney World Resort®, Universal Studios®, and Greater Orlando, 4th Ed.
Everything® Guide to Las Vegas
Everything® Guide to New England
Everything® Travel Guide to the Disneyland Resort®, California Adventure®, Universal Studios®, and the Anaheim Area

WEDDINGS

Everything® Bachelorette Party Book, $9.95
Everything® Bridesmaid Book, $9.95
Everything® Creative Wedding Ideas Book
Everything® Elopement Book, $9.95
Everything® Father of the Bride Book, $9.95
Everything® Groom Book, $9.95
Everything® Jewish Wedding Book
Everything® Mother of the Bride Book, $9.95
Everything® Wedding Book, 3rd Ed.
Everything® Wedding Checklist, $7.95
Everything® Wedding Etiquette Book, $7.95
Everything® Wedding Organizer, $15.00
Everything® Wedding Shower Book, $7.95
Everything® Wedding Vows Book, $7.95
Everything® Weddings on a Budget Book, $9.95

WRITING

Everything® Creative Writing Book
Everything® Get Published Book
Everything® Grammar and Style Book
Everything® Grant Writing Book
Everything® Guide to Writing a Novel
Everything® Guide to Writing Children's Books
Everything® Screenwriting Book
Everything® Writing Well Book